An incredibly powerful and important piece of history, masterfully written and researched. ~ Dave Grossman, Lt. Col. USA (ret), author, *On Killing* and *On Combat*, www.killology.com

This excellent book chronicles the inhuman treatment suffered by young brave soldiers at the hands of a merciless foe. America is still technically at war with North Korea so ignore the lessons of history at your peril. One day American troops might meet these people on the battlefield again . . . ~Phil Chinnery, author of *Korean Atrocity* and historian for the British National Ex-POW Association.

A great book . . . I salute these brave men. I can't imagine what it must have been like for them. It is a miracle that anyone lived at all. No one else can feel their pain and sorrow. Their only salvation is the love they have for each other. ~ Shorty Estabrook, historian and survivor of the Tiger Death March, November 1950.

This book is superbly written. It brilliantly documents stories long buried in the unremembered pages of Korean War History. It has been very well researched and compliments our POWs.~ Samuel L. Clark, a member of the 187th Airborne Regimental Combat Team (RCT), Rakkasans, who participated in the drop to block North Korean Retreat and rescue the POWs in October, 1950

Nothing is more important today than recording the accurate history of yesterday. The *Sunchon Tunnel Massacre Survivors* is a tribute to true heroes. The book and all it entails will be a vital record for our future generations. ~ Charles P. Schantag, P.O.W. NETWORK.

The *Sunchon Tunnel Massacre Survivors* is a book of epic proportion that reveals the near apocalyptic, gut-wrenching experiences of the few remaining Korean Prisoners of War whose lives were forever scarred by the hell of combat and the daily brutality of the North Korean soldiers! ~Lloyd King, author, *From 'Nam With Love* — www.fromnamwithlove.com

They say that war is hell—and yet, God creates His greatest heroes from the shadows of such misery and suffering. This is one compelling story of war that needed to be told; and it is brilliantly done with sensitivity and compassion. This is destined to become a classic book on the Korean War. ~ W. H. McDonald Jr., founder — Military Writer's Society of America, Vietnam Veteran, author, film maker, poet and Veteran Advocate

Sunchon Tunnel Massacre Survivors book is a must read. It has photos of the true heroes of the Korean War. I highly recommend you read this well written and highly documented book that honors those men by telling their stories. They gave above and beyond the call of duty to keep us free. ~ Vincent A. Krepps, Silver Star 8-1-50, editor "The Graybeards", author *One Came Home*

Avery and Faulkner give us both horrors and healing from The Forgotten War with case studies and photos from POW survivors that make this piece of difficult history precise and human. ~Janet Grace Riehl, author *Sightlines: A Poet's Diary* and grand-daughter of Korean Missionaries Anna Riehl and J. Arthur Thompson (who designed the building where the Seoul Peace Treaty was signed)

Pat McGrath Avery and Joyce Faulkner eloquently remind us that every war has events that should not be forgotten, remind us that war is hell no matter where, no matter when. ~Carolyn Howard-Johnson, award-winning author of *This Is the Place* and *Tracings*

Educators today are encouraged to introduce real life situations to their students. This book is a perfect teaching tool for history teachers. Students will be able to visualize the actual suffering of our soldiers. The survivors' vivid recollection of their treatment at the hands of their captors is compelling. This historical book honors these Great Patriots and their descendent families. I can already see the shining faces of the many students who will proudly acknowledge and proclaim to their peers in America's classrooms that one of their grandparents is a veteran of the Korean War. ~ Rudy Garcia, educator, Port Isabel School District, Texas

This book details the human suffering both mentally and physically that most of us wish not to hear . . . but need to in order to understand those heroes among us who are so many times silent about their experiences. Through accounts such as this, you will not be forgotten. For the families that still await word regarding the fate of our lost loved ones, this chronicle hopefully will educate and generate renewed interest in the POW/MIA efforts. Thank you to the authors Pat McGrath Avery and Joyce Faulkner and to the men who were brave enough to tell their stories. ~ Robin Piacine, President, Coalition of Families of Korean and Cold War POW/MIAs

I made eleven tours to Korea to entertain our troops and I love the country. This book gave me a real appreciation of our part in South Korea's fight for freedom. I've met the survivors and I'm happy there's a book that tells their story. ~ Penny Gilley, Entertainer (RFD-TV Network and RFD-TV, The Theater in Branson, Missouri)

Sunchon Tunnel Massacre Survivors

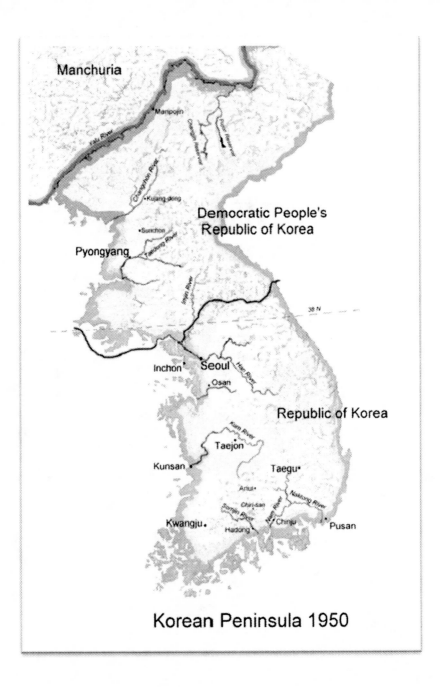

Korean Peninsula 1950

THEY CAME HOME SERIES

Sunchon Tunnel Massacre Survivors

by

Pat McGrath Avery
Joyce Faulkner

Red Engine Press
Branson, Missouri

Published by Red Engine Press

This work is based on extensive personal interviews with survivors, original testimony taken shortly after their rescue, and articles written in the 1950s. The authors of this book are not Korean War historians. Information about the battles is based on the research of others—and presented to provide context for the POWs' experiences.

Library of Congress Cataloging-in-Publication Data

Avery, Pat McGrath
 Sunchon tunnel massacre survivors / By Pat McGrath Avery & JoyceFaulkner.
    p. cm. -- (They Came Home Series)
Includes bibliographical references and index.
  ISBN 978-0-9800064-0-7   (Hard Cover)
  ISBN 978-0-9785158-1-2   (Soft Cover)
1. Korean War, 1950-1953--Personal narratives, American. 2. Korean War, 1950-1953--Participation, American. 3. Soldiers—United States--Interviews. 4. Massacres--Korea. I. Faulkner, Joyce. Title.
 DS921.6.A94 2008
 951.904'2--dc22

                    2007040876

Photos by Pat McGrath Avery, Everett Avery & Joyce Faulkner

Design for POW Museum Statue by William J. Thompson used on cover.

Maps by J. R. R. Faulkner

Printed in the United States of America

Quantity discounts are available on bulk purchases of this book for educational institutions or social organizations. For information, please contact the publisher.

www.RedEnginePress.com

Dedication

To

Allen Gifford
Bill Henninger
Bob Sharpe
Ed Slater
Walt Whitcomb
Jim Yeager
Valdor John
Sherman Jones
George Snodgrass

who came home and to all the others who did not.

Site of Sunchon Massacre *(National Archives)*

Acknowledgements

This book was not easy to write. The suffering of others—especially when you've come to know and care about them—is heartbreaking. George, Ed, Bob, Walt, Sherm, Bill, Valdor, Jim, and Allen allowed us to poke into the sorest corners of their hearts. We know how much our questions hurt—and we appreciate their gallant determination to tell their stories.

Many other people contributed their memories, ideas, information, and kindness to this project—too many to thank each one personally. However, we are going to try.

First, we'd like to acknowledge Nadine Yeager, Linda John, Phyllis Slater, Dorothy Henninger, Richard Reid, and Marsha Eastep. Their support made it easier for the survivors to endure our endless questions. Special thanks to Oleta Jones who began the long journey to create this book about her beloved husband Sherman but didn't live to see it finished. All who knew her grieve her passing—and miss her.

We spent a wonderful day with Nancy Zeman and her husband David talking about her beloved brother Gene Putzier who never came home from Korea.

Shorty Estabrook provided us with information and kindliness. As a Korean War ex-POW and a survivor of the Tiger Death March in November 1950, his input was intriguing and invaluable. Vince Krepps, ex-editor of *Graybeards* and another Korean War Veteran whose twin brother died as a POW in NKPA hands, thank you for sharing your experiences as well.

Valoise Armstrong, Archivist at the Eisenhower Presidential Library, and Randy Sowell, Archivist at the Truman Presidential Library, were important sources of original materials including reports and testimonies.

Christopher Avery served as research assistant and his contributions were much appreciated.

The folks in Branson are integral to this story. We expected their kindness to the survivors. However, their kindness to two writers struggling to tell what we consider the most important story of our lives touched us. Thanks go to the Branson Veterans Task Force—especially Marlyce Stockinger, Steve Weyher, Arlen Lipper, Tom Goldsworthy, and Linda Ward. The Branson Chapter of the Korean War Veterans Association and the Vietnam Veterans Association of Branson are steadfast. The survivors—and veterans of all wars and their families—appreciate your efforts on their behalf. Our admiration for Joe Bryant of the Veterans History Project, who was a reporter during the Korean War, kept us going time after time.

We'd like to thank Marlyce Stockinger for her personal interest in the survivors, her business sense and her willingness to take us by the hand and help us find ways to provide the men with a positive experience in Branson.

Steve Weyher, General Manager of the Branson Golden Corral Restaurant, found solutions, offered advice and became a trusted friend over the last two years as we put this book together.

Many thanks to authors and Vietnam combat veterans Eddie Beesley (*Lucky Enough*) and Lloyd A. King (*From 'Nam With Love*) for their help during the reunions and other events when the authors were busy with interviews. Our love and appreciation go to their spouses, too—Connie Beesley and Paula Breaux King.

Then there are the entertainers and their staffs. Shoji Tabuchi embraced the survivors on several occasions. The Comets, led by Joey Ambrose, evoked happier memories of the 1950s. Allen Edwards allowed the guys to cavort on stage with him—carefree if but for a moment. Jim Stafford reached out to them—and encouraged his audience to offer their appreciation to the ex-POWs. These small acts meant the world to them.

We'd also like to thank Gus and Hannah of 'At Your Service Limousine,' singer Sharon Robinson, and Nancy Smith of the *Branson Daily Independent*.

J.H.Chung, a Korean friend and English speaking tour guide, (Email: anytimeJJ@gmail.com) traveled several hours to take a picture of the memorial near Hadong. He also provided us with some much needed translations of common Korean words.

Many thanks to our eagle-eyed editor Lura Patrick for her work on this piece.

Thanks to Paul and Evelyn Harless for providing a Korean War era jeep for Ed Slater and Sherman Jones to ride in the Branson 2006 Veterans Day Parade—and for the use of Evelyn's marvelous photos of the event.

John R. R. Faulkner spent many hours creating the maps we are using. Everett Avery spent just as many hours taking photos, scanning documents and old pictures, working on the CDs and other assorted jobs. John and Everett kept our everyday lives going while we devoted our hearts and souls to researching and writing this story.

Finally, thanks to Philip O'Brien of the Defense POW/Missing Personnel Office (DPMO) who provided us with major clues to this historical event. He was generous with his time and his ideas. Without his information, this story would not be complete.

"Where have all the soldiers gone . . .

Gone to graveyards every one . . ." — Pete Seeger

Contents

Foreword

Good men served in the Korean War. Many returned to speak of their service and of the deeds of those who had fallen. However, early in the War there are gaps. Men were overrun, men were captured, and men died under circumstances that are still poorly understood, and sometimes, even unimaginable. Take a moment: let us look at just over three hundred men, captured here and there in South Korea during July and August 1950. They move north, at first on foot with wounded in ox carts, and many die along the wayside. Later they board trains and many simply disappear. Bodies are recovered and survivors are found. Some got clear en route, and others escaped from what can only be described as hastily organized murder. Their story has been largely untold. Now it unfolds in more understandable terms.

Pat McGrath Avery and Joyce Faulkner have accomplished a wonderfully humane and a vitally necessary task. They have met, they have befriended, they have gathered, and they have listened. And now a recounting, developed in detail from the very words of those who were there, comes gradually into light. It honors the fallen, and it respects the very important contribution of the survivors. These men, remembering friends and companions, are helping to expand the record of events, and to set it straight. We, at Department of Defense, have often spoken to these men about the immediate facts—but Pat and Joyce have assembled a collective account that tells a larger story in its own right and in its own terms. The personal narratives that they have gathered are also helping us to try to resolve some of these missing-man cases.

Among other missions, the Defense POW/Missing Personnel Office has worked in North Korea, with permission of that government, and hopes to return. We are also following up on investigative leads with respect to Unknown burials at the National Memorial Cemetery of the Pacific in Honolulu, Hawaii. To Pat and Joyce, here's our heartfelt thanks. This is a very big picture, and you have made yourselves a part of it. Your good work speaks for itself, and we will continue to follow up wherever we can. God speed!

Philip O'Brien
Defense POW/Missing Personnel Office
Department of Defense

Introduction

"If the best minds in the world had set out to find us the worst possible location in the world to fight this damnable war, politically and militarily, the unanimous choice would have been Korea." — Dean Acheson, Secretary of State, 1950

This is a story about soldiers—not much more than boys—sent into impossible circumstances more than a half a century ago. Their sacrifices went underreported at the time—except for how they affected strategic military and political issues. Even now, Korean War lore is limited to a long-running, tragicomic television show. The real events were uglier—and more ambiguous.

The survivors are now in their seventies. What happened to them in the summer and fall of 1950 left scars—on their bodies and on their psyches. Born during the Great Depression, they grew up during World War II. People learned about current affairs through newspapers, radios and newsreels. Schooling could be erratic depending upon the needs of the family. Society embraced a world of absolutes—good and evil, black and white, heroes and villains. By definition, they were the 'good guys'—their intentions were noble and their creeds were true. By the end of 1945, American power and prestige seemed endless. Such blessings, they thought, brought global responsibility.

Others saw things differently.

With the end of World War II, Koreans rejoiced. Their long unhappy sojourn under Japanese dominion was over. However, peace continued to elude them as they tried to redefine the core values of their country. World War II allies, mistrusting each other, divided Korea at the 38th parallel.[1]

---

1 An imaginary circle of latitude that is 38 degrees north of the Earth's equatorial plane

Pending the creation of a single government and the subsequent withdrawal of both forces, the Soviet Union occupied the north and the United States the south. Each side fostered their own views on their trustees.

Divided Korean families looked forward to reunification—and in November 1947, the United Nations (UN) passed a resolution calling for the withdrawal of foreign soldiers, free elections and the creation of a UN commission dedicated to the unification of the peninsula. However, the South rejected the proposal and held its own election, establishing an independent Republic of Korea in 1948 with Syngman Rhee[2] as its leader. Later that same year, the Soviet Union sponsored the formation of a Korean government in the north led by Kim Il-Sung.[3]

Both Korean regimes were technically democratic republics—the Democratic People's Republic of North Korea (DPRK) and the Republic of Korea (ROK). Syngman Rhee and Kim Il-Sung each believed that he was the legitimate leader of the whole Korean Peninsula. In the four years and nine months since liberation, it seems unlikely that the citizens of Korea understood or embraced the ideologies of their patrons. That came later. Their issues were local, their animosities regional. The conflict grew out of the structure of Korean society and their own complicated history. Scholars now think that when the North invaded the South, rather than the other way around, it was a matter of timing and resources.

---

2 Syngman Rhee—Controversial American-educated, right-wing, Korean politician. Syngman Rhee remained President throughout the war and for several years thereafter, but corruption and economic stagnation bred discontent. Finally, with ballot box stuffing and other fraudulent election practices in the spring of 1960, demonstrations led to the resignation of the old patriot. He left Korea and died in exile. (*Korea: Its History and Culture*, 1996)

3 Kim Il-Sung—leftist leader of the guerillas in Manchuria during the Japanese occupation of Korea in the 1930s and 40s. (Summers Jr., 1990)

This was not the view of the United States at the time. Most considered socialism a threat to the "American way of life." That the Soviet Union and Red China supported Kim Il-Sung made his Communist government a threat. The bigger picture was even more alarming. In 1950, the "Domino Principle"[4] dominated public opinion. No one wanted to repeat the mistakes that lead to the Second World War. Some historians say that President Harry Truman feared that the next 'domino' would be Japan. It is also clear that by this time, he believed that the US was in competition with the USSR for global domination. Seen through that prism, North Korea's invasion of the South seemed like a provocation on the world stage rather than a simple civil war.

Until June 1950, Truman paid little attention to Korea. "Korea was strategically important enough to preserve for democracy, but not important enough to warrant a major war."[5]

The US population was not interested in Korean politics either. Still weary from the enormous effort of the 1940s, Americans focused on rebuilding their lives. As a result, Allied military presence in the south was minimal on June 25 when Kim Il-Sung crossed the 38th parallel. Believing that the Soviets were behind the invasion, Truman rushed men and equipment to South Korea to hold back the tide until he could gather enough resources to overcome the communist "horde."

The Army that Truman sent to Korea was unprepared for the challenges that it faced. Ammunition was limited. Equipment was aging. The young soldiers were unfamiliar with the terrain and unversed in the native culture and language. They expected the fight to be with a well-defined enemy—as it had been in World War II—clean and morally unambiguous. They came with the best of intentions—to

---

4 Domino Theory—The idea that aggression unchecked would lead to more aggression and that the Communists would take over countries in a chain reaction like a long row of dominoes knocked over by the fall of individual ones in turn. (Summers Jr., 1990)

5 Badsey, Stephen, *Korean War*, pg 13

rescue the South Koreans from communism and to protect American interests.

The situation US soldiers found on arrival was chaotic. They went into battle against a better-armed and numerically superior army—one that had been preparing for war for almost a year. (Mahoney, 2001) The fighting ranged across mountainous areas, creeks and rivers, open farmland, small villages and larger cities.

To American eyes, North and South Koreans were indistinguishable. They looked the same, dressed the same— ate the same unpalatable food. Sharing a common language and a common history, Koreans knew how to scare each other as only countrymen can. To the frustration of Americans seeking absolutes, some invaders put aside their uniforms and blended with locals. Even worse, some South Koreans loathed Syngman Rhee and supported Kim Il-Sung as head of the entire Korean Peninsula. Communist guerillas roamed the area at will. This led to US confusion about enemy and friend. After a few days in country, it was easy to be suspicious of everyone—and to be afraid.

It was confusing to Koreans as well. The first US deployment came from the occupation forces in Japan. Korean antipathy for the Japanese made them wary— especially those coming from the North. They had little experience with Americans. The people in the South, overwhelmed with the frustrations of being in a war zone, focused on trying to get out of the way. While the militaristic DPRK army surged down the peninsula, Syngman Rhee took the opportunity to purge his political enemies. For the ordinary citizen, danger approached in every direction—even from their government.

In the summer of 1950, the first hot battles of the Cold War were intense and bloody. North Korean forces routed, surrounded, killed or captured US troops within days of their arrival. The heroes of our story were among them.

The Sunchon Tunnel Massacre Survivors

Near the Sunchon Tunnel

Dale Blake *
Robert Bomberry*
Myles Cables *
George Davis *
Allen Gifford
Ray Hanchey *
William Henninger
Valdor John
Eugene Jones *
Lloyd Krieder *
John Martin *
Marion Michael *
Joseph Mistretta *
Jose Ortega *
Max Reid *
Raymond Rindels *
Melvin Rookstool *
Harney Rufatto *
Robert Sharpe
Roy Sutterfield *
John Toney *
Sylvester J. Volturo *
James Yeager

Escaped prior to the massacre

Douglas W. Blaylock
Thomas L. Brady
Arlton B. Craig
Robert Morris
Russell Morris
Arlon Mounce
Auvil Parsons
George Snodgrass
Victor Stevens

Near Kujang-dong

Sherman Jones
Ed Slater
Walt Whitcomb

Escaped in Pyongyang

Takeshi Kumugai
William Locke *
Alexander Makarounis *
James Bryant Smith *

* Thought to be deceased as of this writing.

Important Dates

- Bob Sharpe captured July 17—Taejon—Army Medical Corps 19th Regiment, 24th Infantry Division
- Ed Slater captured July 25 (approximately)—21st Regiment, 24th Infantry Division
- Bill Henninger captured July 25—Taejon—34th Regiment, 24th Infantry Division
- Allen Gifford captured July 26—Yongdong—19th Regiment, 24th Infantry Division
- George Snodgrass captured July 26—near Yongdong—1st Cavalry, 7th Regiment
- Major William T. McDaniel captured July 26—Yongdong—Headquarters Company, 34th Regiment, 24th Infantry Division
- Walter Whitcomb captured July 27—Hadong—Company K, 3rd Battalion, 29th Infantry Division
- Jim Yeager captured July 27—Hadong—Company K, 3rd Battalion, 29th Infantry Division
- Gene Putzier captured July 27—Chinju—Company B, 1st Battalion, 29th Infantry Division
- Sherman Jones captured July 28—near Anui—Company B, 1st Battalion, 29th Infantry Division
- Valdor John captured August 5-8—Taejon—Company B 2nd Battalion, 21st Regiment, 24th Infantry Division
- McDaniel's group departs Taejon, September 5, 1950
- POW group arrives in Seoul September 11, 1950
- POWs depart Seoul, September 23, 1950
- POWs arrive in Pyongyang, October 10, 1950
- POW train departs Pyongyang, October 17, 1950
- Sunchon Tunnel Massacre, October 20, 1950
- Kujang-dong Massacre, October 22-27, 1950

One – Sunchon Tunnel
North Korea, October 19, 1950

The train pulled into a tunnel and stopped. Some of the prisoners inside were relieved. The strafing American planes couldn't reach them—and for a few hours, they felt safe. Others were numb. Survival meant another day of suffering. They sat quietly—thinking of food and clean sheets and food and their mothers and home—and food.

Sherman Jones, Walt Whitcomb and Ed Slater were in a boxcar with almost thirty other prisoners. For months, they had been part of a long line of starving scarecrows forced to march north by enemy guards. It was uncomfortable packed together in the train—but at least they didn't have to walk anymore. Disease and abuse had weakened them. They sported wounds received when captured or during 'interrogations'—but they were young and resilient. They knew that the planes meant the Allies were nearby. The guards were nervous. That was encouraging, too. Maybe—just maybe—the end was near.

Walt did not come to Korea hating anyone. He was happy for a change. The military brought discipline and fairness to his life—and oddly enough, peace. He wanted to do a good job—he owed the Army that much. He wasn't in country long before his equanimity vanished. After the North Koreans surrounded his unit, killing or wounding most of his friends and fellow soldiers—and capturing the rest, Walt was scared and angry. Now, after weeks of torment, he despised the guards and was determined to live—to spite them. If he got in a few licks in the meantime—all the better.

Sherman just tried to stay alive. He wanted to go home and see his mother. He wanted to be somewhere warm and safe—somewhere people didn't shoot or torture each other or die of

1

diarrhea or starve to death. Nothing had turned out the way he had planned when he joined the Army in 1949. His eyes were not good enough to fly—and backing over a bank of trashcans stymied his truck-driving ambitions. However, he was happy enough when they said they'd make him an MP and send him to Japan. Who would have thought there would be another war so soon after the last one? Things changed even before he reached Sasebo. Before he knew it, he'd been reassigned and sent to Korea. Sherm was a gregarious boy with a big heart. He made friends easily—and he mourned the loss of each one. In Korea he'd seen a lot of death. Grief and horror had darkened his sunny nature. He fell asleep and awoke hours later. Somewhere someone was shooting. He shivered and prayed that the Allies would find them soon.

Ed was a good-looking, street-wise charmer. He was no stranger to trouble, but being a prisoner of war was trouble he'd never envisioned. Captured, humiliated, starved and terrorized, he used humor to ward off despair. Ed eyed the guards warily. They could be brutal, but they seemed different today—distracted. He hoped that they would feed them soon. The food was bad, but by this point, he ate to stay alive. He closed his eyes as the train started up. He knew that American planes were pressuring the North Koreans. That's why they'd herded the slow-moving prisoners onto the train—to keep the advancing Allied troops from finding them. Ed hoped "those fighter jocks would blow the bastards to smithereens." The only problem with that scenario was that he and the others were in the middle.

As the train left the tunnel, the prisoners saw guards running into the cave and pointing to the sky. A rocket fired from one of the jets hit the train filled with American POWs.

2

Two — Task Force Smith

"We thought the North Koreans would back off once they saw American uniforms." — Phil Day, Task Force Smith

T he Korean War was complicated for everyone involved. Feelings ran high on all sides—and there were many. Anti-communist anxieties ruled politics in the West in general and in the United States in particular. The USSR and the Red Chinese were suspicious of American movements in their backyards—and eager to establish themselves as world powers. Korean hatred and anger for the Japanese after years of occupation simmered. On top of that, North Koreans had centuries of pent-up resentment for their southern countrymen—feeling that they had endured social and political inequities since the Silla Kingdom banded with Tang China to conquer the Northern Goguryeo Kingdom in 668 A.D.

Prior to the outbreak of war, both Koreas engaged in an escalating series of skirmishes. On June 25, 1950, 135,000 North Korean People's Army (NKPA) crossed the 38th parallel near Kaesong. Fueled by the fervor of their regional animosity, they caught the 95,000-strong Republic of Korea Army (ROK) off-guard and routed them. South Korean President Syngman Rhee left the capital and took refuge in Taejon. On June 26, John Muccio, US Ambassador to South Korea, ordered all American Embassy personnel and US dependents evacuated to Japan. (Summers Jr., 1990) Within two days, the NKPA captured Seoul.

The UN demanded that the NKPA return north of the 38th parallel. Lest he be labeled "soft on communism," US President Harry Truman acted quickly and without Congressional approval. He ordered General Douglas MacArthur, Far Eastern Commander in Japan, to go to Korea and evaluate the situation. In the meantime, he offered air and naval support to the ROK along with an artillery battery.[6]

Cautious because of the possible involvement of the USSR, Truman limited American objectives to driving the NKPA back beyond the 38th parallel. He also downplayed the situation—calling it a 'police action' rather than a war.

President Harry Truman *(National Archives)*

Truman's Statement — June 27, 1950

In Korea, the Government forces, which were armed to prevent border raids and to preserve internal security, were attacked by invading forces from North Korea. The Security Council of the United Nations called upon the invading troops to cease hostilities and to withdraw to the 38th parallel. This they have not done, but on the contrary, have pressed the attack. The Security Council called upon all members of the United Nations to render every assistance to the United Nations in the execution of this resolution. In these circumstances, I have ordered United States air and sea forces to give the Korean Government troops cover and support.

The attack upon Korea makes it plain beyond all doubt that Communism has passed beyond the use of subversion to conquer independent nations and will now use armed invasion and war. It has defied the orders of the Security Council of the United Nations issued to preserve international peace and security. In these circumstances, the occupation of Formosa by Communist forces would be a direct threat to the security of the Pacific area and to the United States forces performing their lawful and necessary functions in that area.

---

6 On 29 June, Detachment "X", 507th Anti-aircraft Artillery Battalion, arrived at Suwon and started shooting down enemy planes. (Appleman, 1998) These are the first American ground troops into Korea and theirs are the first shots fired by US Army personnel arriving from Japan. (Evanhoe, *Withdrawl To The Pusan Perimeter: Jun 25 to Aug 3, 1950*, 2002)

At that time, the United States had five hundred advisors in Korea.[7] American combat troops had rotated out of the country a year earlier. Within days of the intrusion, MacArthur visited the site of fighting near the Han River, south of Seoul. Doubtful about the ROK army's fighting ability, he recommended that Truman send two US infantry divisions into Korea. He thought that would be sufficient to put an end to North Korea's aggression.

Truman agreed and on June 30, MacArthur ordered Major General William F. Dean to deploy the 24th Infantry Division to Korea. That night, the 1st Battalion, 21st Infantry Regiment, 24th Division—less A and D companies, flew to Korea. This group, led by Lieutenant Colonel Charles B. Smith, became "Task Force Smith (TFS)." Their goal was to stop the NKPA before they reached Osan, a few miles south of Seoul.

Task Force Smith arriving in Taejon *(National Archives)*

Early in the morning on July 5, Task Force Smith set up an ambush north of Osan. The 52nd Field Artillery guns dug in

7 KMAG—Korea Military Advisory Group

to the rear of them. Colonel Smith expected air support, but bad weather denied him that cover. The defenders had no tanks and little ammunition for the guns and rifles they did possess. The men shivered in the rain, waiting for the war to begin.

A little after seven A.M., a North Korean tank column approached. The 52nd Field Artillery fired at them. The barrage was accurate but ineffective. Taking bazooka rounds, thirty-three Russian-made T-34 tanks rolled past Task Force Smith and continued south toward Osan.

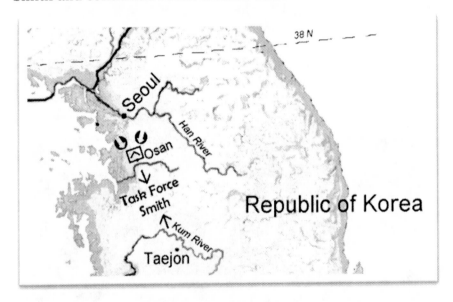

Battle of Osan, North of Taejon

At mid-morning, a column of enemy trucks and infantry, several miles long and led by three more T-34 tanks, approached the TFS position. Task Force Smith mortars and machine guns fired. Trucks blew up throwing NKPA soldiers into the air. However, the undamaged North Korean tanks turned their guns on the American troops who were crouching in ditches and rice paddies. The enemy infantry reorganized—and flanked Task Force Smith on both sides in a maneuver known as a "double envelopment." To make things worse, a huge North Korean reserve waited on the road. The

US soldiers had few options. Colonel Smith gave the order to fall back.

This was the first defeat for American forces in Korea. During the battle and the subsequent retreat, one hundred sixty-five men and officers were lost—killed, wounded or missing. (Appleman, 1998)

John Muccio *(National Archives)*

John Muccio, as Ambassador to Korea, had an integral role in South Korean and UN relations when the North Koreans invaded Korea. He strongly supported Truman saying "On Korea, I was 100 percent with Truman who showed great wisdom and courage."

Muccio described Syngman Rhee as a "very intelligent person, who . . . became the symbol of the struggle against Japan and the struggle for independence. He was known to all Koreans. That was his political strength.

"Rhee was a very determined willful person . . . an isolated man. He had been a guerrilla for forty-five years, a guerrilla and revolutionary leader. By the time he became President after quite an honest election and recognized by thirty odd countries of the Western World, Rhee was too old to appreciate and keep in mind the difference between a revolutionary independence warrior and a head of a duly recognized state."

Oral History Interview with John J. Muccio, Special Representative of the President to Korea, 1948–1949, Ambassador, 1949–1952, recorded in Washington DC, 2-10 and 2-18-1971, Jerry N. Hess and Dec 7, 1973 with Richard D. McKenzie (*Truman Library*)

Three — Ed Slater

3rd Battalion, 21st Infantry Regiment, 24th Division

In 1950, Ed Slater was twenty years old. His family—like many other people living in the Midwest during the Great Depression—was poor. His dad was a plumber but they often relied on welfare in those difficult years.

Ed did not like school. It seemed like a waste of time when his family's basic needs were so pressing. He worked a series of odd jobs in his hometown of Quincy, Illinois, scrapping junk, selling bottles, setting pins at the bowling alley—anything to make extra money.

Everyone deals with hard times differently. Ed had a sharp wit and a quick tongue. In stressful situations, he vented his frustration with caustic comments that made people around him laugh—and defused tension. An intelligent and rambunctious teenager, he got into trouble with the police a few times. In the late 1940s, people believed that the Army was a viable option to 'straighten out' problem kids.

Ed: "When I was seventeen, I was a little hoodlum. The police gave me a choice—service or reform school. I asked, 'What branch do you want me to go to?'"

In 1948, his father signed for him and Ed headed for Fort Ord, California, for basic training.

Ed's first assignment was Haeundae, South Korea, guarding an ammunition dump. After a few months, he transferred to an infantry unit on the 38th parallel.

Ed: "I was there until they took the troops out of Korea—except for a short stint in Japan. When I was in Seoul, I guarded big warehouses. This guy I worked with had dogs—and he wanted me to take one of them. I said, 'No,' because I'm afraid of dogs. Anyway, this dog had more medals than anyone I knew. So I was busy guarding the dump and talking about dogs when this idiot came down the other way—and someone said, 'Quick, draw!' and this guy drew a forty-five and shot me through the gut—so I went to Japan to recover."

When Syngman Rhee became President of South Korea, the military sent him to another infantry unit at Camp Wood in Japan.

Ed Slater — 1950

When fighting broke out in Korea, Ed was married and a father. Assigned to the 3rd Battalion, 21st Infantry Regiment, he went back to Korea with the rest of the 24th Division the day after Task Force Smith. Raucous crowds cheered them as they climbed aboard a train to Taejon, a mid-sized city seventy-five miles south of Seoul. From there, trucks carried them north to support Task Force Smith.

Four — Bill Henninger
34th Infantry Regiment, 24th Division

Bill Henninger was born in St. Paul, Minnesota, on January 20, 1924. He was the oldest of three children.

Bill: "My family moved to Florida where my dad worked as a mailman. Then, in 1930, my mother died and we moved back to Minnesota."

Bill's dad got a job driving a truck. His grandparents helped raise him, his sister, and brother.

When Bill graduated from high school in 1942, war consumed most of the world. Bill and a buddy figured that Uncle Sam would soon draft them. Like many young men, they had things they wanted to do before becoming soldiers—so they took off hitchhiking. Their adventure didn't last long. They made it to Oklahoma before a letter from home informed them that the Selective Service was looking for them.

Bill: "We hadn't registered before we left home."

The boys headed back to Minnesota. However, it wasn't until 1943 that Bill received his draft notice.

Bill: "I had to report for duty on my sister's birthday."

After basic training, Bill's first assignment was an engineering unit. He became the company bugler—but that duty was short-lived. He went to England in support of D-Day troops. As a replacement soldier, he wasn't part of that fight, but he did help with field artillery. Throughout the attack, he never fired a weapon.

Then, about a week before Christmas, he joined the 95th Division—and on New Year's Day, he participated in the fight for Saarlautern in Germany.

After the war, Bill left the Army, got married and had a son—but he couldn't find a decent job. Civilian life was complicated and he yearned for the simplicity of a soldier's life.

Bill: "I had problems getting up in the mornings and adjusting to life in general. After three years, I re-enlisted and went to West Point as a mechanic in the motor pool. However, I goofed up and the Army sent me overseas in April of 1949, assigned to the 24th Division."

Bill was in Sasebo, Japan, with the 34th Regiment, enjoying occupation duty when his life changed again. In response to the North Korean attack, the 34th Regiment rushed to Korea. Landing in Pusan on July 2, Bill headed north to Taejon. Within three days, the 34th engaged the enemy in support of Task Force Smith's withdrawal from Osan.

Five — Falling Back

"Once I was a soldier and I fought on foreign lands for you." — Tim Buckley

Task Force Smith (TFS) was on the road to Osan when Major William T. McDaniel and Bill Henninger arrived in Taejon with the 34th Infantry Regiment. They moved north to set up defenses at Pyongtaek and Ansong, ten miles south of TFS's temporary stand. Their job was to block two roads heading south.

Outgunned and outnumbered, they, too, went into battle without reserves or support. After Task Force Smith's disastrous confrontation with the NKPA, General Dean re-evaluated his approach. He ordered the 1st Battalion, 34th Regiment to hold only until the enemy threatened to envelop them—and to use delaying tactics as they fell back.

At dawn on July 6, soldiers from the 1st Battalion, 34th saw thirteen T-34 tanks headed their way through the rain and fog. While they fired their mortars at the tanks, North Korean infantry began flanking them.

The 1st Battalion's response to the NPKA pressure was inconsistent. One company fell back, leaving their weapons and radios behind. Their more determined comrades threw what they had at the enemy, but the situation made delaying tactics difficult to implement. The American line drifted south to Chonan. To the east, the 3rd Battalion was forced back, too.

On July 7, the remainder of the 21st Infantry Regiment arrived in Taejon. They continued on to Chochiwon to support the 34th. Ed Slater's unit, the 3rd Battalion, 21st Regiment, blocked the highway six miles northwest of Chochiwon while A and D Companies of the 1st Battalion, 21st Infantry moved south on the Chonan–Chochiwon road and took up defensive positions near the town of Chonui.

At daybreak on July 8, North Korean tanks and infantry units entered Chonan from the east. The T-34s roamed the town destroying any US positions they found. Communist infantry soldiers moved south to block an American retreat. By afternoon, Chonan was in enemy hands. Only one hundred and seventy-five men and officers from the 3rd Battalion, 34th, escaped from the town.

When notified of the loss of Chonan, General Dean ordered what was left of the 34th Infantry Regiment to fight a delaying action as it moved down the road leading to the Kum River. The 21st Regiment was to contain the enemy north of Chochiwon for at least four days. At the same time, the 3rd Engineer Combat Battalion set up roadblocks along the 34th Infantry's withdrawal route at Kongju, and prepared all the bridges over the Kum River for demolition.

On July 9, A and D Companies, 1st Battalion, 21st Infantry, were on a low ridge southeast of Chonui. The 3rd Battalion, 21st Infantry set up a mile to the south. In mid-afternoon, eleven T-34s, escorted by infantry, appeared on the road north of Chonui. American air strikes, mortars and artillery destroyed five of the eleven tanks and pushed back the North Korean infantry.

The next morning, NKPA forces circled the US held hill, and attacked the mortars, overrunning them at seven A.M. About the same time, North Korean tanks came out of Chonui, passed through American lines and headed toward Chochiwon. It was so foggy that the defenders heard the tanks, but could not see them.

When the fog lifted, North Korean infantry moved out of Chonui and attacked the 1st Battalion, 21st Regiment on the hill. The young American soldiers beat them off twice, but a combination of enemy action and friendly fire from US artillery forced them to withdraw to Chochiwon.

Later that afternoon, the 3rd Battalion, 21st Infantry, retook former 1st Battalion positions. They found six US soldiers lying in a ditch, hands tied behind their backs, shot in the head. The 3rd Battalion stayed in former 1st Battalion positions until midnight and then withdrew to a point six miles north of Chochiwon.

Murdered US soldier (*National Archives*)

On July 11, Task Force Smith's B and C companies rejoined the 1st Battalion at Chochiwon. Reinforced, the 1st Battalion then set up two miles north of the town. The 21st's 3rd Battalion was already engaged up ahead. Using the now familiar double-envelopment tactic, NKPA troops surrounded the 3rd Battalion and overran them.

Ed Slater: "At the end, fighting was hand-to-hand. Every-one scattered, trying to cross the river behind us. The enemy shot people in the water or captured them as they came up on the other side."

Horrified, Ed found a way behind the North Korean attackers. After crossing a couple of hills, he found a 2nd Lieutenant and several soldiers including a sergeant with a wounded ankle in a riverbed. Searching for safety together, they came upon an enemy machine gun nest on the other side of the river.

Ed: "As we approached the machine gun nest, all hell broke loose. I turned and ran up the hill in front of the gun on the right. There was another GI running with me, along with the wounded sergeant . . . I kept running and never saw the sergeant again. The other kid was still with me. We ran over a couple of large hills before we stopped. We saw Koreans at the bottom of the hill pointing up in our direction and yelling. The kid got excited and pulled a hand grenade from his belt. He started crying and said he was going to pull the pin on that thing because he wasn't going to let them get him. I told him if he was going to pull the pin to wait until I got out of there. I crawled to the top of the hill and ran down the other side. A short time later, I heard a large explosion, which I'm sure, was the other GI."

Only three hundred twenty-two out of six hundred sixty-seven men found their way back to their units. Ed Slater was not one of them. He disappeared into the unfamiliar Korean countryside.

Six — Robert L. Sharpe

US Army Medical Company, 2nd Battalion, 19th Regiment, 24th Infantry Division

Bob Sharpe was a soft-spoken southern boy. His patriotism was both idealistic and intellectual. He enlisted in the Army in July 1949—right after his high school graduation. Basic training was at Ft. Jackson, South Carolina. Practical by nature, he endured the intense regimen—accepting discipline as a core value for a soldier.

Bob: "Our drill sergeant, appropriately named Roar, told us that the water in the canteens belonged to him and we would drink when he told us. Once I had to go with an empty canteen for two weeks."

After basic, Bob shipped to Japan for occupation duty. Army leadership told the young soldiers to treat the Japanese as they would like to be treated. That was easy for the tenderhearted young soldier—however, there were situational opportunities that were hard to ignore.

Bob: "One time, I traded a bar of soap for a weekend at a hotel. We bought cigarettes for eighty cents a carton."

When the North Koreans invaded South Korea on June 25, Bob's unit was on maneuvers. When they returned to camp, he transferred to the 19th Regiment, 24th Division as a medic. They landed in Pusan on July 4 and moved north to blunt the advancing Communist army.

Bob: "As we understood it, at first, the South Korean Army was to do the fighting and we were to do the mopping up behind." (R. L. Sharpe, 1951)

Seven — The Kum River

"It looks like World War III is here—I hope not—but we must meet what-ever comes—and we will." — Harry Truman, President of United States (1945–1953)

To the west on the Chonan–Taejon highway, the 1st Battalion, 34th, fought a series of delaying actions as it withdrew, crossing to the south bank of the Kum River, which became the new defensive line.

Kum River protecting Taejon

There were two roads the NKPA could take from the river to reach Taejon. General Dean faced a dilemma. The 34th had suffered two weeks of combat disasters—and the 19th, led by Colonel Guy S. Meloy, Jr., was untried. On the other hand, the few men at his disposal now had bigger guns and more ammo, which increased their effectiveness. Circumstances didn't offer Dean many options. He split his forces to cover both routes. However, in the end, it didn't make much difference. The North Koreans came at them with fifty tanks and roughly twelve thousand men.

Bob: "As a medical corpsman, I arrived in Korea with little equipment, and, of course, I was unarmed. But we heard of the

17

massacre of medics . . . so before we went into action, we were issued an M-1 rifle and plenty of medical supplies." (R. L. Sharpe, 1951)

On July 14, the North Koreans overran the 34th Regiment again. That left the 19th Regiment on the right flank, covering thirty miles of river with two battalions. The attack came early in the morning of July 16. T-34 tanks covered an infantry assault across the Kum River. By daybreak, over a thousand North Koreans were on the south bank launching their standard double-envelopment. By mid-morning, they had established a roadblock on the Taepyong-ni–Taejon road. Over the next several hours, 19th Infantry positions were overrun and American troops began retreating, leaving their dead and wounded behind.

Bob: "As an aid man, I stayed red all the time from the heavy casualties. The Army didn't have helicopters at that time. All I could do was stop the bleeding, bandage wounds and give morphine shots."

One man that Bob attended had a bad chest wound. The young soldier thrashed around crying. Bob opened his clothes and found a picture of a young woman.

Bob: "She was a pretty girl and the bullet that had killed him went right through her chest too. I took the picture, rolled it up and put it in my kit. I was going to find her if I got back—to tell her about him . . . ." (R. L. Sharpe, 1951)

On July 17, the enemy surrounded Bob's unit. The red cross on his helmet made him a target. The enemy shot at medics to keep them from returning the wounded to the battlefield. It offended Bob's sense of morality—and added to his horror—as the North Koreans breached the perimeter and advanced toward him. There were so many wounded men and there was only so much that he could do. He worked until the last possible moment.

Bob: "A bullet struck my helmet and knocked me unconscious. When I woke up, I saw North Korean soldiers plunging bayonets into bodies. I prayed and played dead."

Bob was covered with blood.

Bob: "My arms were soaked to the elbows. I had bent my head to listen for heartbeats in the wounded men until my hair was matted with blood and it was dried on my face." (R. L. Sharpe, 1951)

The first North Korean soldiers to approach Bob must have thought he was dead. One sat him up and unlaced his belt. Another took his boots. Bob remained unresponsive and the enemy moved on.

Bob: "It was horrible lying there in the mud with my buddies all dead or dying around me. I buried my face in the mud and lay there for a couple hours until the sun went down."

Sometime in the night, Bob crawled over to check on the others. Three were alive. They drank from a scummy pond and retreated into the hills. They needed to move toward American lines but the other men wouldn't leave their hiding places. On the fourth day, Bob was so hungry that he left the others and walked down a road until he found a farmer working in a rice paddy.

Bob: "He didn't want to have anything to do with me . . . finally he agreed to give me something to eat and took me to his little shanty on the mountain side."

The farmer and his wife gave Bob some kind of mush. He gobbled it down. At first he felt fine—full. Then he got sick. His benefactors were nervous and urged him to leave. Not wanting to get these people in trouble, Bob headed back for the mountain where the others were hiding.

He didn't get very far. A bunch of North Koreans dressed as civilians rushed him, screaming. They were armed with grenades and rifles with bayonets. Bob expected them to kill him but the fatal blow never came. Someone slapped him across the face and asked him if he understood Japanese. When he answered in the affirmative, the man hit him again and began asking questions.

Bob: "They cuffed me around—but they didn't hurt me much."

They stripped him—taking his watch, wallet and the picture of the pretty young girl with a bullet hole through it.

Bob: "I slipped most of the money into my mouth. I'm glad I did because later on I was able to buy a cigarette butt for ten dollars. Another fellow paid two hundred dollars for a half slice of bread."

Bob became a prisoner. He was one of the six hundred fifty men of the 19th Regiment lost defending the Kum River.

Eight — Lost

"Lost in the night all alone
With nowhere to hide, crying inside
A wild heart looking for home." — John Denver

E d Slater was lost. He met a young boy, probably seven or so, on a path in the mountains.

Ed: "I figured I had the choice of killing him so he couldn't yell out—or running like hell to save myself. I chose to run."

Days passed. Ed was on the move—trying to avoid the enemy while searching for the American lines. He lost his canteen. It was July and the temperature reached the nineties. Thirsty, he looked for running water—or wells. There were Koreans all around him—but he wasn't sure who was friendly or hostile. To avoid detection, he slid on his butt down steep gravel slopes. Finally, at the foot of a mountain, he found a cave with water.

Ed: "I ran and fell in it on my belly with my head in the water. As I raised up to get a breath, I saw huge rats staring at me . . . I jumped up, pushed my helmet down into the water so I could take some with me—and ran as fast as I could back up the mountain. The water didn't last too long since I slipped and fell a couple of times. I was too tired to run and too scared to sit still."

He found another cave. Crawling inside, he curled up and fell asleep. He woke to the sound of footsteps on gravel. Afraid that the enemy might have discovered him, Ed was surprised to see a little girl about six years old, staring at him. He offered her a harmonica that he had in his pocket. She took it. He tried to communicate his need for food and water. She ran away and came back with an old man who gestured for Ed to follow him.

They went to the old man's home. After an argument with his wife (probably about the advisability of having an American soldier in their house), they fed him and gave him a place to sleep.

Before daylight, Ed woke to people screaming for him to get out. He knew the North Koreans would shoot the family if they found him there, so he headed down the mountain with a little pack of food they gave him.

That night there was a rainstorm. Ed sat under a small bush, listening to the thunder and watching the lightning.

Ed: "The next morning, the sun came up real hot and before I knew it, I was licking the leaves on the bushes and trees to get water."

That afternoon, Ed sat in the shade at the edge of a rice paddy. Suddenly, he heard screaming in a nearby village. Two soldiers ran across the field toward him. At first, he thought they were South Korean and he relaxed. Then one of them fired a rifle over Ed's head and told him to raise his hands.

Fear tightened Ed's throat and thumped in his ears.

He stood and lifted his arms.

Ed: "The two guards were a hell of a lot more afraid of me than I was of them. The little one wasn't as tall as his rifle."

They prodded him with their bayonets and, sensing that their fear made them more dangerous rather than less, he went with them.

As they walked along a ridge, about twenty feet above the rice patties, they reached a level spot where a dark-skinned man was tied to a tree with his arms behind his back. He had nothing on but his shorts and was bleeding from puncture wounds all over his body.

Ed: "I panicked and threw my arm to the left, knocked the little guy down and took off running. As I ran, I looked back and saw the other guard running the other way. I wished I had the carbine I'd lost in the river. I ran as fast as I could right off a fifteen or twenty-foot ridge. I dropped into a rice paddy at the bottom."

An American plane fired at the hill Ed had just left.

Ed: "I think the guards saw the jet before I did. The pilot was coming in low. It seemed like he was coming right at me when he opened his guns. I wanted to point to where I thought they were, but I was afraid he would mistake me for one of them."

The pilot came around again and fired at another hill. That's when Ed took off again. He didn't look back but he hoped that those rounds got the two men that had captured him. He managed to get back to the mountains before dark.

It had been a close call—too close.

Ed: "I thought about that man tied to the tree and could only hope that he was dead or had died fast. He must have suffered a lot. Over the years, I've seen that man a thousand times in my mind. I still see him in my dreams—and in my thoughts."

Nine — Valdor John

Company B, 2nd Battalion, 21st Infantry Regiment, 24th Division

Valdor John is an Oneida Native American. He was born in 1931 in Oneida, Wisconsin—not too far from Green Bay. His family lived there until his father came home from World War II. Then they moved to Milwaukee.

Valdor John — 1948

In 1948 Valdor left school and volunteered for the Army. He was the only male child in his family and his father wasn't happy with that decision. After induction at Ft. Sheridan, Illinois, the Army sent him to Ft. Knox, Kentucky. Being a soldier seemed like a great adventure. Valdor looked forward to seeing new places—learning new things. He even enjoyed basic training.

Valdor: "I loved running up and down hills—and crawling in the mud. It made me feel like a grown man."

Valdor shipped to Japan, but had to return home because of his age. Eventually, he received a release and went back to Japan. At first, he worked with the Graves Registration recovery team, retrieving bodies from WWII. However, Valdor dreamed of being a professional soldier. To him, that meant the infantry. When he got the chance, he transferred to the 11th Airborne.

When the Korean troubles surfaced, Valdor knew little about what was going on—but he was willing to do his duty like everyone else.

Valdor: "In 1950, they told us that we were going to Korea. I didn't even know where that was. We flew there on what we thought was a thirty-day assignment. We set up camp, moved and set up camp again. We finally joined an infantry outfit in the hills—the 2nd Battalion, 21st Regiment. A couple of days later, North Koreans surrounded us. They were like ants coming down the hills on all sides. There were only about two hundred of us. We tried to fall back but they surrounded us again."

Ten — The Battle for Taejon

"A sour little war." — Averill Harriman, Secretary of Commerce 1946–48

Reinforcements were on the way. General Walton Walker moved the Eighth Army headquarters to Taegu southwest of Taejon. Despite heavy American losses up to this point, General Walker intended to stop the Communist invasion somewhere on the road between Taejon and Taegu. The 1st Cavalry, 25th and 7th Divisions were coming from Japan. However, it took time to get soldiers and equipment in position once they arrived. On July 16, General Walker instructed General Dean to hold Taejon for two days until the 1st Cavalry could relieve them.

Machine gun position near Taejon — July 1950 *(National Archives)*

It was a tall order. General Dean had only remnants of three battle-weary regiments. After Osan and Chonui, the 21st Infantry could barely man a single battalion. After weeks of reverses, the remaining men of the 34th Infantry were exhausted and demoralized. The fight at the Kum River had decimated the 19th Infantry.

In 1950, Taejon had a population of about 130,000 and was the second largest city in South Korea. One hundred miles below Seoul and one hundred and thirty miles northwest of Pusan, the Kum River formed a semicircle around the north side of Taejon. General Dean placed the 24th Division in a defensive arc—the 34th Infantry on the left, the 19th Infantry on the right and the 21st Infantry in reserve. By positioning elements of the 34th at Kongju, twenty miles northwest of Taejon, Dean hoped to slow the North Koreans as they crossed the Kum River and pushed on toward Taejon. Since the division had about 4,000 men, he understood that the 24th could not stop two enemy divisions.

During an intense two-day period, the NKPA penetrated the 34th and 19th Regiments' positions on the south side of the Kum River. Hoping to give General Walker more time to beef up the American lines near Taegu, Dean

General Walton H. Walker

Commanding General of the 8th Army, he was born in 1889 and graduated from West Point in 1912. He served in Vera Cruz Expedition in 1914, on Mexican border patrol, WWI, and WWII before leading his troops in Korea in 1950.

During WWII, he took part in the Normandy Invasion, the capture of Metz and the liberation of Buchenwald. Once in Europe, Walker was assigned to Patton's Third Army, where he established his reputation as a "Bulldog." In 1945, he was promoted to Lieutenant General. He was a tough commander, not given to sentiment and was not popular with his troops.

In Korea, he commanded the 8th Army. His defense of the Naktong Line in Korea is regarded as a military classic.

On December 23, 1950, he was killed in a jeep wreck. He is buried in Arlington Cemetery.

General Walker was awarded the Distinguished Service Cross with Oak Leaf Cluster, the Distinguished Service Medal with Oak Leaf Cluster, the Silver Star with 2 Oak Leaf Clusters, the Legion of Merit, the Bronze Star and the Commendation Ribbon.

Sources:
www.arlingtoncemetery.net/whwalker.htm, The Center for Military History, United States Army and *Patton's Bulldog: The Life and Service of General Walton H. Walker* by Wilson A. Heefner.

pulled his regiments into a tighter defensive perimeter.

Valdor John: "Our officers had told us before we got to Taejon that we were going to stay there and fight until the last man. We knew that we weren't going anywhere because we were already surrounded." (Carlson, 2002)

The North Koreans launched their attack on July 19. The 24th Division had just received a new weapon—the 3.5-inch rocket launcher. The hand-carried launcher fired a two-foot-long, eight-and-a-half pound rocket with a shaped charge designed to burn through any tank. US soldiers destroyed ten enemy tanks in Taejon on July 20, eight of them with their new launchers.

Valdor: "We took quite a pounding for about five days. By then, the North Koreans had just about leveled Taejon, and we didn't have that many people left." (Carlson, 2002)

At this time, Major William T. McDaniel was engaged in an action that earned him a Silver Star (See sidebar).

It was to no avail. The enemy overran Taejon within a day.

Bill Henninger: "During the battle, I got shrapnel in my arm. I used the tobacco from cigarettes to make a poultice and then pulled out six pieces of metal."

Valdor: "I awakened to the sound of a big old tank driving right by me. It made it to the aid station, out of gas. The driver told us a lot of Russian tanks were coming, and our tanks were overwhelmed."

Taejon 1950 *(National Archives)*

General Dean gave the retreat order and led a group of American defenders south from Taejon in a motor column. Along the way, he picked up seven walking wounded and loaded them into his jeep. The General then climbed aboard the prime mover of a howitzer.

Bill: "I was on point with a guy from Baltimore. When we came back, our unit had pulled out in retreat."

Valdor: "We tried to break out, but it didn't do any good. They hit us on a road leading out of Taejon." (Carlson, 2002)

Major General William F. Dean
(National Archives)

Born on August 1, 1899, in Carlyle, Illinois, Dean graduated from the University of California at Berkeley in 1922. Commissioned as a Second Lieutenant in the California National Guard in 1921, he was tendered a Regular Army commission on October 18, 1923. Promoted to Brigadier General in 1942 and then to Major General in 1943, Dean served first as assistant division commander and later as division commander of the 44th Infantry Division.

In 1944 while serving in southern Germany and Austria, his troops captured 30,000 prisoners and helped force the surrender of the German 19th Army. He won the Distinguished Service Cross for bravery.

In October 1947, he became the military governor of South Korea. He took command of the Seventh Infantry Division in 1948 and moved it from Korea to Japan. After serving as Eighth U.S. Army chief of staff, he took command of the 24th Infantry Division, then headquartered at Kokura on the southern Japanese island of Kyushu.

When the Korean War began in June 1950, the 24th Infantry Division was the first American ground combat unit to be committed. General Dean arrived in Korea on July 3, 1950. He established his headquarters at Taejon.

At an enemy roadblock, the NKPA wounded Dean's aide and his interpreter. The convoy kept moving until a stalled truck stopped it permanently. Dean ordered the vehicles abandoned—and led the men on foot into a bean patch.

That night, as the men worked their way south into the mountains, Dean dropped behind to get water for a wounded man. His aide, Lieutenant Arthur Clarke, waited. When the General didn't return, Clarke continued on—reaching American lines three days later. Others were not so lucky.

Valdor: "I was on a truck when they shot the driver. The truck crashed. The driver fell out and a jeep ran over his legs. He crawled into a rice paddy. The North Koreans found him and killed him. I lay there until it was dark."

The enemy went around with lanterns killing any one they found. Hit in the hip, Valdor used a stick to help him get to his feet. Hoping that no one would see him, he hobbled away from the area. Along the way, he met another soldier by the name of George who had a wound on his foot.

Valdor: "I saw General Dean and four others running, but we couldn't keep up."

Valdor and George found a little hamlet up in the hills. They approached someone to ask for food and water. The villagers went to get it for them but North Korean soldiers arrived and captured them.

Valdor: "An enemy soldier, who spoke English, told us that communism was good. We scoffed. He got mad and pulled back the bolt on his carbine—but he never shot us."

Bill Henninger walked across a rice paddy and hid behind bushes trying to figure out where he was. He walked to a river and crossed it. On the other side, he met a South Korean who told him that he was going the wrong way. He put a rag on his head to look Korean and headed down some railroad tracks with the man.

His orders were to fight a delaying action against the advancing North Korean People's Army. Although he planned to withdraw from Taejon, he was asked by General Walton H. Walker to hold that city until July 20, 1950, in order to buy time necessary for deploying other American units from Japan. His regiments had been decimated in earlier fighting. Dean personally led tank killer teams, armed with the newly arrived 3.5-inch rocket launchers, to destroy the attacking North Korean T-34 tanks. He gained acclaim by such exploits as attacking and destroying an enemy tank armed with only a hand grenade and handgun.

On July 20, General Dean became separated from his men. He hid alone in the woods around the countryside during the day and traveled at night for over a month. On August 25, 1950 after a hand-to-hand struggle with fifteen North Koreans, he was captured. He remained a POW with the North Koreans until his release on September 4, 1953. He was the highest ranking prisoner in the war.

In 1951 Congress voted General Dean the Medal of Honor for his actions during the defense of Taejon.

www.militarymuseum.org/DeanCMH.html

A couple of civilian guerillas stepped out from some bushes about five miles out of Taejon. Bill's companion told him to run. Bill froze. The guerillas shot the South Korean as he tried to get away.

That night the guerillas marched Bill back to Taejon.

On July 22, the 8th Cavalry replaced the 21st Infantry Division at Yongdong. The 1st Cavalry took responsibility for defending the Taejon–Taegu corridor. In the seventeen days since the 'ambush' at Osan, the NKPA had pushed the 24th back over one hundred miles. Thirty-six hundred US soldiers were dead, wounded or missing in action.

Eleven — Allen Gifford

Medical, Company H, 19th Regiment, 24th Division

Allen Gifford was born in Pemberton, New Jersey, on January 13, 1930. He grew up with four brothers and a sister.

Allen: "Although it was during the Depression and times were tough, I had a good home. My parents always took care of us. My Dad was a forest cutter—he cut trees down for around seven dollars a week."

By the time Allen was fourteen or fifteen, he'd worked the berry farms in the area. German WWII prisoners held at Ft. Dix labored alongside the local farmers. As Allen learned about the war, he wanted to join the service. When he was sixteen, his older brother enlisted.

Allen Gifford -- 1950

Allen never finished school. After eighth grade, he felt he needed to get a job to help support the family. In July 1948, he enlisted in the Army. By this time, trouble was brewing with Russia. After taking basic training at Ft. Dix, he could choose four years in Germany or three years in Japan. He chose Japan. At the time, he didn't know war was brewing in Korea.

He boarded a train in Trenton, New Jersey.

Allen: "I remember boarding in my uniform, finding a seat and as the train moved away, taking a pillow, burying my face and crying.

33

I was a boy leaving home far behind. An older man asked me "Soldier, what's wrong?" I told him I'd never been this far from home. He comforted me and told me I was doing the right thing."

The Army sent Allen to Seattle for three months. He worked in a chicken factory while waiting for the next leg of his journey. Shortly after his arrival in Yokohama, Japan, he went to Camp King, which had been a Japanese Army barracks during World War II. It was only twelve miles from Tokyo.

Allen was first assigned to the 1st Cavalry, 8th Regiment. He joined the bugle corps. After about six months, he transferred to Beppu on the island of Kyushu. He reported to Able Company and after screening, chose to work in the mountains with the 6th Battalion medical corps. There, he received training in first aid and ambulance driving.

Allen: "I drove from Beppu to Kokora, where the 118th Hospital was stationed and to Fukoka, to the 128th hospital. I gathered water and blood samples—and took them back for testing."

When war broke out in Korea, Allen transferred to the 19th Regiment of the 24th Division—and on July 4, he shipped to Pusan.

Allen: "We were kids landing there. The sounds of shooting and smell of smoke scared us all. I loved the service but never expected to be in a war. I traveled by truck to Taejon. I joined the front line and we were successfully pushing back the North Koreans. For two or three days, we kept pushing them."

The tide turned and Allen's Regiment fell back to Taejon. They became part of General Dean's effort to hold the city until General Walker could set up defensive lines on the road between Taejon and Taegu.

The NKPA surrounded the city, blocking escape routes. In Taejon, the North Koreans invaded buildings and climbed

34

into towers where they could shoot down on the GIs[8]. At one point, they shot at an ammo truck and hit an American soldier.

Allen: "I jumped up on it to give first aid. Major McDaniel ordered me down. He said if the truck was hit, it would explode and I'd be dead. I dragged the guy off the truck. I don't remember whether or not the truck was ever hit."

Everyone scattered. Allen went around a hill and up the other side to see what was going on. He saw a soldier crying for help. He tried to reach him with his hand, but couldn't.

Allen: "I took my belt off and was able to save him. I put him on my back and ran down the hill. For this, I received a Silver Star."

Allen took off his helmet and dove under some brush. A North Korean soldier came right at him, but someone called to him in Korean and he left. Allen knew that he had to get away and started moving. He ran into Corporal Stevens. They looked around and found Major McDaniel. He asked Allen, "Aren't you the one up on the truck?"

When Allen told him that he was, Major McDaniel said he was in the wrong place on that truck.

Allen: "We understood each other and became buddies."

They spent several days up in the hills. They drank rice paddy water, rested during the day and moved at night.

---

8 GI originally stood for "general issue," it became the nickname for American foot soldiers during World War II.

Twelve — Ed Slater's Capture

"Fear of monsters attracts monsters." — Unknown

Ed Slater: "It was stupid to travel during the daytime, but the night in Korea is so black you can't see anything. I knew I was headed south and that's where I wanted to go. I finally found a place where I could rest. I thought I was safe."

When Ed awoke the morning after seeing the black man tied to the tree, he was famished and dehydrated. An American plane approached. Ed jumped up and waved his arms trying to attract the pilot's attention. The airplane vanished over the horizon. As the sound faded, Ed sat down.

Ed: "The bad lonesome feeling I got as the plane flew out of sight—made me cry again. I decided that I was going to a village that night to get something to eat. I spent most of the day feeling sorry for myself, wondering how many days I had been running and how far I had to run. I wondered how much longer I could keep this up."

That evening, he slipped into a village to forage. He knew there were enemy troops in town. It was dark. He crawled up to an extra-large house. There was activity inside. He could smell food and see the shadows through the rice paper doors. Someone set bowls of food on the floor close to the door. He figured that he would slide that door open a little, grab a bowl and go.

He took a breath and slid open the door.

A North Korean soldier stared back at him.

Ed screamed and everyone in the house panicked, falling over each other to reach their guns.

He slammed the door shut and ran back up the hill. Enemy gunfire followed him, but he got away clean.

Several days later, hunger drove him back. He entered a house—frightening an old man and woman. He felt bad about scaring them, but he asked for something to eat anyway. Again, North Korean soldiers chased him out of the village.

Ed: "As I sat in the hills that night, I wondered if this would ever end. I thought about the soldiers chasing me and wondered if they were the same ones that had been following me all this time."

The next morning marked eleven days that Ed had been alone on the mountain. His face was sunburned. His throat was raw and his stomach ached. He had to do something.

Ed: "I slid down the hill, out from under the brush I was hiding in. I planned on getting something to eat and drink, no matter what."

Once again, Ed entered a house and scared the occupants. However, this time the couple whose home he invaded offered him a large bowl of rice and a can of water. A hot sauce covered the rice—burning Ed's tender mouth and raw digestive system—but he ate all he could.

Two men came in, sat down and stared at him while he ate.

Ed: "I wondered why they weren't out there doing their own fighting—and why I wasn't at home, like I should be."

Spooked, Ed finished eating, stood up and said, "Now I go." Before he could move, the two men grabbed his arms.

Ed: "I heard rifle bolts click all the way around the wall."

Soldiers came over the wall that encircled the house, threw open the gate and aimed their guns at Ed's head.

Ed: "I was almost relieved that I didn't have to run anymore."

A soldier hit Ed across the back and knocked him to his knees. He fell on his face. His tormentors picked him up and set him on the porch again.

Ed: "They questioned me and told me to eat more rice. I said I couldn't. They stuffed a fist full into my mouth and aimed a gun at my head. I tried to eat, but I just couldn't do it. They made motions like those that they were going to fatten me up and cut my throat. One of them held my head back while two others crammed rice in my mouth. They laughed all the while they were doing this. I vomited all over one of them. He hit me in the face with his fist. I saw stars and vomited again."

They grabbed Ed by the collar and dragged him through a gate out into the open.

Ed: "They tied my hands behind my back and this time I thought I had had it because I had seen some of the guys with their hands tied behind their back and shot in the head."

The NKPA soldiers took turns hitting and kicking Ed. They even stomped on his feet. Another soldier came through the gate. He must have been an officer because the others stopped beating Ed and stood at attention.

The leader walked up and said to Ed, "Where is your radio, where is your radio?"

Ed: "It seemed like that was all he could say. Every time I shrugged my shoulders or said something, he hit me across the back with a club. He asked my rank. I told him I was a private and he hit me again. They pulled my whiskers and said I must be an officer if I had a beard. I must have blacked out after a while because I woke up laying face down in a yard with a grave dug next to me."

A low-level officer interrogated Ed in English. "Where did you leave your radio? Why did MacArthur send you here? Are the Japanese coming over here?"

Ed did not have a radio and he had no idea whether the Japanese were returning to Korea any time soon. When Ed could not provide the North Korean soldiers with the information they required, they positioned him at one end of the grave and raised their rifles.

A moment ticked past—and another.

Ed squirmed.

Finally, a guard struck him and he fell into the hole.

Ed: "I fell on my right shoulder and thought I crushed it. As I moved, they laughed and started shooting around the top of the grave."

Trembling, Ed opened his eyes.

The firing squad was a ruse meant to torment rather than kill. After they'd had their fun, the soldiers lifted Ed out of the hole, tied his hands behind his back and put a stick through his arms.

Ed: "We went to a big shrine or house. I stood at the bottom of a stairway. Two guards stood at attention beside me. A high-ranking officer came out and looked at me for a long time. My left eye was swollen shut, my lips were split and bleeding—and I thought my nose was broken."

Speaking English, the officer asked the same questions as the others, "Where is your radio? Why did MacArthur send you? Are the Japanese coming over here?"

Noting Ed's bruises, he said, "Who did this to you?"

Ed told him that the guards were responsible.

The officer said that he would take action because they had orders not to do this. He told Ed to sit down and rest.

Ed: "He sat in a large chair and told me his name. He was a General. He asked my rank and I told him my serial number and rank. When he asked my job, I told him I worked in supply. I'd never tell him I was a machine gunner's assistant. He asked if my officers explained why we were there. I told him I thought it was a sneak maneuver and that we knew nothing about any kind of a war."

Satisfied with Ed's responses, the general told his men that they should not have beaten Ed. He talked about going to school in America and then said, "Your trouble will be over real soon and you'll be able to go home—but right now we're going to put you with some other prisoners."

Then he said, "Good luck" and left.

It was July 25—somewhere north of Chonan.

Thirteen — George Snodgrass

1st Cavalry, 7th Regiment

Born in Aurora, Missouri, George Snodgrass grew up on a farm. By the time, he was seventeen, his family had moved to Illinois. Influenced by WWII patriotism, he grew up wanting to be a soldier—so he left high school and enlisted in 1949. He was seventeen.

After basic training, George shipped to Ft. Lewis, Washington, to await an assignment. The Army offered him a chance to go to Japan. Occupation duty sounded great to him—and he accepted, but the Korean War began before he left the States.

George Snodgrass — 1956

At Camp Drake in Japan, he joined the 1st Cavalry, 7th Regiment. After a couple weeks of training, they went to Pusan and started pushing inland toward the sound of artillery.

Navy guns sounded different from Army guns. That's how they could tell how close they were to shore.

George: "I remember seeing Army trucks and smelling a horrible odor. The trucks were loaded with dead bodies, row upon row of American soldiers. It scared me."

They moved past the bodies and got into position. Moving from spot to spot, they reached Yongdong the evening of July 25, 1950.

Fourteen — Yongdong

"All wars are popular for the first thirty days." — Arthur Schlesinger, Jr., US Historian

During the night of July 25, the 7th Cavalry Regiment received a report of an enemy breakthrough to the north. Believing that the enemy was enveloping them, the 2nd Battalion of the 7th Cavalry Regiment withdrew from their position east of Yongdong to the vicinity of No Gun-Ri.

George Snodgrass: "We were getting hammered. Another guy and I were on an outpost. We got hit, so we stayed there all night. The next day we went back to join our unit—it was gone. Apparently, they received orders to move out and no one came after us."

George and his friend walked out of a wooded area off the hill, looking for their unit. Not too far away, they saw a bunch of soldiers. As they got closer, George realized that they were North Koreans. Feigning nonchalance, they turned around and went back into the trees. The enemy must not have realized who they were.

Relieved, the frightened young men wandered up the slope of a small hill where they ran into trouble again.

George: "I heard someone yelling in Korean. When I got close enough, I shot him—and started to run. My buddy ran around one side of a hill and I ran around the other. We never saw each other again. I heard gunshots."

Fifteen — Walt Whitcomb
Company C, 29th Infantry Regiment, 24th Division

Walt Whitcomb was born on an Indian reservation in New York State. His mother was a Seneca Indian. His father was a violent man who drank and was abusive to his family. Walt's mother loved her children, but she was passive and couldn't protect them from her husband.

Walt Whitcomb — 1950

Walt: "My family wasn't particularly religious. We went to church because the neighbors required it. My father was a hypocrite. He'd tell me, 'Don't steal.' Then he'd bring home tools from work. He'd say, you should have only one wife, but he'd go out catting around. It was confusing."

Walt didn't like how his father treated him. His brother and sister could go to ballgames, but Walt would have to stay home and take care of the neighbors' kids because his family needed the money.

The unhappy young boy ran away from home again and again. Small in stature and embittered by the way his father treated him, Walt picked fights—some that he could win and some that he couldn't.

Walt: "I was little and crapped on. I was quick-tempered but really I was just looking for equal treatment—what was fair and just."

By the time Walt was a teenager, he began drinking, too.

Walt: "When I was thirteen, I went to a church bazaar and got hold of a couple quarts of wine. I got loaded whenever I could. At the bowling alley, I'd get tips and use them for shots. It got to be a habit to drink while working—and it was more fun to work than to be at home."

He was also passionate about the opposite sex. As a very young man, he fell in love. He asked his sweetheart to marry him and she agreed.

However, fate got in the way. When Walt was seventeen, he and a friend stole a car and went for a joy ride. The cops caught them. The parents of the other boy bailed him out right away, but Walt's father left him in jail for eight months until the case was adjudicated.

Walt: "I was nudged by the judge. He said I could choose prison or the Army. My dad said that I could go to jail but he wouldn't let me be a soldier. That sealed it for me. I joined the Army in 1949."

Everyone wanted Walt to marry his fiancé before going overseas. However, after he was in the military, he heard about adulterous relationships on some of the bases and he refused to get married for fear that she would see other men while he was gone.

Walt: "It was old style thinking. My father was always suspicious of my mother, so I had that fear built in from an early age. It was based on insecurity and it took me a long time to get over it."

The Army sent Walt to Stockton, California. After basic training, he shipped to Okinawa.

Walt: "I liked the Army. The same rules held for every-one. It was fair."

On July 20, 1950, Walt left for Korea, landing in Pusan. Fighting had started in June and already the North Koreans were as far south as the Pusan Perimeter.

Sixteen — James Yeager
Company C, 29th Infantry Regiment, 24th Division

Born in 1930, Jim Yeager was a sensitive, imaginative boy living on a farm in Colorado. He dreamed of being a soldier. His traditional parents supported this goal. When he was twelve, his father built a firing range in their basement and taught him to shoot. Encouraged to eat what was available rather than just what he liked, he learned to kill and clean game for dinner. From grade school on, he focused on all things military—enlisting first in the Naval Reserves when he was seventeen and then transferring to a National Guard unit. In 1949, he joined the US Army—determined to serve his country and make his parents proud.

James Yeager — 1949

At Camp Funston in Ft. Riley, Kansas, Jim met John Toney—another ambitious young man. They saw eye to eye and became close friends. During basic training, the two young men were in the 4th Platoon. Jim became the Squad Leader of the Second Squad and Toney was his assistant Squad Leader. About half way through training, the Platoon Sergeant called Jim into his quarters and asked if he would have a problem with Toney becoming the Fourth Squad Leader.

Jim: "I told the Sergeant I thought Toney would make a good Squad Leader, and it was done."

45

After basic, Jim was gratified to learn that the Army had selected him for Leadership Academy. That Toney had also been chosen for this honor made the experience even better. Intelligent and gung-ho, it seemed possible that Jim would soon achieve another dream—to be an officer.

John Toney — 1949

Upon completion of Leader-ship Academy, Jim and Toney received orders to go to Okinawa for occupation duty. They sailed from San Francisco on the USS *General Walker*.

Jim: "Toney and I stood on the main deck watching the shore line glide by—and as we passed under the Golden Gate Bridge, I told Toney, 'We will be home by Christmas.' Toney looked at me and said, 'Are you nuts? We have eighteen months duty to do before thinking about coming home.' My reply was, 'Wait and see.'"

Seventeen — Hadong

"The whole art of war consists of guessing at what is on the other side of the hill." — Arthur Wellesley

In the middle of July, Major Tony J. Raibl, Executive Officer of the 3rd Battalion, 29th Infantry, learned that the regiment would need at least six weeks' training. They were seriously under strength. To prepare for action in Korea, command reestablished two battalions taking men from the 2nd Battalion to fill the 1st, commanded by Lieutenant Colonel Wesley Wilson, and the 3rd, led by Lieutenant Colonel Harold Mott. Four hundred recruits fresh from basic trained reinforced the units.

On July 20, the Far East Command told Major Raibl that the 29th would not come to Japan but would sail directly to Korea, where they would receive at least ten days of intensive field training before being committed to battle.

The USS *General Walker* arrived at Okinawa with the expected recruits—including Jim Yeager, John Toney, Walt Whitcomb and Sherman Jones. They disembarked and went to the battalion areas where they received their company assignments, guns and field equipment.

Lieutenant Alexander Makarounis, a veteran of World War II, became the commander of Company I of the 3rd Battalion, 29th Regiment.

Jim and Toney were in Company K of the 3rd Battalion, 29th Regimental combat team—as scouts and observers. Again, the two friends were in the same platoon. Jim was excited. It was his turn now—time to fulfill his destiny—and show everyone what he could do.

Walt Whitcomb ended up in Company K as well.

Sherman Jones and Gene Putzier were in B Company, 1st Battalion.

On July 21, the two battalions, now at full strength, boarded the *Fentriss* and *Takasago Maru*, and sailed for Pusan.

When Major Raibl arrived at Taegu on July 22, he was dismayed to find that despite the regiment's lack of battle-readiness, the 29th would have only three days at Pusan to draw equipment and zero-in and test fire their weapons.

However, it was worse than that.

When the 29th arrived at Pusan on July 24, they had orders to proceed immediately to Chinju where they would be attached to the 19th Infantry Regiment. Instead of the six weeks of training first agreed upon, they found themselves going into battle—rifles not zeroed, mortars not test-fired, and their new .50-caliber machine guns still packed in cosmoline.[9]

The young recruits arrived with little knowledge about Korea. However, it didn't take long for them to realize the grave situation that they faced.

Jim Yeager: "Toney and I were on train station guard. We saw two guys from 19th come in—all emaciated, no weapons, dirty, hungry. Around two A.M., a train from up north pulled in—and they started unloading wounded. So help me God, blood was running out of the back of those ambulances."

On July 25, the 29th arrived in Chinju. That night, Colonel Moore, commanding the 19th Infantry at Chinju, ordered Colonel Mott to seize Hadong, thirty-five miles southwest of Chinju. (Ent, 1998) They were to engage about two hundred or more guerrilla forces that were disturbing the citizenry and recruiting for the North Korean Communist Army.

---

9 An oily substance used to protect weapons from rusting while not in use.

48

A disgraced South Korean General, Chae Byong Duk, explained the strategic importance of the area and asked to join the 3rd Battalion as an interpreter and guide. He was a controversial character. Fired from his position as Chief of Staff for the ROK Army after losing Seoul to the NKPA, he was looking for a way to get back into the good graces of Syngman Rhee.

At dusk, the men learned about their mission. It was the first military action for Jim Yeager, John Toney and Walt Whitcomb. They were excited and nervous.

Walt Whitcomb: "I didn't have anything against those people—but the Army had been good to me. I wanted to hold up my end of the deal. I was there to do what I was told."

Near midnight, they started toward Hadong. Thickly wooded with pines and known for its green tea crops, the region is mountainous and beautiful. The crystalline Somjin River winds through it.

Leaving Chinju, the column detoured from the direct road to Hadong because of an impassable ford. As a result, they spent the night negotiating the narrow road and pulling vehicles out of rice paddies.

Around daybreak, they met a truckload of wounded ROK soldiers who claimed to be the only survivors of Hadong's local militia. Colonel Mott had no radio communication with 19th Infantry Headquarters, so Major Raibl returned to Chinju by jeep to tell Colonel Moore that the North Koreans now held Hadong. The troops set up camp at Wonjon and had breakfast while they waited.

Raibl suggested that the 3rd Battalion, 29th Infantry take up a defensive position on the Hadong road. However, Colonel Moore re-emphasized the need to seize Hadong. Just before noon, Raibl returned to Wonjon to report Colonel Moore's instructions to Colonel Mott.

With their mission clarified, the 3rd Battalion, 29th Infantry marched on, stopping three miles from Hadong for the night. There they discovered that the Air Force TAC radio was defective. This left Colonel Mott with no way to call in airstrikes or to communicate with Colonel Moore in Chinju.

The S-2, Captain William Mitchell, selected Jim Yeager, John Toney and an interpreter—and they went forward to

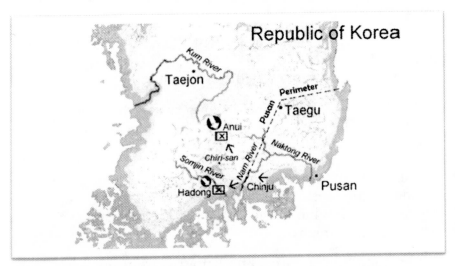

Action at Hadong & Anui

recon the area. In talking to a local farmer, they learned that they had to cross enemy lines to go over the pass. Through the interpreter, the old man told them that there was going to be a "big battle."(Ent, 1998)

Jim: "We could see the glow of many cigarettes in the darkness."

Suspicious-looking men dressed in white clothing stood alongside the road. They offered no information, but didn't interfere with the patrol in any way.

Jim and Toney returned to the battalion position around two A.M., and Captain Mitchell made his report to the command group.

The next morning, July 27, the column moved out before nine A.M. Captain George Sharra and L Company, with a platoon of the Heavy Weapons Company, led. The command group came next. Captain Joseph K. Donahue with K

50

Company and Captain Hugh P. Milleson with M Company followed. I Company with Lieutenant Alexander G. Makarounis was in reserve.

About a thousand yards from the top of Hadong Pass, a patrol of North Korean soldiers started down toward them. The Heavy Weapons platoon fired but missed. The enemy turned and ran back over the pass.

Captain Sharra ordered L Company to secure the area. They ran to the top and positioned themselves on either side of the pass. To the north, a high peak overlooked the road. To the south, a hill sloped down to some rice paddies extending down to the Somjin River. The view was stunning. The Hadong pine forest is one of Korea's national treasures.

About ten A.M., Captain Sharra received orders to dig in and wait for an air strike on Hadong.[10]

General Chae Byok Duk

(Fat Chae) was born in 1915 in Pyongyang, where he attended primary and secondary schools. In 1932, Chae was accepted by the Japanese Military Academy. In April 1933, Chae moved to Japan and enrolled at the Academy. Because of this, he lost the respect of his own people.

By August 15, 1945, he rose to the rank of major in the Japanese Army. In 1948, Chae became Chief of Staff of the ROK Army. When the North Koreans attacked South Korea, Chae led forces who lacked equipment and training. Although they exhibited bravery, they were victims of complete surprise. They had no weapons and little organization. They could only react to the invasion.

General Chae *(National Archives)*

In his book, *This Kind of War: The Classic Korean War Story*, T.R. Fehrenbach says, "Since the South had been heavily infiltrated with line crosses and Communists agents, the NKPA without exception knew the location of every South Korean defense unit and sent superior forces against it. And almost with exception,

---

10 The air strike never came. The Air Force Forward Officer had no radio contact. Later he became embroiled in the battle and was killed. US aircraft flew back and forth over the area, but left without making an attack.

Colonel Mott and most of the battalion staff along with General Chae and his party, hurried toward the pass. Raibl, at the rear of the column, received orders from Mott to join him. As the battalion command group gathered, Captain Sharra, thinking that they made an attractive target, flattened himself on the ground near the gunner of a light machine gun.

When Raibl arrived, he saw unidentifiable troops climbing the peak to the north. Colonel Mott told him that it was K Company. These were actually North Korean soldiers. (Johnson, 2003)

Colonel Mott pointed down the road toward a column of soldiers. Some wore American green fatigues while others were in the mustard brown of the North Korean Army. When the approaching men were about one hundred yards away, General Chae shouted to them in Korean, asking them to identify themselves. The column scattered and L Company opened fire.

At that moment, enemy machine gun, mortar and small arms fire hit the pass from the high ground to the north. A hidden North Korean machine gunner killed General Chae and hit Major Raibl, Colonel Mott, Captain Mitchell and the Assistant S-2. The rounds destroyed several US Army

52

vehicles, too. In the first bloody moment of the battle for Hadong, the NKPA severely damaged the 3rd Battalion staff.

It was later determined that instead of the two hundred guerillas they thought they would find, the 3rd Battalion, 29th Infantry ran into elements of four North Korean divisions that were making their sweep to form along the Pusan perimeter defense. Having the high ground and arranged in a rough U shape, the enemy fired down on the 29th.

Hadong Pass (*National Archives*)

As the attack progressed, Raibl, wounded a second time by mortar fragments, went down the hill seeking a medical aid man. Grazed by a bullet, Colonel Mott left the pass to get out of the line of fire. Later that morning, someone dropped a box of ammunition on Colonel Mott's foot and broke it. A soldier dug him a foxhole. As the fighting grew fiercer, everyone in Mott's vicinity was either killed or wounded or had withdrawn down the hill. For a while, Mott lost contact with his staff. Around noon, someone found him and carried him to safety. He told Sharra to take command of the 3rd Battalion and get them out of danger.

Sharra ordered a retreat, but enemy soldiers had dug in behind them. As the various companies of the 3rd Battalion fell back, mortar and machine gun fire pinned them down in the rice paddies. They could not move. Hundreds died—including Captain Donahue and Captain Milleson. NKPA troops came down and captured the rest including Lieutenant Makarounis, the commander of Company I, who was bringing up the rear of the retreat.

Makarounis was shot in the back as he lay in a rice paddy. The only medical attention he received for his wound was a bandage from a fellow prisoner who was an American aid man.

Jim Yeager's jeep was the fourth in line when the battalion convoy moved forward that morning. He savored the sense of adventure. This was how he'd always seen himself—a soldier seeking out the enemy. They advanced down a narrow dirt road with a mountain on their right, a rice paddy with mountains behind it on the left.

At nine A.M., they heard firing. The battalion staff went forward and the sounds of combat intensified.

Jim: "Toney and I piled out on the right and took cover in the ditch."

A captain jumped up on a truck behind their jeep and charged a .50-caliber machine gun. Before he could get off any rounds, he fell off the truck—shot dead.

Jim: "I told Toney that we better get away from the road before they started dropping 120-mm mortars on us."

Before they could act on that idea, a Master Sergeant sent them up the hill. They were fifty yards away when a shell hit their jeep.

Jim: "We went up to the military crest. There was a squad just out on the flat ground in front of the pine trees. All were dead—shot to hell."

Jim and Toney fought all day on the hill. Toward dusk, there was a lull in the firing. A group of about fifteen headed down the road.

Jim: "All I saw were dead American troopers."

Chased by the enemy, they ran up a hill and sprawled on the ridge, trying to catch their breath.

Jim: "Three North Koreans killed an Air Force Forward Observer who was sitting an arm's length from me, panting from the run up the mountain. I was lying at the base of a bush and they didn't see me."

The men behind Jim ran off the mountain to the right while he fired at the enemy—killing all three of them.

Jim: "Toney and I proceeded out on a point of the ridge. Off to the right, we saw a large rice paddy and when I glassed[11] it, I saw some of our men trying to make it to a river in the distance. Looking down, we saw a small dirt track. The men who had left us were moving up it towards a finger of ground. Behind this finger, I observed intermittent machine gun fire on the men in the distant paddy. The men below us didn't have their weapons. Toney and I decided we had to stop them before they got to the machine gun position. We ran down the mountain and when we got within about twenty–thirty yards, we yelled at them. At this point, two camouflaged North Koreans with burp guns[12], jumped up out of the ditch behind the men and shouted at us, 'You had better throw down your rifles.' Everything seemed to be in slow motion. Toney and I knew if we tried to shoot it out, we'd get our men killed. We threw our weapons down—good thing because a number of North Koreans, with lots of weapons rose up out of the grass behind us at that point." (J. Yeager, "My Trip to Hell and Back", n.d.)

---

11 Viewed it through binoculars.

12 Nickname for two Soviet-made submachine guns used by the North Koreans. Designed in 1941, the PPsh was replaced by the PPS, which was designed in 1943. A **submachine gun** is a firearm that combines the automatic fire of a machine gun with the cartridge of a pistol. It is carried and used as a personal weapon. A **machine gun** is a fully-automatic mounted or portable firearm, usually designed to fire rifle cartridges in quick succession from an ammunition belt or large-capacity magazine, typically at a rate of several hundred rounds per minute. (Summers Jr., 1990)

The situation was equally horrifying for Walt Whitcomb.

Walt: "We were trapped in a gully. It seemed like everyone around me was running—and the enemy was shooting at us. We zigzagged across a muddy field. I was loaded down with mud. There was nothing but blood and guts all around. The smell of death drifted up into my nose. I'd gag—and start to slow down and then someone else would die—and that would impel me into action again. I don't know how I got across that field. God must have had me by the hand. It didn't seem real. I knew a guy who got killed— we shot pool together—and then, bang—he was out of life. I hid in a rice paddy. When I got to the river, there were so many bodies in it that it ran red with blood."

The North Koreans went downstream and hid in the rocks.

Walt: "During the battle, my old self surfaced. I thought, 'I got to get even.' I learned to hate all over again."

Walt made it to another rice paddy, crawling for several hours. When he stood up, enemy soldiers surrounded him. They offered him a drink from a canteen. Thirsty from his efforts to escape the carnage around him, he took a big gulp— only to choke as the liquid burned his esophagus. It was sake.

Over three hundred green recruits died that day—many others went missing. Jim Yeager, his friend John Toney and Walt Whitcomb were among those taken prisoner.

Eighteen — Gifford and McDaniel

"All hope abandon, ye who enter here!" — Dante

On that same day, Allen Gifford, with the 19th Regiment, 24th Division and Major McDaniel with Headquarters Company, 34th Infantry Regiment, 24th Division faced capture. They had been wandering around the hills since they evacuated Taejon on July 20. Once in awhile, they found some discarded C-rations—usually crackers. Even so, after a few days, they had to look for food.

Allen: "We saw people traveling in white gowns and hoods. Major McDaniel said we needed to keep away from them. Everything seemed to be quiet. We were headed south. We decided to go down out of the hills and ask for food. That's where North Koreans surrounded us. We had no weapons. We tried to run. They shot Corporal Stevens when he ran."

They were in Yongdong County.

Allen: "I was belligerent. I had a knife. A North Korean Lieutenant pointed a gun right at my eye. Major McDaniel called to me, 'Al, come on, they got us.' They had tied him to a post. His guard spoke to the lieutenant holding a gun on me. I could see the change in his eyes—I knew he would shoot me. I dropped the knife. The Lieutenant walked up and slapped me. Another soldier kicked me in the back of my right leg and started pushing me around."

They put Corporal Stevens on a stretcher and told Allen to carry him. A civilian picked up the front of the stretcher and Allen took the back. They took him into a building and stayed there a few hours. Stevens had taken a bullet in his pelvic area and couldn't urinate. He was in a great deal of pain. The guards put him on an oxcart. Allen never saw him again.

Nineteen — Sherman Jones
Company B, 1st Battalion, 29th Infantry Division

Sherman Jones came to Korea through a fate-driven circuitous route.

Sherman Jones — 1950

He was born in Spade, Texas. A generous, playful boy, he grew up in a loving family. As a teenager, he found it easy to get good paying summer jobs—working cotton or the oil fields. In the fall of 1948, he quit school.

Sherman: "I kept thinking, 'What's the sense of me going to school when I can make that kind of money?' I thought I knew more than the teacher anyway."

Sherman kept working until September 1949, when he decided to go into the Army. No one thought it was a good idea.

Sherman: "My brother had been in World War II. He told me that if I'd finish school, he'd pay my college tuition. My brother-in-law was a recruiter for the Air Force. He filled out papers for me and put me on a bus. I said, 'I want to fly.' He said, 'You are wearing glasses. You can't fly.' I said, 'If I can't fly, I don't want the Air Force.' I went to the Army because they said they'd give me anything I wanted. I talked my mom into it and signed up."

After basic, the Army sent Sherman to Ford Ord. At first, they were going to make him a surgical technician and send him to Rhode Island to train. However, that didn't work out—and Sherm went to Okinawa—still without a specific job.

Sherman: "They took us on a ferry to San Francisco—and put us on a big ship. We got about a mile out and they let us go up on the top deck to see the Golden Gate Bridge. After an hour, I got seasick. Everything started going round and round, so I went downstairs and fell asleep. That night, I got in line for supper and they gave me peaches for dessert. I threw them up and then everyone in that line started throwing up. They put me on KP. For four days, I'd wash dishes in one sink and throw up in the other one."

Sherman cured his seasickness by going up on deck and breathing in the sea air. He got to Okinawa on March 15. At that point, the Army put him in a service company.

Sherman: "They were going to make me a truck driver, but when I backed up into trash cans, they said, you are no truck driver—and they transferred me to Company B. On July 27 at midnight, they said take your mattresses off and tie them up. We are going to Japan for MP duty."

Sherm traveled from Okinawa on the *Takasago Maru*, which was a horse ship. He got seasick again so he went up on the top deck. It wasn't long before he heard that they weren't going to Japan after all.

Sherman: "When we got close to Pusan, they said we got an enemy submarine—and they dropped depth charges. I grabbed my M1. I guess I thought I was going to sink that submarine with it."

The next day, Sherm boarded a train. They passed Taegu and went up to Chinju. At that point, the 1st Battalion, 29th Infantry Regiment divided—and Company B went on to Anui.

Twenty — Anui

"Older men declare war. But it is the youth that must fight and die." — Herbert Hoover

On July 28, B and D Companies, 29th Infantry were attacked at Anui. They tried to withdraw to high ground across the Nam River but only two officers and sixteen men made it before North Korean troops enveloped them. The remainder of the two units fought in the streets of Anui until midnight when those who could, slipped into the hills and tried to walk to safety. Approximately half of the two companies were either killed or missing in this battle.

Gene Putzier

Sherman Jones: "We ran out of ammo in no time. They told us to go down a hill. I carried two hundred and fifty rounds in each hand. Another guy had five hundred rounds too. Our platoon sergeant said not to fire until we saw the North Koreans advancing toward us."

The sights and sounds of battle overwhelmed the unprepared young soldiers. Sherm saw the first sergeant shot in the stomach—and a bunch of bodies lying around.

Sherman: "They promised tank and air support but then the radio went out. Around dark, someone said that it was every man for himself."

Sherm and five others—including his friend Gene Putzier— were separated from the rest of their unit. The six of them

60

were walking in the river. A PFC in the group wanted to go back on the road. When they did, they encountered enemy fire. In the darkness, they heard someone shouting, "We ROKs"—but they were NKPA and they captured Sherm and Gene. The enemy tied their hands behind their backs—and took their boots and clothes.

After someone gave them gray flannel pants, a white shirt and some shoes, the enemy interrogated them and returned them to Anui. The NKPA captured about two hundred GIs that night. The guards made them stand for hours—then marched them to Taejon.

Twenty-One — The March from Hadong

"It is well that war is so terrible, or we should get too fond of it." —
Robert E. Lee

As the North Korean soldiers approached Jim Yeager and John Toney near Hadong, Jim took off his helmet and threw it in the weeds. He had maps inside his helmet and he knew that if they found them, he would be in for a hard time.

The enemy moved Jim and Toney down onto the road with other prisoners and searched them.

Jim: "They ripped dog tags off the men in front of us and threw them in the rice paddies. I slipped mine off and tucked them in my waistband. When they got to me, they couldn't find them but, in the process, they stripped me of my fatigue shirt."

As darkness fell, the North Korean soldiers marched the new prisoners into Hadong and quartered the seriously wounded, including Lieutenant Makarounis, in a building near the center of town—and the ones who could walk, stayed in a church.

Walt Whitcomb: "There were about forty other captives there. To this day, I remember the layout of that church."

The guards ordered the men to strip to their undershorts—and then they took their clothes and shoes.

On July 28, a Korean officer interrogated the men kept in the church.

Jim: "They lined us up in a column and we had to stand in front of an officer at his desk. I was the fourth one in line. The first man was a master Sergeant. The officer asked him where our artillery was located. The sergeant stated his name, rank and serial number. The officer asked him the same thing again and once again, the man gave his name, rank and serial number. The officer yelled something to the guards in Korean. They took the sergeant and pushed him up against the wall. The officer took out his pistol and shot him in the head, splattering brains, bone and blood on the wall. The officer called the next man and asked him the same question. This man told him that we had a regiment and gave him a false location. (We had no artillery with us.) The officer called the next man up and asked him the same question. This man told the same story, so he motioned him to move on. Then it was my turn. The officer jumped up, jabbed his fingers into my chest and asked, what is your job? I replied, 'Me jeep driver' and made a motion like driving and turning a steering wheel. He said, "You lie, you die," and hit me several times. After I recovered, I yelled back at him, saying I was a rifleman, made a motion of firing a rifle and said it is too bad I didn't kill more of you. At this point, the guards dragged me to the wall and I thought they were going to kill me like they did the sergeant. They knocked me unconscious instead. When I woke up, the interrogation was over. I crawled to my spot on the floor and lay there." (J. Yeager, "My Trip to Hell and Back", n.d.)

In the early hours of the day, the North Korean soldiers herded the town's people past the church. They looked through the open window, jabbering and pointing at the prisoners.

Jim: "We couldn't understand what was being said, but it was evident the NKPA was showing us off for propaganda purposes."

Around noon, the parade stopped. There were eighty men lying on the floor either sleeping or resting. The day was hot and humid. Shortly after noon, the town was rocketed and strafed by Allied planes. A rocket came in the front of the church by the pulpit.

Jim: "I was on the right-hand side, three-quarters of the way back, lying with my left ear facing the front. Noise from the explosion left me deaf. It took several days for my hearing to return."

Walt: "The rocket came through the building right above my head and blew one of the captives out the door."

The roof collapsed. Timbers and masonry rained down on the men. Jim had a difficult time getting the debris off his body, but managed to crawl through the hole in the left wall before the next strafing run.

Jim: "I can still see the carnage. There were body parts all around me. One man, split wide open with his guts hanging out, was still alive."

Twenty of the eighty GIs died there. The North Koreans rounded up the rest of the prisoners, ran them through town and up the side of a mountain, while US planes continued bombing and strafing the area.

Early that evening, the North Koreans separated the critically wounded from those who were ambulatory.

Jim: "One man had taken a hit above his left ear. His skull had a large hole in it and you could see his brain. They told him they were going to take him to the hospital. He disappeared into the darkness with the soldiers. A short time later, there was a rifle report. The guards returned and separations continued, finally leaving thirty to forty men."

The North Koreans began marching the prisoners north. After an hour, they turned off the narrow track into a farmyard. The guards pushed, kicked and butt-stroked the terrified young men into a small building. The next morning, they each received a small rice ball. The prisoners passed a sake bottle of water around.

Jim: "After 'breakfast,' they roused us up and we stumbled on. The roads were only wide enough for a jeep. This became our routine—sometimes we stayed in barnyards and slept on the bare ground. We walked from daylight till late at night. Toney and I felt that our jobs as scouts and observers were still in effect. Almost nightly, columns of NKPA troops passed us."

Walt: "We tried to drink out of streams, but if caught, we were punished. One of my buddies, a Mexican named Johnny, was shot for that offense."

The guards told them that they were going to Taegu and that there would be food once they arrived. They walked at night from town to town. Walt, Jim, Toney and Sherman had only been in country a few days. They understood very little Korean. Street signs were in Hangul.[13] They had no idea where they were or where their units were located. They'd seen their friends blown apart. They were disoriented, hungry and anxious.

Walt: "My feet were numb. After the second day, my legs began to swell too. The guards promised they'd get me medicine, but they never did. At night, we slept close to each other to keep warm. As we passed through towns, the South Koreans tried to give us food."

Their route twisted and turned over the war-torn countryside. They detoured to avoid troop movements or to march through villages for propaganda purposes. They avoided battlefields and sought out schools and barns for shelter. As they got closer to Taejon, Allied air strikes became more troublesome. The guards would yell "hongo hongo"[14] and everybody dove off the road for cover.

Jim: "Numerous times, empty shell casings sprayed us. The pilots had no idea who we were."

Walt: "I thought about all kinds of things while we were marching. Things were bad, but I didn't want my parents thinking that I'd done a dumb thing again. I was determined to get through to prove I did everything right. I was still resentful. I'd gotten rid of my life insurance so no one could get ahead if I died."

---

[13] Hangul is the Korean alphabet.

[14] "Bihaenggi" means airplane in Korean.

65

One day, they stopped in a vineyard on a mountain. Hiding under grape vines to avoid an air strike on a town in a valley below, they gulped down as many grapes as they could. After it was over, the guards forced them into double time down the mountain, headed for a town.

Jim: "When we reached the valley floor, we could see that there had been a ferocious battle. The guards ran us through a bare piece of ground where arms and legs protruded from shallow graves. Some had American uniforms covering part of the limbs. The air was heavy with putrefaction. Clearing this, we turned down a street at a slower pace and ended up at the police station. This was Taejon where General Dean had been taken prisoner a month before."

Meanwhile, back in Hadong, the US Air Force continued pounding the little city. The ambulatory wounded who had been too ill to make the march north endured the daily bombing and strafing along with the citizenry. The guards moved the prisoners up to the hill, which was to the rear of a large concrete building where they were staying. They hid in the trees, and in two or three caves that were in the area.

After several days, Lieutenant Makarounis decided to escape rather than die by friendly fire in Hadong. He waited until dark and then slipped away with two other soldiers from I Company.

Twenty-Two — Other Roads to Taejon

"You discover what your enemy fears most by observing the means he uses to frighten you." — Eric Hoffer

The soldiers took Ed Slater to a building where there were other prisoners—South Korean civilians. The guards put a rope down the middle of the room and told everyone to stay on their side and not to talk.

During the night, they took people out and beat them. Ed heard the sound of flesh being pummeled—and the cries of the victims. Toward morning, an officer rushed in, shrieking at a prisoner. Suddenly, he pulled a pistol and shot the man in the head. His body crumbled to the floor.

The soldiers began beating the others again.

They beat Ed, too. It went on for a couple of days. They always asked the same questions, "Where is your radio?", "Why did MacArthur send you here?", "Are the Japanese coming here?"

Ed: "They played the good guy and the bad guy. One fellow gave me cigarettes. Another one hit me in the head for having them. Their favorite thing, I think, was to take one of their rubber shoes that looked like a canoe, put a rock in the toe of it—and then hit you with that. It didn't make any difference where they hit you, you'd get a big knot come up."

The torment took many forms. Guards took people outside. Gunfire startled Ed out of his exhaustion. Those prisoners never returned—leaving Ed to ponder their fate and wonder if he would be next.

Ed: "They did give me some food, but they didn't give the political prisoners anything but beatings. Most of them sat there crying, moaning or talking quietly."

On the second afternoon in this location, the guards yelled, "Hongo, hongo!" Ed heard an explosion and then a jet roared by overhead. One bomb was so close that it threw rocks and gravel against the metal shed. After several passes, the planes left. The guards were even more vicious after that attack.

Ed: "They brought in an American GI. The poor kid was scared to death—and even more so when he saw me. They had already worked him over pretty good. He kept asking me what he should tell them. I asked him what his job was and he said that he was a BAR man.[15] I told him to tell them that he was an aide, but he had already told them about the BAR. That afternoon, they came in and told us to take off all of our clothes. They laughed at us as we undressed. They kept everything but my pants. One guy sat down right there and put on my boots so I knew they were gone. They even kept my shorts. They took the kid out the door struggling and kicking as they were beating him. I never saw him again, but a short time later, I heard shots. All I could do was pray for him."

The guards told Ed that they were taking him to a camp where he would be with his own people. They walked all night. As they walked through villages, people threw him things. One woman tried to give him something to eat, but they threatened to shoot her.

---

15 BAR — Browning Automatic Rifle.

Ed's feet were cut and bleeding. He asked for something to wrap around them, but the guards ignored his request. By the time they reached the other camp, Ed was hurting all over. He sat down against a building and started crying. All the other prisoners seem to be wounded, in pain and filthy. They were all Americans. One told him that most of them were captured in Taejon.

○○○

After his capture near the Kum River, enemy soldiers put Bob Sharpe in a collecting area at a police station.

Bob: "The mental torture was worse than the physical brutality."

Not just the intelligence office questioned Bob -- all the soldiers did and the civilians too. They showed him a cache of American weapons and asked him where they could find General Dean.

Bob: "Of course, I didn't know but they thought I did. They had the general's helmet with the two stars painted on it—and they had the silver stars from his jacket too." (R. L. Sharpe, 1951)

Bob figured that General Dean must have thrown away his insignia to keep from being identified and kept on fighting with his men until the end.

Bob: "They kept me around for a couple of days and then sent me to a POW camp in Taejon. There were about seventy Americans there."

Many of them were wounded and had had no medical care. Bob ripped up uniforms and made bandages and did the best he could.

○○○

Allen Gifford and Major McDaniel were captured on July 26 near Yongdong. The North Korean soldiers marched them to a schoolhouse where there were two other prisoners.

Allen: "Our food, mostly rice balls, didn't agree with some of us. The wounded men received soup. Sometimes we received hot sauce, which many of us couldn't stomach."

After a while, the guards herded the prisoners back toward Taejon. As they walked, they picked up more frightened, frustrated and hungry American soldiers.

Allen: "By the time we got there, there were about one hundred of us."

Roy Sutterfield,[16] was one of them.

OOO

After hiding out in the hills around Taegu for several days without rations, George Snodgrass came out for food.

George: "I'd been drinking creek water, but I couldn't find anything to eat. An old man in a village, motioned for me. I thought it would help me get away if I wasn't wearing my uniform. I found some old clothes, put them on and tied a rag around my head. I had light hair and knew that could give me away. I stored my broken-down rifle in my pack."

George went down to the creek to get a drink. As he bent over, he saw the reflection of people in the water. They were North Korean soldiers hiding from American planes under a railroad bridge. They started talking. George turned to walk away, but he knew they'd seen him. Someone knocked the rag off his head and motioned for him to put his hands in the air.

George had a knife in his shirt pocket. The soldiers saw it— and attacked him. A NKPA lieutenant pointed at George's eyes—and grabbed his dog tags. The captors took turns beating the terrified young man—and humiliating him.

George: "I kept telling them I was only seventeen and didn't know anything. One asked if I was a farm boy. I said yes. Things got bad.

---

16 Another Sunchon Tunnel survivor.

They beat me—and worse. They buried me once. I'd lose control of my bodily functions and they'd laugh. It was a game they played with me."

The band of North Korean soldiers spent days moving from one place to another. They picked up another prisoner, Bond, and then in a few days, added Spencer and Jerome.

OOO

About five days after his first escape from Hadong, twenty miles as the crow flies, local militiamen captured Lieutenant Makarounis and his companions in a small South Korean village as they broke into an empty doctor's office. They were trying to find fresh dressings for the wounds they'd received during the Battle of Hadong.

They were turned over to the police who then sent them to Kwangju and then on to Taejon.

OOO

A civilian vigilante group captured Valdor John and George. They took Valdor's shoes. During one of the many beatings that he endured in the fall of 1950, his captors broke the arches in his feet.

OOO

Melvin Rookstool[17]: "I was taken prisoner on July 27. We'd been fighting for a day and a half when the North Koreans simply overran us. A half dozen or so of us were going down this road, thinking we were heading in the right direction. Some North Korean on the hill must have yelled 'Americans' because all hell broke loose. I was lying in a shallow stream and bullets were hitting the water all around me. That's a good way to wake up in a hurry. I started running down this stream trying to get away—and I got hit in the shoulder. Then I ran into one of their machine guns and I said to myself, 'Hell, I can't outrun that,' so I just threw up my hands and climbed out on the bank." (Carlson, 2002)

---

17 Another survivor of the Sunchon Tunnel Massacre.

71

Twenty-Three — Assembly in Taejon

"The miserable have no other medicine but hope." — Friedrich Nietzsche

Jim Yeager, John Toney, Walt Whitcomb and the other men coming from Hadong arrived in Taejon after several torturous days. The guards put them in a building with a long hallway in the center. South Korean prisoners filled the cells on either side. The exhausted boys went up a stairway to what appeared to be a courtroom filled with GIs.

Walt Whitcomb: "Taejon is where we met up with another bunch that included Slater and Valdor John. That's why the group got to be big as it did—they consolidated smaller ones."

Two soldiers lay on rough boards placed on top of desks. Korean medics had amputated the left arm of one man. The other had lost his right foot at the ankle. Several prisoners had shrapnel injuries. Each morning, someone sprinkled sulfa powder on their wounds.

Several men were partially clad. Their captors stripped them—because they needed the clothing and to discourage escape. Those who had arrived first advised newcomers to cut up their clothes and shoes so that the North Koreans couldn't use them. Lieutenant Makarounis ripped his jacket and cut the toes from his shoes to dampen anyone's interest in them.

Jim Yeager: "The North Koreans took our combat boots and socks. The guard who took mine gave me his tennis shoes in exchange. His shoes were a size five—my boots were a size ten. I used a C-ration can opener to cut the toes out of the shoes so I could wear them. I made triangular bandages out of rags and used them for socks. This was my footwear until I returned to Japan. The long march over primitive roads, dirt, rocks and gravel beat up my feet."

After the long march from Anui, Sherman Jones and Gene Putzier were relieved of their shoes in Taejon.

Over time, their feet and legs swelled. Those who had shoes chose not to take them off for fear they couldn't get them on again. Those who ended up barefoot often died on the march north because the road tore up their feet.

The jail reeked—by this time, almost everyone had diarrhea. Unable to go out except in the morning or evening, GIs relieved themselves in the room. Filth covered the floor.

Jim Yeager and Sherman Jones were on honey pot duty together—carrying buckets of human waste to dump in a field.

It was equally difficult for those coming to Taejon from other directions.

Ed Slater: "Just after dark, a guard who spoke some English came in and told me I was being taken to a camp with some of my own people. That was the best news I'd heard in a long time."

They walked all night on gravel roads. Ed's feet were cut and bleeding. He asked the guards to give him something to wrap around them, but they ignored his request.

Ed: "We came to a town. My captors turned me over to other guards and told me to find a place to sit down. I sat against a building and cried. Everyone there was wounded, laying in that dirty, dusty clay and trying to help each other. I saw a Tech Sergeant who was shot in the lower leg and I wondered it if was the same man I had been with that first day when I got lost. He was in a lot of pain so I didn't ask. I tried to find somebody from my outfit. Someone told me that most had been captured in Taejon. That was how I found out where I was. Those thousand miles I thought I'd walked over and around the mountains was a lot shorter than I thought. I could have taken the road and walked it in two days. I sincerely believe that had I known what was ahead of me, I would have shot myself—if I could."

Allen Gifford: "I met Ed Slater and Bob Sharpe in Japan. They were the only two prisoners I knew. I looked for others in my company, but never found out what happened to any of them."

Melvin Rookstool: "They had us carry some boxes—ammunition, I think—up this hill where they kept gathering more and more prisoners. After that, they headed us toward Taejon." (Carlson, 2002)

After their arrival in Taejon, the enemy questioned and photographed Lieutenant Makarounis and his companions before placing them in the big room on the second floor. This was the first large group of prisoners he had seen since his capture two weeks before. The North Koreans in charge divided them into groups—and assigned a specific guard to each one.

When Valdor John and George arrived in Taejon, the guards put them in a six-foot-by-six-foot jail cell with six others. All were wounded and gangrene was setting in. They spent ten days in that cell. They knew there were other prisoners in other rooms.

A civilian collaborator visited Valdor every day—perhaps because Valdor spoke a little Japanese. He'd give a "report" on the war. "The US troops are getting closer—I'll have to kill you," he'd say. "I'm sorry,"—and then he'd laugh at his own little joke.

Valdor: "He'd pull the bolt and put his gun to my head—day after day. Sometimes he'd harass me all night—just to keep me from sleeping."

Melvin: "Like everyone else, I was asleep on the floor. This guard came in—and I don't know whether he tripped over me or what, but I came up off the floor right quick. I guess he thought I was going to jump him. He had a pistol in his hand and he hit me with it on the side of the face—and took out my eye." (Carlson, 2002)

The men were horrified by the sight of Melvin's dangling eye.

Ed: "No one knew what to do about it."

In Taejon, Bob Sharpe met Ed Slater. They became good friends—and swore to stick by each other.

After five days, the North Koreans told the men that they were going to Seoul where they would find airplanes waiting to take them home to America. Bob knew it was a lie, but some of the men believed it.

The guards told other prisoners a different story.

Jim: "We stayed in Taejon about a week. Finally, they said that they were taking us to a POW camp and marched us out of the city, headed north."

Twenty-Four — The March from Taejon to Seoul

"Do or don't do. There is no try." — Yoda

After a few days in Taejon, the North Koreans rousted everyone from their second story rooms. The men fell out and stood in front of their police station prison. The guards paced up and down the line, counting.

Someone asked how many could walk twenty-two miles. He said they were going to Seoul and that after they marched twenty-two miles there would be a train—and they would go on to Seoul in that. Seoul was about fifty miles or so beyond. "The camps in the north are better," he said.

Roy Sutterfield: "They didn't force us to march from Taejon. All the guys that were possibly able to walk did try to go."

Fifty men couldn't march. The guards held them aside—hit them with rifle butts, gagged them and knocked them unconscious. Then they took sixteen, including Sherman Jones, out for special treatment.

Sherman Jones: "They threw me on the ground—spread-eagled— with one guard on each leg, arm and on my back. Then they ground bayonets into my spine."

Three died. The guards then put axle grease on their wounds and told them "don't tell."

Hurt and angry, Sherman joined the ranks marching to Seoul.

Ed Slater: "They told us to get on our feet. The healthy ones could help the wounded. I was one of the healthy ones."

Melvin Rookstool's eye was still attached and it bounced against his cheek when he moved.

Bob Sharpe: "We knew it must hurt him terribly."

However, being left behind seemed more dangerous than the uncertainty at the end of the road to Seoul. Melvin marched.

George Snodgrass: "They seemed in a hurry to move us out. We left Taejon, headed to Seoul. We walked all the way, in columns."

Valdor John: "Most of us marched barefoot until we were able to wrap our feet in rice bags."

The guards put some of the American prisoners in cattle cars—packed in so tight that they couldn't move. Many had dysentery.

Allen Gifford: "We relieved ourselves where we stood. It seemed like hours before the train moved. We were in the train for five or six hours and probably didn't go more than a mile or two."

The guards formed the rest into columns of four abreast and marched them out of the city. In addition to the GIs, there were South Korean prisoners. Before long, the men began seeing evidence of the fierce battles that had taken place around Taejon. Burned out half-tracks littered the road along with piles of ammo—and bodies.

Jim Yeager: "The smell of decomposing bodies overwhelmed us. The bridge across the Kum River had one end blown, the remains hanging down in the river. The North Koreans bypassed the bridge with a makeshift one just above the water."

After several hours, the guards unloaded the men on the train and forced them to join the long line of prisoners marching through the hilly countryside. They walked the twenty-two miles that first night—but there was no train waiting for them.

Allen: "There were so many bodies—American and Korean. Tanks were burning."

Ed: "The only break came when someone would yell 'hongo hongo.' Then we had the chance to sit down in the ditches. We rested in the fields that evening for a couple of hours. Then they said, 'walk, walk.' The officers and non-coms complained but the guards said it would be better to walk at night and rest during the day. 'Besides, the train will be in the next village in the morning.' This train story went on and on for months. Once they told us that trucks would be waiting in the next town."

The guards were brutal with their charges. The prisoners understood that any infraction of the rules meant death.

Allen: "I was in the third group and we saw guys who had fallen out of the first two. I saw guys who had been bayoneted. They were left there for us to see."

George: "If anyone fell out of line, they were shot or left there along the road."

For the wounded, the march was torture.

Melvin Rookstool: "I carried my eye around in my hand for sixty-three days. This is difficult to explain, but I grabbed that eye and pinched it real hard between my thumb and fingers. You know you have cords—I'll call them that—running back into your head from your eye. Each time I'd bounce up and down while I was walking—man, that would hurt. After pinching it so hard, it would go numb. My eye eventually came completely off from my cutting those cords with my fingernails." (Chinnery, 2000)

The civilian collaborator who had been harassing Valdor John in Taejon followed them almost to Seoul.

Valdor: "I don't know why finally he stopped—or where he went."

Sometimes, if the men encountered a guard when he was alone, they might have a civil conversation. However, if another guard showed up, the first one would revert to his previous, violent behavior.

Valdor: "This was no particular guard—just the guards in general. One on one, they could be human."

Bob: "It was part of the system. They used peer pressure to get people to behave in certain ways. Everyone was always looking at everyone else—wondering if that guy over there was a snitch."

The men were lost in a foreign country without weapons or tools. They didn't speak the language or understand the culture. Friends and foes were indistinguishable. They had no maps—and nowhere to go. Most were wounded or sick.

Ed: "Most of the people in the villages threw rocks and cussed us. I tried to stay in the center row. I was embarrassed because the whole rear-end of my pants was gone from sliding down hills. Strange how that bothered me when I had a hell of a lot more to worry about. They had taken my shorts so that left my bare rear showing. The guards laughed and pointed at my rear with their guns."

For all the prisoners knew, the American forces had been pushed back into the sea. Their only hope lay in the planes that roared overhead from time to time. However, they were terrified lest death come from friendly fire.

Bob: "The guards were happy to see us strafed but they didn't take to it themselves." (R. L. Sharpe, 1951)

Ed: "Someone up ahead would start yelling 'airplanes, airplanes.' Then there'd be Navy Corsairs diving right at us. They came over the mountain with the sun behind them. Everyone yelled and waved their arms. Most of us hit the deck as they came in and opened fire. The planes killed about a dozen of the badly wounded on oxcarts. Others died while sitting in the ditches before the pilots recognized us. When they came around again, we all thought, 'This is it,'—but they tipped their wings in acknowledgement that they knew who we were. I still see that terror in the faces of those guys—screaming. I get sick when I think about it. The only good thing is that they knew where we were from then on."

The men were hungry—and the enemy exploited that fact. The Koreans chewed on oxen bones. When they discarded them, the prisoners picked them up. If a guard noticed someone eating, he beat him. One time when the column stopped, a guard threw down an apple core. If anyone grabbed for it, he hit him.

Melvin: "This Korean woman was sitting alongside the road holding some apples in her lap. I jumped out to get one and the guards shot me in the foot." (Carlson, 2002)

Once someone gave them some green peaches.

Bob: "Oh, they were good, but they turned our insides out."

Jim: "We were lucky if we received anything to eat or drink— usually a lump of rice about the size of a golf ball twice a day."

To the dismay of the prisoners, the Koreans often mixed barley into the rice.

Walt: "It wasn't that it tasted bad—it didn't agree with our systems. We were almost always sick after eating it."

Valdor: "Food was the same every day. We were given little metal bowls. Rice wasn't that plentiful so they gave us millet balls. Then there was an awful-tasting gruel they dripped over the balls—it was like a paste and many of the guys wouldn't eat it at all."

Despite these torments, some of the men managed to get pepper, salt, and other spices as they walked through the villages. It was dangerous for both the POWs and the people who threw them food. However, as the days passed, hunger forced the prisoners to risk prolonged beatings or immediate execution for the tiniest of morsels.

Ed: "I had already lost so much weight that I had to tie my pants with a rice rope. It was the third day before we received any food. They threw a bunch of rice in a large pot and boiled it until it was sticky. Then, they dug it out with a teacup and smoothed off the top so that we all received the same amount. They dropped it in our hands. Some of the guys found old newspapers and tore them up to put their rice on. It was just as dirty as our hands, so what difference did it make?"

Bob: "Dysentery hit and the men were mighty sick, passing blood nearly all the time . . . one man had several feet of his entrails on the outside of him and he lived for awhile with his insides tied to his leg so that they wouldn't swing while he walked."

After leaving Taejon for Seoul, the prisoners' general state of health degraded. Some of the men were hurt in the battles that led to their capture. Under the unsanitary conditions that followed, their wounds became infected. Others were injured during "interrogations" or beatings.

Valdor John: "I had a broken leg during the entire march from Taejon to Seoul."

All of the men imprisoned with Valdor, including George Lucas, died during the march.

Ed: "My legs and feet were swollen and ached constantly. The bottom of my feet looked like big blood blisters. Sometimes I thought they would burst from the swelling."

Parasites and other insects added to their misery. Within days of capture, body lice covered the POWs. Even though the men picked them off and squished them between their thumbs and forefingers, there was no way to get rid of them completely.

Bob: "For every one that I picked off, there were a hundred that I missed."

Maggots worked in their wounds. Shuddering, they tried to scrape the writhing larvae off with sticks or bits of paper. Then, someone passed the word back through the column that the maggots kept torn flesh clean. Disgusted, they tried not to look at the moving dark gray masses on each others' bodies.

Valdor: "The maggots on my legs kept me alive."

Allen: "I remember a guy—we called him Gale—who had been shot in the head. The bullet had gone all the way through. We could see the maggots inside. A doctor took a steel pick and wiped it through the guy's head to get the maggots out."

Ed: "There was a guy who had the whole lower muscle of his arm blown off. Once I saw him eating a big yellow maggot that crawled out of his arm. I didn't get sick. I just felt a sudden flash of fear. I didn't look at him again."

Starvation, water fouled by human wastes and exposure degraded their immune systems. Stress further burdened their overloaded bodies. Disease was the natural consequence. The men began dying—from malnutrition, beriberi or from giving up. Most of the prisoners had dysentery.

Ed: "If we got a drink of water, it ran right through us. The guys would let Mother Nature take her course, right down the back of their legs. I was no exception. Sometimes the guard looked at me, laughed and pointed their guns at me. I could hardly stand the humiliation."

One day, the guards let the men rest in a large field. An American bomber came over the hills right on top of them. The pilot came in at about 5000 feet, circled around and opened his bomb doors.

Ed: "I thought 'Oh, my God, he's going to bomb us right here in the open field.' Bob (Sharpe) and I fell to our knees and covered our heads, trying to get as close to the ground as possible. When we looked up, all the guys were cheering and waving their shirts. Little parachutes were coming down all over the place. It was Red Cross bundles."

The guards yelled and shot into the air. They wouldn't let the starving men have the packages. It was a huge letdown, but still the incident gave the men reason to hope.

Ed: "They knew we were here. They were following us. I just knew that they would send helicopters in to take us out."

The prisoners fumed as they watched the North Koreans enjoy their Red Cross cigarettes and goodies. The next day, to add insult to injury, the guards stuffed their pockets with the candies, cookies, soap and whatever else was in the boxes.

Ed: "I heard one of our officers yelling at the guards that it was supposed to be ours and mentioning the Geneva Convention, but they were too busy taking it away from us to hear that."

The North Koreans continued to urge the men forward with promises of food just down the road—or a train ride just over the hill. One night, they went into a village and sure enough, there was a train. They told the prisoners that this was their train and told them to board it. There were boxcars and gravel cars with small sides on them.

Ed: "I didn't have the strength to step over a railroad track and fell on my face. My only thought was that if I didn't get that train, this was going to be the end. Bob and another guy helped me to my feet and to the ladder of the car. How in the world am I going to get on this train? No one is going to lift me up over the top with dried feces all over me and my ass sticking out, but someone did lift me up and threw me onto the train."

Ed struggled to his knees, crawled to the side of the car and sat down leaning against it. Gunfire broke out and something hit Ed in the right leg.

Ed: "I looked down at the calf of my leg and saw that it started to bleed. I checked the other side of my leg, hoping that whatever it was went through. I couldn't see anything—and it didn't hurt that much anyway. I was too preoccupied to think about it because they said 'everyone off the train. This train is going the other way.'"

Disappointed, the men started marching again. By daybreak, Ed's leg was hurting and he had a bad limp. With every stop, pain ran up his leg and seemed to be tied to something under his arm. The next afternoon as they were resting, Ed looked at his calf. It was dark grey all around it and he presumed that gangrene had set in.

Ed: "Then, I saw that it was maggots—millions of tiny grey ones. I took a stick and tried to brush them off but couldn't. My pants were too short to pull down over it because I had torn them off to wrap around my feet. I could squeeze the wound but couldn't see anything. My only hope was that it would work out by itself. With guys dying every day, or being beaten to death, I didn't have anything to complain about."

One day, they stayed in a schoolhouse with many small rooms. The guards crowded them together and made them sit on the floors. Several Russian officers came down the hall and looked at them. One of the guys had a prayer book and the Korean guard asked for it. The kid held it to his chest. The guard asked for it again and the kid refused. The guard raised his rifle and asked one more time. When the kid refused, the guard pulled the bolt back and started counting. They kid just stood there crying.

Ed: "I wanted to yell, 'Give him the damn book!'"

The Russian said something and they walked away laughing.

The prisoners had known the excitement of battle and had seen friends die. When captured, they'd felt despair and dread. Now, although beaten down and physically depleted, each man searched inside for the will to face whatever came next.

Most of the men were young—boys really. Many were new to the Army. Some were only a few months from the warmth of their mothers' kitchens—others had been on their own for years. Each reacted to their new circumstances differently.

Most—religious or not—prayed. Tears muddied the dirty faces of many others. They'd lost so much—home, security—control. Some fantasized about women—or food. Others worried about their parents. Did telegrams bearing news of lost sons lie crumpled on dining room tables across the country? One man agonized about his wife. Was she still true to him? Would she be there for him when he came home? Another seethed with hatred and vengeance.

Walt Whitcomb: "The important thing now was to survive—to be stronger than they were—to let them KNOW that I was stronger than they were. My feelings for my father resurfaced. When I was twelve, he beat me up with a two by four—so I started hating him. A person filled with hatred can endure an awful lot of pain. So now, as a prisoner, I reacted like I did at home. I put one foot in front of the other, thinking 'my turn will come—eventually it will be my turn.'"

George: "I survived by telling myself that I was a soldier—and that's what soldiers do."

Exposed to death and the threat of bodily harm on a daily basis, they were torn between needing each other and not wanting to face another traumatizing loss. Still, it seems only natural that some of the prisoners formed close relationships.

Ed Slater and Bob Sharpe marched together whenever they could. Ed's pithy sense of humor made Bob laugh even when it seemed that things couldn't get any worse. Bob was determined and easygoing. His companionship made Ed feel less alone.

Bob: "One of the guards began beating the prisoners with a rubber hose. There was a long line of us. Ed says, under his breath, 'I sure hope that guy gets tired before he gets to me.' It was a bad scene, but you couldn't help but laugh."

Ed: "The guard did wear out, but I think that is when we both realized we were half out of our minds. We certainly had no reason to laugh."

Jim Yeager and John Toney were a team. They stuck together on the long marches, shared food and plotted escapes. Their friendship gave them constancy and support during the most difficult times of their lives.

Fate threw Sherman Jones and Gene Putzier together in the 1st Battalion of the 29th Infantry. They endured the hell of Anui—then their capture and the long marches. They were teenagers but shock and horror forged their friendship.

Others found themselves with strangers as buddies died or disappeared. The fortunate ones made new attachments that helped them deal with their daily realities. The unlucky ones lost touch and drifted away.

Walt: "I made friends easily and I bonded with my fellow prisoners. The last thing I wanted was to be off by myself."

Bob: "At one time, I thought of taking the easy way out. I had dysentery—very bad. My friend Ed Slater kept me from it. Good Lord, Slater has some strength in him. We took turns keeping each other moving forward."

Walt: "I remember Jonesy.[18] We talked a couple of times. He and Yeager carried the honey bucket together. They used to talk for hours."

Jim: "There were only a few guards. Toney would wait until they were several yards away—and then he'd count cadence in Donald Duck's voice. That really pissed off the guards and gave us all a good laugh."

Companionship and humor weren't the only survival strategies used by the prisoners. Some focused on food—searching the sides of the road for pumpkin rinds or peppers. Others watched for enemy troop movements and plotted ways to escape. They all relied on the officers. Major McDaniel was

---

18 Sherman Jones

the ranking officer and he wore the leadership mantle easily—even under the most difficult of circumstances.

Ed: "Our officers were Captain Locke, Lieutenant Makarounis, Lieutenant Smith and Major McDaniel. Captain Locke didn't realize it, but I watched everything he did. I would try to do the same. Although I never talked to them, I was always close and would do anything they did. I figured if anyone made it, they would."

Bill Henninger: "I couldn't walk by myself and Major McDaniel got guys to help me. The next morning, we got to talking and I told him I was going to take my trousers down and let the sun warm me up. He was okay with that and it helped my legs."

Somewhere between Taejon and Seoul, an airplane strafed a rail yard. Everybody ran for cover. After the attack was over, the guards directed the prisoners off road and through some fields. They found a path and trudged down it toward a village. It started raining and water cascaded off the thatched roofs as they passed.

Jim: "I stopped to wash myself, as I was filthy dirty. A couple of guards beat me with their rifles. I finally managed to get up and back into the column."

As they marched down the street at Yong Dong Po, several P-51s strafed the area. Everyone broke into a run seeking cover. After the attack, the guards rounded the prisoners up and moved them into a theater. Russian propaganda movies were showing.

Jim: "There were lots of flag-waving people, but we couldn't understand what they were saying. After the film was over, we went down to the Han River, which separates Yong Dong Po and Seoul, and boarded a ferryboat to cross the river."

On the other side, North Korean guards marched the prisoners up out of the riverbed where they boarded old-fashioned streetcars and rode to the capital building. There, they unloaded and formed another column at the base of the steps while photographers snapped pictures. Humiliated, they could only hope that their families would see that they were still alive.

Afterwards, the prisoners marched to a northeastern section of the city. The guards quartered them on the second floor of a schoolhouse, which had been an annex girls' school of the University of Seoul.[19]

---

19 Moo Hak school

Twenty-Five — Seoul

The long line of captives meant that people at the front of the line had different experiences than men in the rear. On the march from Taejon, more men joined them. By the time they got to Seoul, there were three hundred and seventy-six prisoners.

Ed Slater: "We walked into the city at night. It was so cold I thought we would freeze to death. It sure didn't look like the same street that I had walked down when I was here before—the busy shoppers, merchants, motorcycles and the smoke coming out of the small shops. The North Koreans had totally ruined the city. There were very few buildings, no streetlights and everything was dark. People came out and threw things at us."

Lieutenant Makarounis had a different experience. He arrived in Seoul about eight in the morning in the middle of an air raid. Jets were strafing some of the streets, but fortunately, the pilots didn't see the prisoners—or if they did, they recognized them as Americans.

The streets were crowded despite the raid. Lieutenant Makarounis and his group marched into a courtyard created by three buildings. Hundreds of American men leaned out the windows and called down into the square. Lieutenant Makarounis recognized some of them. They were from his unit. Somebody shouted, "How's the food situation," and one of the men in the window said, "Soup twice a day and bread twice a day." "It isn't so bad," someone else said. "We wash twice a day, too—and there's plenty of water to drink, but no Red Cross and no chance to write letters."

Lieutenant Makarounis: "I heard this voice, 'Get the hell away from those windows, you bastards. And stay away.' Now that was my

89

introduction to Mr. Kim, who was the man we hated most of all. Mr. Kim, who had been a newspaper man in Seoul before the war started, was an ardent Communist."

Mr. Kim made an unpleasant first impression—rounding up the men and herding them into the building. Shoving and yelling, the guards processed the men and placed them in a room with about forty-five enlisted men and five officers.

Lloyd Krieder:[20] "He called [us] no good animals, and dogs, and everything else. He was not even human in his actions, but he said if he had it his way he would have us shot. That's why I figure he wasn't really in charge of the camp." (Krieder, 1953)

A light-haired, Air Force captain greeted Lieutenant Makarounis, "I'm Captain Locke."[21] He introduced the other officers—a Lieutenant Blaylock and a Lieutenant James Smith. He also told Makarounis that Major McDaniel was the senior officer—and currently in charge of the POWs.

Bob Sharpe: "Captain Locke married a girl from my home town, High Point, North Carolina. I talked with [him] as much as we dared."

The prisoners viewed Mr. Kim as their chief tormentor. He stood out from the other North Koreans. Instead of a uniform, he wore a white suit.[22] Some said that he was a civilian—a reporter for a leftist newspaper. There were rumors that he was a mess boy with the 7th Division during World War II—and that he was a South Korean. Someone heard that he was a schoolteacher. Someone else thought he was a spy. Clearly, he was educated. No one seemed to know how he came to be responsible for the American POWs. Most

---

20 Lloyd Krieder was another POW who survived the Sunchon Tunnel Massacre

21 Captain Locke was leading a flight of fighter aircraft on the 17th of August 1950, in the vicinity of Yongdong when his plane was hit and caught on fire. He crash landed into a rice field where enemy troops took him prisoner. (Locke, 1953)

22 Communist interrogators wore white. (O'Brien, 2007)

assumed that the North Koreans appointed him to that position.

History has clarified Mr. Kim's role slightly. Before the war, he was a South Korean civilian employed by civil administration. An opportunist, he worked to appease whoever was in charge. With the success of the North Korean invaders, Mr. Kim turned against his American contacts and made the best deal that he could. The North Koreans took many thousands of people north. Since Kim Il-Sung considered himself the leader of the entire Korean Peninsula, these people were automatically citizens of his regime. Some even became soldiers. Mr. Kim went out of his way to serve his new masters—seeking to ingratiate himself with a North Korean rear guard Major who was in charge. (O'Brien, 2007)

Bob Sharpe: "Kim was an SOB. His best English was cussing. He knew all the bad words—and he'd use them, but he wouldn't let you cuss. He was arrogant."

Whatever his background, Mr. Kim became a daily part of the men's lives during the final, tragic weeks of their Korean sojourn. Ideologically passionate, he took every opportunity to berate and abuse the prisoners. He disrespected them on many levels. For their part, the POWs loathed him—and imbued him with the characteristics of the "communist boogey-man."

Allen: "Mr. Kim was about five-foot-nine, had a fat face, brown eyes and black hair. He wore glasses. He had the Communist look in his face."

Roy Sutterfield: "He had a little bit of gold in his teeth . . . on one side. He had a bad habit of putting his hands in his back pockets when he was talking." (Sutterfield, 1950)

Allen: "He cursed and yelled a lot. I saw him slapping guys in the face and hitting them in the back. There's a story that he put a lit cigarette in a Sergeant's eye, but I didn't see that. He ranted propaganda. We just listened."

Lieutenant Smith: "He always wanted to be called Mr. Kim. You had to be very polite to him. The fellow that was with me made a little error as he came in and he called him 'boisun.' Kim just blew his top when he said that." (Smith, 1953)

Valdor John: "Kim encouraged the town residents to come out and heckle the prisoners. Residents were afraid to help."

In Seoul, a new platoon of North Korean soldiers—a unit of the Security Guard Bureau, Home Affairs, led by a major—took responsibility for the prisoners. Aside from Mr. Kim, the men spent the most time with two guards in particular—a beefy fellow nicknamed "Johnny" and a smaller, unpleasant man that they called "Buck."

Jim: "Buck—so named because he had buck teeth—was the meanest of them all. He looked for any excuse to beat, bayonet and club with his rifle. He was about five-foot tall. Everyone hated him with a passion."

Allen: "The guard looked like an ape with big buck teeth. I remember he had a little scar on his right cheek and his eyes were squinty."

The major remained a shadowy character. The real bad guy was Mr. Kim—or so it seemed at first. It was clear that Mr. Kim planned to use the POWs to promote his communist agenda to the South Koreans—and the rest of the world. It wasn't long before he ramped up the interrogation sessions.

Bob Sharpe: "Trained Communist interrogators questioned us repeatedly. Many had limited English skills. They separated the POWs into reactionaries or progressives. They classed me as a reactionary, one they thought they couldn't convert."

If a prisoner didn't understand a command, the guards rifle-whipped him until he did.

Valdor John: "I learned the Korean language from being beaten."

The interrogators could be worse. They had a political agenda to promote—and they used American social inequities to push their ideologies.

Lieutenant James Bryant Smith was a black man. His interrogations seemed to focus on racism.

Lieutenant Smith: "He said, 'You don't seem to have done very much hard labor. Your hands are soft.' That is one thing they did all along the line, they would look at your hands. I guess they were trying to find out whether you were a machine gunner, a worker, or laborer, or capitalist, or something of that type. He wanted to know who my relatives were, and if I knew Paul Robeson, if I ever went to see him, and if I ever heard him, and if I had ever been a member of the party. He always got negative answers and seemed to be very disturbed." (Smith, 1953)

They knew the troubled history between Native Americans and the United States government. In fact, they knew more about it than Valdor John did.

Valdor: "They wanted us to become communists. They would run down the American government—and being an Indian, they'd say to me, 'Look how you've been treated.' I tried to tell them that I wasn't into politics, that I didn't know anything, and that I joined the Army because I didn't have anything else to do." (Carlson, 2002)

The interrogators told him that someone had reported that he witnessed a massacre. Apparently, NKPA troops had captured about twelve UN soldiers. Rather than take them captive, they tied their hands behind their backs with barbed wire and shot them. Valdor's tormentors gave him electric shocks under his fingernails to get him to confess to witnessing this act. However, he had only seen photos of the event in Stars and Stripes and had nothing to tell them.

Valdor: "When I refused to give them the admission they wanted, they pulled off my fingernails—one by one. The first one was horrible —each succeeding one, I became more and more numb to the pain."

Mr. Kim and his helpers knew many ways to hurt a man.

Valdor: "They stripped me naked, dunked me in cold water and hung me up by my hands until my shoulders dislocated."

Valdor wasn't Mr. Kim's only victim—however, the treatment seemed arbitrary. Bill Henninger wasn't tortured nor did he see anyone tortured.

These sessions provoked deep anger in some of the POWs.

Jim Yeager: "The North Koreans tried to brainwash us. Kim demanded that everyone stand at attention. I remained sitting cross-legged on the floor. Kim screamed at me and I stayed sitting. A guard with a burp gun came over and waved it in my face. He grunted, making motions for me to get up. I looked him straight in the eyes and it raced through my mind, 'you take one foot closer and I will take your damn gun and kill you all.' He must have thought I was crazy, because he backed off."

94

The questionnaires seemed out of touch with the lives of the young Americans. Modeled after Russian questionnaires designed to elicit information from prisoners brought up in Eastern Europe, the information collected in this matter had dubious utility. (O'Brien, 2007)

Ed: "They took us a few at a time and asked questions. I'm sure none of us told the truth on the questionnaire. They gave us books to read. If you didn't act like you were reading them, they would stop by and slap the hell out of us. They gave me *Mary Had a Little Lamb* or something like that. I couldn't figure out what this was all about."

Lieutenant Smith: "First, he asked me if I had ever been lynched, and I wondered how he expected me to be there." (Smith, 1953)

The Communist operatives took themselves and their mission seriously. Their command of American idiom was hilariously literal. Some of the men took advantage of the wide cultural gap to get back at their captors with sarcasm and down-home humor.

Walt Whitcomb: "When we had to fill out those questionnaires, I said that my father was Clark Gable and my mother was Jane Russell. For 'Why did you come to Korea?' I wrote to kill gooks. Of course, it cost me a few teeth."

The questioners took pictures of each POW and stapled them to the forms. "These are going to Moscow," they warned. "If you escape and we capture you again, we'll kill you."

Lloyd Krieder: "All the boys turned out to be farmers after a while. That was the only way they could keep living they thought. If they had a car or anything else, they wanted to shoot you. They wanted to shoot me once when I said I had a car, so I forgot about the car." (Krieder, 1953)

The men walked away smirking. Getting one over on Mr. Kim made everyone feel good.

By this point, the men had developed a great deal of affection for American officers Major McDaniel, Captain Locke and Lieutenant Makarounis. They knew that they were paying a physical price for looking out for them.

Major McDaniel was in his thirties—old to most of the men who were in their late teens and early twenties. He was tall with a military bearing.

Jim: "He was all business."

As the men came in at different times from different areas, the Major made it his business to meet as many of the prisoners as possible. He was the boss but he became more than that to the men. They saw him as a hero—someone to look up to—someone with character. He took an interest in many things—like the distribution of food, the organization of the camps, who was in each squad, and what jobs they should be doing. It's likely that Major McDaniel himself felt that he was doing his job. It was what the Army trained him to do—and what they expected of him. However, the men admired him for confronting the North Koreans on their behalf. They felt that he went the extra mile for them—and they appreciated it.

Ed: "One day in Seoul, Major McDaniel walked by and someone said, 'He's in trouble. They are going to beat the hell out of him.' When he came back, they HAD beaten him. He was struggling like he had bad legs, but he never complained."

McDaniel and Locke had some disagreements. McDaniel thought that Locke was too outspoken and that he might get others hurt. However, the men loved Captain Locke's outspokenness. It made them feel less helpless.

Captain Locke was a veteran of World War II and a fighter pilot. He provoked Mr. Kim and the guards—calling them names, demanding better food, more clothing and more downtime. His bravado under pressure kept morale high.

Ed: "We were in a small school that had solid doors on the rooms. Someone drew pictures on the blackboard of an army deuce and a half running over North Koreans—that really got them upset. I suspect that Locke did it. Another time, Locke said, 'Slater, put your head up by the door and see if he's out there.' Therefore, I'm listening and I said, 'Yeah, there's someone out there.' Then, Locke ran and hit the door with his shoulder, which knocked over the guards on the other side. That ticked them off and they came in and beat up on us."

Jim: "Mr. Kim thought Captain Locke was bonkers. He knew that Locke was an officer and that it was his job to stand up to the North Koreans and try to intimidate them. However, even though they were enemies, I think that Kim respected him."

Bob: "Captain Locke would come around to the classrooms where people were staying and point to his head—meaning, 'Think!' He was a smart guy but he played dumb as hell."

Walt: "Major McDaniel kept the guys together. He and Lieutenant Makarounis—those guys were the real heroes. They did something for everyone."

Mr. Kim and his helpers seemed to have two goals—to get a prisoner to admit something embarrassing to the Allied Forces and to forward his communist message.

Valdor: "I blocked all that stuff they were telling us out of my mind. It was like a tape recording—every day it was the same thing. To try to warm up to you, they'd say 'Here's a cigarette'—and if you resisted, they got tougher and tougher."

Bob: "They tried to turn us against each other. Like any prison situation, there was a system of snitches. We were in their system. Eventually, you began to look at your buddy and wonder if you could trust him."

Mr. Kim told them that American troops had given up and were killed. The men didn't believe that. However, they had no idea what was the truth. They clung to the hope of rescue—

but they had no idea how long that might take—or how long they could hang on.

Lloyd: "Mr. Kim was the chief interpreter at the camp at Seoul and at that girl's school. He gave us a radio in our room. Every night about seven or seven-thirty, he wanted us to listen to Sioux City Sue. They broadcast every evening for about half an hour, propaganda, how they were winning, how the North Korean Army was conquering all Korea, and all that." (Krieder, 1953)

Lieutenant Smith: "We called her Rice Ball Kate." (Smith, 1953)

Others called her "Rice Bowl Maggie" or "Seoul City Sue." She was the Korean War version of Tokyo Rose. She played American music on her radio program dished up with Communist propaganda. Like her Japanese counterpart, Sue's listeners loathed her but listened to her daily broadcast.

One day, the POWs were shown a propaganda movie with a column of GIs holding up banners written in Korean.

Ed: "I looked for someone I knew. The only one was Sergeant Haley,[23] my first Sergeant. I heard he died as a POW."

A day or so later, the guards herded the prisoners down the stairs to the end of the building where a barber cut their hair and shaved their faces—forehead and all with a straight razor. After they returned to their rooms, three guards came in and gave everybody a shot, from a syringe.

Jim: "He went from one man to the next, just shoot-squirt-shoot-squirt—no sanitary procedure at all. One of our men was on his deathbed, but that didn't bother the shooter. The poor guy got his shot too. They told us it was for cholera."

---

23 Haley was 1st Sergeant Richard A. Haley—captured on 12 July 1950, he died on August 11, 1950 in Pyongyang. He was born in 1920 in Auburndale, Massachusetts. (Estabrook, 2007)

Some of the men didn't have shirts, so they received Korean army shirts. They couldn't imagine why they were suddenly receiving all the attention.

Eventually, they understood.

Their captors assembled the prisoners in the gym behind the school. Sitting on one side was a long row of Korean men and women, dressed in fine white clothing (the basic formal attire). Vases of flowers sat on tables decorated with banners with Korean writing on them. On the opposite wall, a line of Korean guards with burp guns and rifles stood at the ready. The POWs sat between these two groups.

Allen: "They seated us in a room. North Korean soldiers and Russian civilians came to take pictures. The Major (McDaniel) brought our group to attention when the North Korean soldiers came into the room. He said this would make the American side look good."

Mr. Kim and a couple of other Koreans in business suits and Captain Locke sat on the stage. Over on the side where the guards were standing, were several news cameras.

Jim: "The ceremony started. Kim gave a rambling speech in both Korean and English."

Captain Locke reading propaganda papers

Bill: "I remember Mr. Kim yelling a lot."

Jim: "The basic subject was about the capitalist imperial aggression against the peace-loving Korean people, etc. Finally it was Captain Locke's turn—he read from some papers the same communist line but in closing, good old Captain Locke said, 'You may have us prisoners but our troops are going to kick the hell out of you.' Mr. Kim and the other communists were visibly shaken."

Later on, they heard that Major McDaniel, the ranking POW officer, had refused to give that talk and that Kim had him beaten.

After the ceremony in the gym, the guards ordered the prisoners to form a column in front of the school. They forced some of the men to carry large posters with communist slogans in English and Korean. Two POWs supported the dying man who'd received his cholera shot along with the rest. They marched from the school to the capital building and back, which took the rest of the day. Photographers took pictures of the spectacle.

Along the way, the sick man died and his buddies had to drag him back to the school.

While living conditions in Seoul were better than when the men had been marching, they were still prisoners in a strange and hostile land. Ravaged by dysentery, they now exhibited diseases brought on by malnutrition—things like beriberi and scurvy. Infections, sickness and depression took their toll—and men died every day. Medical Aid man Robert Sharpe was on burial detail. He performed this sad duty more and more often now.

Ed: "My leg was still killing me. I thought it was infected. I could now squeeze it and see some metal in the wound. When I tried to pull it out, the pain was unbearable. I asked the guy next to me if he would jerk it out when I turned my head. He jerked as hard as he could and the tears rolled down my cheeks. On the second try, it came out. It was flat and had stick things on it like little hooks that held it in my leg. My leg was bleeding a lot. I couldn't afford to lose much blood."

Jim: "We were crowded with barely enough space to lie down. Everybody had diarrhea. During the night, the call of nature would strike. We would try to get up and make it to the bathroom. A lot of us didn't even make it to the door of our room."

It had been weeks since the men had eaten a proper meal. During the day, they made up menus of what they were going to have for Thanksgiving if they ever made it home. Others talked about how the food tasted in last night's dreams.

100

Jim: "At that time, our ration was a small piece of bread and a bowl of soup made from radish greens and fish. The major persuaded them to let our own cooks handle the show. That helped, but when he saw the Reds were shorting us on food, he raised hell with them."

Lieutenant Smith: "What we received was a water soup. The soup was made from the tops of the vegetables. The Koreans would eat the beets and turnips. They would take the bottom part and they would cut the tops off and give it to our GI cooks to boil in water and that was our food. It had a very low calorie rating and it was just keeping you alive. That is all." (Smith, 1953)

Allen: "In the building, they kept a big tub filled with rice. When another bomb hit the side of the building, the windows shattered and glass fell in the tub. That was our meal. We picked out the big pieces of glass and ate our rice balls."

By this point, the men had been with their captors for several weeks and had begun to deduce some of their fears and weaknesses.

Jim: "One day, we decided to try and shake up the North Koreans, so we concocted a story about how the Japanese were going to liberate us by dropping in a large unit of paratroopers. We leaked it to some of the guards. From observing reactions of Mr. Kim and his men, it was apparent that they were not discounting the possibility of this happening."

Then one day in September, something did happen.

Jim: "We heard a noise—like bump, bump. At first, we thought the guards were playing in the gym, but that wasn't it. It finally dawned on us that it was heavy artillery fire."

In the weeks since their capture, Allied Forces reinforced their numbers in southern Korea with well-armed, well-trained troops. Their presence stopped the NKPA advance in a fierce bloody confrontation at the Pusan Perimeter.

Inchon Invasion *(National Archives)*

In support of this effort, MacArthur devised Operation Bluehearts—a scheme that was considered too risky earlier in the war because American troops weren't prepared to carry off such a complex maneuver. The idea involved an amphibious landing at Inchon on Korea's West Coast just below Seoul. The Marines and the 7th Division were to cut enemy forces off from the north and reduce pressure on the defenders of the Pusan Perimeter.

In the days before the invasion, things began changing for the prisoners and their guards in Seoul.

Bob: "Air activity became intense, navy corsairs were everywhere."

Ed: "We saw a lot of strafing and bombing. We watched the planes dive down, bomb the city, disappear and come up on the other side. They were literally destroying Seoul. We heard rumors that the Americans were coming and that there were ships at Yong-Dung-Po and maybe Inchon."

On September 15, hundreds of US Navy ships, landing craft and airplanes participated in the landing. Seventy-thousand soldiers and Marines along with two ROK infantry regiments came ashore at Inchon. Resistance was light—perhaps because of the naval bombardment—perhaps because the NKPA had dismissed the possibility of an attack from that direction.

American forces pushed the enemy back toward Seoul and captured the Kimpo Airfield on the south shore of the Han River two days later.

Bombed train near Seoul in 1950 *(National Archives)*

It didn't take long before the prisoners got an idea of what was happening. The guards brought several Marines in starched fatigues into one of the POW rooms. About the only thing the men were able to get out of them was that there had been an amphibious landing. They had been on a patrol, gotten lost, and then captured.

Lieutenant Smith: "We started trying to figure out what was going on. We couldn't figure our troops being that far north. Anyway, we knew that Kim and the lieutenant in charge there, and another officer, were burning papers during the day. So we figured that we were getting ready to be moved out, that they were going to move us north someplace." (Smith, 1953)

George: "The North Koreans were anxious to get us out of there. I remember them taking a man out to bury him and he wasn't dead. People would be dragged out of the building and I'd hear shots. Others were dying of starvation and dysentery. I watched Jerome die. Spencer died during the march."

Jim: "I can't recall the time frame between the original firing to the night that we all moved out of the school and marched north. I do know that Toney and I had planned on trying to escape that night."

American troops from Inchon crossed the Han River and entered Seoul. After three days of bloody street-to-street fighting in which large numbers of civilians died, they took the city on September 26.

By that point, the POWs were gone—but many left their names on blackboards in the schoolhouse. At least someone would know they had been there, they hoped.

Twenty-Six — Pyongyang
"If you are going through hell . . . keep going." — Winston Churchill

Seoul was in chaos. American troops fought a bloody, street-by-street battle for the city. It was after dark on September 20 and the men were getting ready to sleep. Suddenly, the North Koreans broke into the rooms and herded everyone outside into the courtyard.

Mr. Kim gave a speech. He said that it was becoming too dangerous in Seoul. The front was getting near and it was time to go. He inspected the sickroom and sent all of the men who were capable of walking out to join the column. At about nine P.M., the prisoners started out of the courtyard heading north.

The men were nervous. They'd already marched hundreds of miles. Weakened by disease and starvation, their physical reserves were low. They knew that something big was happening—they saw how anxious their captors were and they heard the battle going on around them. If they stayed in Seoul, perhaps they would be rescued soon—and of course, no one wanted to go to North Korea with winter approaching.

Lieutenant Makarounis: "I wonder if you can know how that made us feel—that the Americans might be entering the city at any time."

There was one other thing—something that filled the men with dread. The guards on the march from Taejon to Seoul had been civilians. Now, rear guard soldiers took over that duty—that could not be good news.

Ed Slater: "Some men refused to leave Seoul. That led to a lot of beatings and shootings."

Their captors kept the men off-balance. There were no hard and fast rules. The same behavior that instigated a beating one day was ignored the next. Sometimes, if they tried to escape, they were recaptured and told not to do it again. Sometimes, the guards shot escapees on the spot. Uncertainty left the men in a state of constant wariness. As long as it was possible to survive—as long as they could hope, they obeyed. Those convinced that they were going to die anyway had little reason to comply. (O'Brien, 2007)

As they were going through the outskirts of the city, Captain Locke told Lieutenant Makarounis that two of the lieutenants had escaped from the column. They started out with three hundred and seventy-six prisoners—now they were down to three hundred and seventy-four.

Valdor John: "About one hundred captives came from the Inchon Invasion—mostly Army 7th Infantry Division and a few Marines."

George Snodgrass: "As we left Seoul, they loaded some of the sick and badly wounded on oxcarts."

Allen Gifford: "Mr. Kim stayed with them. There were forty-five put on the carts, but only twenty-five made it to Pyongyang."

They walked five miles straight north at a fast pace. After about an hour, a North Korean army officer on horseback rode up and shouted to the guards. They'd almost run into an artillery barrage.

They turned the column around and marched the men back into the city the way they'd come—and took another route out of Seoul.

Lieutenant Makarounis: "I kept saying 'By tomorrow at this time the Americans will be in Seoul and we'll be on our way back to the States in a week.' That's what I said, and that's what I believed. Instead, we got almost back to the building where they'd kept us, when all of a sudden, they switched us on to another road and we went on into a forest. I felt weak inside and discouraged—discouraged as I ever will be."

106

Kim and his helpers ran up and down the line clubbing the men, trying to get them to move faster. Soon they were out of immediate danger, but they headed north toward the land of the enemy. It was a chilling prospect. As bad as things were in South Korea, would they be worse once they crossed into North Korea? Would the Allied Forces be able to find them there?

Lloyd Krieder: "They moved us out from Seoul at a fast rate. They were afraid, I guess, of us getting liberated, they didn't want us liberated to the States. I guess that is why they moved us out so fast."

They walked all that night and most of the next day without resting.

The guard said there was no more rice. Instead they gave the men crackers that were square, about the size of a quarter and hard as rocks. They couldn't even bite them.

Ed: "They cut my mouth and gums when I tried to chew them. Men were dropping out from malnutrition and wounds."

Allen Gifford: "We were starving. I stole food from the fields every chance I had."

Captain Locke: "We passed by numerous cornfields that had fresh corn that we would have been glad to eat. Potatoes were being harvested. Apple orchards were loaded with apples and we begged for this food and they would not give it to us because they said the farmers under the communistic way of life were responsible for their harvests, and so much was expected to be turned into the Government and it was not for us to have." (Locke, 1953)

Lieutenant Makarounis: "The Communist guards never shared the same food that they doled out to us. As we would go through villages, they would go off into a village and get chickens, for example, and corn. They would bring this back and eat it with relish right in front of us, offering us none of it." (Makarounis, Subcommittee on Korean War Atrocities 1953)

One day as the prisoners crossed a river, an American jet flew over. The pilot saw them, circled around and attacked. The bullets ricocheted off the road in front of the column. The guards stepped into line with the POWs. The men shoved them back out again.

Ed: "I was out in the middle of the bridge. I sat down and wrapped my arms around a concrete post. The plane came around again and tipped his wings. Then he flew away. We had a pilot with us, Captain Locke, who had been shot down before he was captured. He said the plane was taking pictures of us while they were shooting. I guess they knew who we were all along. A couple of guys pried my arms loose from that concrete post. That scared me so much more than anything on the march did. I still have dreams about those jets."

After a while, the officers encouraged the men to signal to the planes.

Jim Yeager: "We were on the road with bare open ground all around, when all of a sudden the guards cried, 'Hongo, Hongo!' Major McDaniel yelled to stand fast and wave. The guards crowded in among us, taking off their hats and waving towels that they used for sweat rags. Two Marine fighters zoomed past about fifty to seventy-five feet off the ground. One pilot waved at us."

The rest of the day, they continued marching north. Airplanes flew over them wagging their wings. The men took heart, realizing that the American forces still knew where they were. That evening, they arrived at the Imjin River and crossed the 38th parallel into North Korea.

Jim: "One of the men who had been a fresh-water sailor on the Great Lakes had it in his head that they would never take us across the 38th parallel. Upon reaching the North Korean side, he went crazy. We marched down the road, leaving him thrashing around in the sand."

A short distance down the road, they turned into a schoolyard. As the rest of the men settled into their accommodations for the night, Mr. Kim told Jim Yeager and John Toney to get into the bed of a dump truck. None of the men liked being singled out. Who knew what Kim might have in mind? They'd seen comrades murdered. Some had simply disappeared.

Jim: "Toney and I were worried about what was going to happen. The truck stopped near the man who had gone nuts. He was still thrashing around on the riverbank. The guard had us dismount and indicated that we were to place him in the truck bed, which we did. He motioned us back in the truck."

Mr. Kim met the truck in the schoolyard. He had a guard escort Jim and Toney to one of the second-story rooms where the other POWs were. They never saw the crazed soldier again.

Jim and Toney were still plotting ways to escape. One night, Jim decided to check things out and asked to go to the bathroom.

Jim: "The shed with the squat hole was fifty to sixty feet back of the school. Behind it were rice paddies that backed up to a mountain range. On my return to the school, I managed to get in one building where I discovered a jar of bean paste. I had my rice bowl in my pants pocket so I whipped it out and filled it up. Scouting around, I found some small potatoes. At first, I couldn't figure out how I could get them past the guards. Then it hit me, blouse your trousers and fill up the pant legs. I still had my blousing rubbers in my pocket."

He walked past the guards and returned to his sleeping place, next to Toney. Jim shared potatoes and bean paste while discussing possible escape routes.

The next morning, a B-29 bombed the school and the guards wouldn't let anyone out of the building during the day. The prisoners' room had a door that opened out onto a porch. Since they had to get permission from the guards to go to the bathroom, they put some straw out on the porch so they could relieve themselves. One of the guards patrolling around the base of the school caught them—and they fired on the next person to drop his pants. They missed him, but he was a mess as he dove back into the room.

Jim: "After dark, the guard let a few men go to the toilet. One of them was a fourteen year old kid who had lied about his age. He was always taunting Mr. Kim who hated him. The kid discovered a door ajar on the ground floor. Inside he found bags of rice crackers and cigarettes. He filled up his pockets and inside his shirt. When he returned, he passed out smokes and crackers."

Jim and Toney scheduled their escape for the next evening. However, about an hour before dark, the guards herded the prisoners out into the schoolyard. It was too late. They were moving on.

Mr. Kim marched up with the kid who'd shared his stolen bounty with the others.

Jim: "Mr. Kim delivered a ranting speech about stealing from the Korean People's Republic while the kid held two large rocks in his outstretched hands. Every time the boy moved, the guards hit him in the face with a rifle barrel. Mr. Kim gave orders for us to move out. We turned and marched to the road. The last time I saw the kid, the guards were still beating him."

They marched at night to avoid the planes. The road to Pyongyang was busy. Long columns of enemy soldiers detoured around the straggling line of POWs. Soon they noticed that not all the soldiers they saw were North Koreans. Railroad tracks ran parallel to the road. They saw three flat cars pushed by a steam engine.

Jim: "The flat cars were loaded with blue-quilted uniformed men. This puzzled us, as these men didn't look like Koreans."

As they moved further north, the conditions became more dreadful. Sometimes there wasn't anything to eat for days—and now it was deep in the fall and nighttime temperatures were uncomfortably low.

Ed: "As the sun came up, we'd see frost on our chests and clothing—from our breath, I guess."

Every night, they marched long distances. More and more men began dropping out.

Lloyd: "They would say 'putty-putty,'[24] and the men were falling, and they wouldn't want us to pick them up. They didn't want us to carry them with us. They said one rotten apple would spoil the bunch. As we went along, each man got weaker and weaker—and no one could walk any more, hardly any of us."

The guards began shooting the ones who couldn't walk.

Lloyd: "About half way between Seoul and Pyongyang a few fellows stayed at a village, and this one fellow came back and he was shot in the leg and he said they shot everybody." (Krieder, 1953)

Lieutenant Smith: "(Major McDaniel) had various officers get to the end of the column every now and then to try to keep down that type of thing—by trying to ask the men to keep up in line, and also to give him reports on what went on there. He had officers at the end of the line and the front of the line and in each group."

Lieutenant Makarounis: "Major McDaniel would always head the column, trying to keep the pace slow."

Major McDaniel's efforts encouraged the men and kept them moving forward.

Walt Whitcomb: "All my life, I was taught I could make it through any problems. That helped me survive. I kept telling myself I could make it just a little bit more."

Death came in more shocking forms. One evening, Sherman Jones fell. The man behind him fell on top of him. A

---

24 Putty-putty — Lloyd is mistaken. 'Ppali Ppali' means 'hurry up' or 'fast fast' in Korean and that was what the guards were probably saying. (Chong, 2007)

guard shot the prisoner above Sherman and cut off his head with his bayonet.

Allen: "Usually the sick were in the rear. The guys who could walk tried to help the ones who couldn't make it on their own. I remember one guy who was falling down from exhaustion. I saw a guard shoot. It turned my stomach."

Friends implored each other to get up and keep going.

Walt: "I'd pick at people—try to make them mad. Anger will get you up and going just a little bit longer."

Occasionally, they stopped so that troops, supply trains and motorized vehicles could pass, all going south.

Jim: "I started stealing dry fish off the supply carts as they passed by. Toney and I ate them—flesh, bone and all. Somewhere I picked up a Pall Mall cigarette package. From this point on, Toney and I picked up cigarette butts, stripped them and placed the tobacco in the cigarette package."

Walt: "Prisoners stole food from each other, or traded it for cigarettes. I could never understand that—giving up your food for a smoke."

There was no toilet paper, so the men improvised. Whenever possible, they took pleasure in stealing propaganda posters and using them for that purpose. It was a small, rebellious gesture, but it made them feel better.

Lieutenant Makarounis: "Major McDaniel made a little speech. He said that even though we were prisoners and had lost a lot, we should retain our pride as Americans. At the time it was just the right thing to say."

Gene Putzier was sick—and getting worse as they marched north. His friend Sherman Jones stayed close—trying to keep Gene on his feet.

Late one evening, Ed spent more time with Mr. Kim than he wished. The guard was feeding the men when Ed noticed that they were skipping some of the prisoners—including him. Right away, he knew that something was up—and that Mr. Kim was behind it.

Ed: "Mr. Kim told Lieutenant Smith to pick out the worst wounded and the weakest. He said that he would take them back to a village and let them rest a couple of days. I told Lieutenant Smith I didn't want to go back, because I knew what was going to happen to us. If I was going to die, I would do it right here in front of my men and let Kim answer for it later."

They loaded eight or ten of the worst wounded on an oxcart and started south.

Ed: "I was reluctant to go, but Lieutenant Smith said I would be okay and slipped me half of his rice ball. Kim looked at me and said, 'Come on you.'"

Mr. Kim spoke English. Ed figured that he'd probably been educated in the USA like the North Korean general he'd met earlier. They walked late into the night. The mist was cold and the moon was bright. The carts moved slowly—but Ed still had a hard time keeping up. He tried to convince Kim that he would catch up with the column if he would let him rest for a while.

Mr. Kim refused and ordered Ed to walk up straight.

Ed: "I was holding on to a post that was stuck in the corner of the cart for support. He started talking about America and our government. I wasn't paying much attention to him until he started talking about President Lincoln. He said he was the only good American, and would be a Communist if he were here today."

Ed was sick, hurt and frustrated. Since coming to Korea in July, he'd been lost, beaten and starved. He figured he was being marched back to a village to be murdered in cold blood and buried in a shallow grave. He didn't have much to lose and he'd had just about enough of Mr. Kim and his politics.

Ed: "I told him that was bullshit. If this were communism, I wouldn't want any part of it."

Mr. Kim got so upset that he lost his English. Cursing in Korean, he hit Ed across the arm with his fist, knocking him down. He told Ed to get up or he would shoot him.

Ed managed to get back up and start walking, but Mr. Kim wouldn't let him hold on to the cart anymore. Ed was in a cantankerous mood and pushed Kim as far as he dared, asking if he could ride because some of the men on the cart had already died. Mr. Kim didn't answer.

They came to a village with four buildings. The North Korean guards threw the bodies off the cart—and put the sick and wounded POWs in one of the larger structures that had straw on the floor. They promised the exhausted men that they'd feed them. The prisoners huddled together—hoping for something to fill their aching bellies.

The guards put water in an old bucket with concrete in it and boiled some fish heads. In the end, there was nothing there but scales, bones and eyes.

Ed: "The eyes were the only things we could eat."

The guys lay down and covered themselves with straw to keep warm. They'd been asleep about an hour when Mr. Kim came in, pistol in hand and said, "Okay, let's go."

Afraid that this was the moment of their execution, some of the men hid. The guards bayoneted the straw, hitting a couple of them.

Ed: "We walked until we caught up with the column the next evening. I knew they thought we'd all die overnight. I don't know how many made it back, but I'm sure it was just three or four."

Eventually, Major McDaniel talked to Mr. Kim and persuaded him to march during the day. At first, the prisoners were terrified. They'd all had close calls with friendly fire. However, now—at the request of their officers, when

American planes flew over, the men stood their ground and waved rice bags.

Jim: "A jet would roar over the column, go into a steep climb, execute several rolls and go out of sight. All eyes were fixed on him when three more jets buzzed us, firing their guns, the rounds hitting the road. The planes peeled off to the right, left and center, executing the same routine as the leader. Then the leader would do another run and they would all leave. It finally dawned on us that they were keeping track of us, maybe even taking pictures."

Bob Sharpe: "Captain Locke found a mirror and started signaling the aircraft."

Sometimes Mr. Kim allowed the prisoners to sit down in a field or a building like a school or town hall. Once they sat on concrete floors from daylight until dark. They couldn't lean back on their hands, lean forward or stretch out their aching legs.

Ed: "When dark came, they made us lie down and not get up until daylight. Everyone would lay in the fetal position close together for warmth. We were in lines of about thirty or forty men. When one of us turned, all of us had to turn. We were in this one place for several days. One morning, everyone turned to the left. The guy next to me didn't turn. I nudged him but he didn't move. He had died during the night. His face was about six inches from mine. He had a blank stare and maggots were already crawling out of his eyes."

Ed recoiled. What had been human the night before had become horrific only a few hours later.

Ed: "I'll see that face for the rest of my life."

Survival depends on many small, practical decisions. Ed took the dead man's boots.

Ed: "Before they took him away, Bob gave me his shirt. He was on burial detail that day."

Valdor John had a similar experience that still haunts him. In Seoul—and again in Pyongyang, the Koreans gave the prisoners hard bread that they hoarded and tried to keep warm in a sack. When one of the prisoners died, Valdor took his bread.

Valdor: "I drank for years to escape the guilt of stealing food from a dead comrade."

Some of the sick and wounded men were near death. Major McDaniel persuaded Mr. Kim to get oxcarts for them.

Bombed out tank near Pyongyang
(National Archives)

While they were loading the dying men, a column of wounded North Koreans approached the POWs from behind. Some were on crutches, others hobbling along—going north. As the carts started moving, they headed to the ditch on the right side of the road. The Koreans passed on the left side, bunching up behind the last cart.

A Korean on one crutch, his left leg and right arm in casts, struggled to keep up. One of the POWs placed him on the cart with the sick and wounded American prisoners. He didn't get to ride more than a few feet before one of the guards saw him, knocked him off the cart and beat him unconscious. This brought the Korean column to a halt.

The long line of POWs moved forward, leaving the Koreans and the oxcarts filled with American prisoners behind.

About two days later, one of the wounded POWs managed to catch up with the main body. Jets had strafed the Korean column and ox carts. He was the only one left alive.

Lieutenant Makarounis: "Captain Locke told me that four American planes strafed the oxcarts and killed all the prisoners on it, a

Korean driver and six oxen. The Korean guards were mad at one lieutenant who kept saying how terrible it was that the oxen were killed."

The prisoners were in such bad shape that they could walk only twelve miles a day, sometimes no more than five.

The North Korean lieutenant said they've have to move out again. He didn't care how cold it was—from then on, they'd march at night.

Lieutenant Makarounis: "Major McDaniel, who was from North Carolina, had a real southern drawl and never raised his voice, said, 'Many men will die, Lieutenant.' The lieutenant said, 'Goddamn it. I'm giving the orders here and I say we go now.' We did. We marched all that night."

The next morning Captain Locke argued with the lieutenant and convinced him again that they should travel in the daytime.

Six men couldn't walk. Major McDaniel asked the guards if they could be left behind and picked up by oxcart.

Lieutenant Makarounis: "At this point, the lieutenant broke into a big grin. He said, 'Sure, sure, leave them here—but if you do,' he said—in that singsong English of his—'if you do, I'll have to shoot them.' He started fingering his gun. 'I already have shot twelve of your men.' He seemed proud of that."

Allen Gifford: "The North Korean lieutenant was fairly good-looking. He carried sort of a grin on his face."

Roy: "This lieutenant was the cruelest thing there was. He was real short—not a bad looking guy. He was a clean-cut young fellow. You would think by looking at him that he was generous, I mean just that appearance of face." (Sutterfield, 1951)

Major McDaniel and the other officers pleaded with the lieutenant to stop and let the men get water and rest—but the lieutenant just pushed them harder.

Along about that time, the men noticed that one of their tormentors was no longer with them.

Bob: "Mr. Kim talked crazy about communism all the time. The North Koreans supported him at first, but somewhere along the way, things seemed to turn against him. He was having a tough time and the last time I saw him, he was hobbling a lot. I heard rumors they were going to put him on the oxcart. We still hated him—even when he seemed to be more like us. I don't recall seeing him at Pyongyang. Maybe they killed him or left him behind somewhere."

Roy: "Mr. Kim stayed with us until his feet got so bad he had to stay back." (Sutterfield, 1950)

The march exhuasted the men. As they approached Pyongyang, they looked forward to staying in a warm building where they could rest and recover their strength.

Allen: "The trip from Seoul to Pyongyang took fifteen days. When we got there, there were only two hundred and forty-three of us left."

Jim: "On the outskirts of Pyongyang, we encountered two Russians in a jeep. They wore field green uniforms with the high Russian-style riding boots. One of them stepped out of the jeep, came over and spit on us."

On October 10, the men marched through the city to still another schoolhouse—the Fourth National Grammar School.

Bob: "We had a new set of guards—a bunch of South Koreans who'd been 'converted.'" (R. L. Sharpe, 1951)

Just the day before, Junior Lieutenant Lee Hae Do joined the Security Guard Bureau, Home Affairs squad assigned to guard the POWs.

Lee Hae Do: "The names of other guards I can remember are: Major Chong Myong Sil, Sergeant Kang Myong Sik, Sergeant Kim Bak Ching, Private Chae Chang Ho and myself." (Lee, 1951)

Kim Chung Un of Pyongyang lived in the Fourth Primary School quarters where the US POWs stayed.

Kim Chung Un: "Junior Lieutenant Lee Hae Do was a member of the North Korean Security Forces. I saw him inspecting his men in and around the quarters. The members of the POW guard were from a platoon of the 316th Unit, Security Guard Bureau, of Pyongyang City Home Affairs. A Platoon Leader, the Company Commander and a Major used to come around too." (C. U. Kim, 1951)

Conditions were primitive compared to Seoul. Candles lighted the school.

Ed: "The building was not only dark, it was cold."

As poor as the food had been in South Korea, there was even less of it in Pyongyang. Supper was a piece of rice cake about the size of a Fig Newton—but even divided that small, there wasn't enough for everyone.

It had been more than thirty-six hours since they'd had anything to eat.

Their fat stores were gone. Walt Whitcomb, already slight, was down to sixty-three pounds. Bill Henninger lost one hundred pounds.

Roy: "I think the Major (McDaniel) finally talked some of the soldiers into getting some medical supplies and a few rolls of tape and bandages. They bandaged up some of the feet." (Sutterfield, 1951)

Valdor: "The prisoners were dying—dozens at a time."

Roy: "Everybody began to have colds and sore throats." (Sutterfield, 1950)

Ed: "I sat thinking about my family and my two year old son. I wondered if this would ever end and if I'd get to see him again. Mostly we thought about food. That's all Bob and I talked about. I was now spitting up blood from the crackers I had swallowed."

Lieutenant Smith: "The major (McDaniel) had me in charge of the sick up there in Pyongyang, the sickroom. Each officer was assigned a room, one of the schoolrooms, with a group of men. The men were dying pretty fast there, and he asked me to go along with them and see that they were decently buried as much as possible, under the supervision of the North Korean guards, and also to make a record of where they were buried."

Lloyd: "While we were there a few men would die each day, and we would take them out to a Pyongyang graveyard and bury them. They took me as an interpreter, and that is how I got food. The civilians would give us apples and money." (Krieder, 1953)

Each loss, coming one on top of the other, traumatized the men further. Gene Putzier, Sherman Jones' friend, died in Pyongyang. At the end, Gene lay in Sherm's lap and cried out for his momma.

The men were eager for information about the progress of the war.

Lieutenant Smith: "While we were working during the day, every now and then we would get a pamphlet from one of the civilians, pamphlets that had been dropped from airplanes . . . It said, 'Do not harm the prisoners of war.'-It was signed by General MacArthur-'Or you will be brought to task for it. The war is lost. Surrender and treat our prisoners well.' We would carry these back and show them to the major. We would try to figure out what was going on. We figured maybe our forces were coming north, or maybe going to plan another end sweep. We found out they had landed at Inchon because three marines were added to our group as we traveled north and they told us about the landing at Inchon." (Smith, 1953)

Everyone knew that the end—whatever it was—was near. Some of the men started making plans to escape.

Lieutenant Smith: "They all concluded they would not travel north, that they couldn't make it. The Major (McDaniel) said that was fine, that they had his blessing but that he would stick with the main group so that he could try and see them through."

After they'd been in Pyongyang for a few days, Captain Locke approached Lieutenant Makarounis and asked him if he'd like a chance to "bug out," which meant "escape" in the parlance of the day.

Lieutenant Makarounis: "On October 13 . . . we were soaking up what sun we could get. Actually, what we would be doing in all these schoolyards during the daylight would be taking the clothes off our bodies and killing the lice with our fingernails, which was the only way we could kill those. For a minute, we were more or less to ourselves and the captain said to me in a low whisper, 'If you had a chance to bug out, would you?' I think I stopped breathing for a minute. Then I got myself in hand and I said, 'Captain, I definitely would.'" (Makarounis, Subcommittee on Korean War Atrocities 1953)

Makarounis asked for details of the plot. Locke explained that a Japanese-American soldier who was a translator had arranged an escape for himself and two officers.

Lieutenant Makarounis: "Captain Locke said that Sergeant Kumagai, one of our prisoners, had been contacted by a North Korean. This Korean had told the sergeant . . . that the whole bunch of us were going to be moved out any day to the other side of the Manchurian border. He added that this was a long distance and few, if any, of the men would survive. This Korean said that he would hide three men that would take a chance on escaping. No guaranties, understand, just three men that would take a gamble, if you can call it that."

The original plan was for three Korean teachers, who were underground operatives, to hide Major McDaniel, Captain Locke and Sergeant Kumagai, the translator. However, the major declined the opportunity—telling Captain Locke that he felt, as the senior officer, it was his responsibility to stay with the men. By this time, McDaniel had pneumonia.

Lieutenant Makarounis: "I might say here that the Major, a West Point officer, the S-3 of the 34th Regiment, was one of the most courageous men that you will ever find in the United States Army, one of the most courageous men I have ever met." (Makarounis, Subcommittee on Korean War Atrocities 1953)

When Major McDaniel chose not to participate in the escape, the group decided to ask Lieutenant Makarounis, who accepted the offer. Sergeant Kumagai had already made contact with the underground schoolteachers and had instructions.

Other plans were less clear-cut.

Lieutenant Smith: "Four of us in the burial detail figured if we could move out at night we could bolt out of the column as they passed an alley, the alley being one adjacent to the school compound." (Smith, 1953)

On the evening of the 14th, there were no guards in the corridor. Captain Locke, Lieutenant Makarounis and Sergeant Kumagai took this opportunity to slide down the rear stairway—to one of the numerous large rooms in the building. There was a trapdoor about one foot square in the corner. The sergeant moved a table and the three men crawled into a small space under the floor.

Captain Locke: "The trapdoor was concealed by all the desks in the room being torn up and shoved over into that corner of the room. Evidently the Communist guards did not know about it because they were new to the place the same as we were. They had brought us all the way from Seoul and probably had never been in the building before." (Locke, 1953)

John Martin:[25] "Just before we moved out, I decided to move into the sick room. That was a room set aside for the men that were

---

25 John Ervin Martin was another survivor. A member of Company K, 29th Infantry, he was captured near Hadong.

either dead or dying. They were all suffering from dysentery and exposure, starvation and everything else." (Martin, 1950)

A few hours later, NKPA soldiers awakened the other POWs. They were especially cruel—telling them that they were going to Manchuria and that they would never go home again. It was mid-October and it was freezing cold outside. The prisoners had already marched hundreds of miles. Hunger made them lethargic—and rebellious.

John Martin: "The rest of the group fell out. A South Korean traitor, known only as 'Johnny,' brought a bunch of guards up and began beating and kicking the sick men and trying to move them out of the room." (Martin, 1950)

Lloyd: "I would say one-third of the men couldn't possibly stand up, they were so weak. So some of them came out, we carried them out and some we couldn't even get off the floor. The North Korean guards went in there and said, 'Let them go," and they hit them over the head with the butts of their rifles and they were possibly killed." (Krieder, 1953)

Ed: "Everyone wanted to refuse. Some did. There was shooting but I don't know if anyone was killed. I scooted into the hall, reached the banister and started to raise myself up when a guard told me to get out. There were flashing lights and shooting inside the building now. I managed to get up and hold on to the banister. One of them pulled me down on my knees and hit me with his rifle butt. When I told him I couldn't get up, he kicked me in the back and I rolled down the stairs. I landed at the bottom about half-conscious and tried to shake it out of my head and get to my feet. I couldn't make it. I cussed the guard and told them to just shoot me. They poked me with the barrels of their guns. Somebody grabbed me and helped me to my feet. By this time, they were forming a column outside again. We started marching and I thought if I didn't get shot, I would freeze to death."

In the chaos, other men tried to escape.

Lieutenant Smith: "We got out of the column—and the column and the guards at the rear passed by us—and didn't see us. We ran our way through the town, and ran into some soldiers once and got away from them, and then ran into a roadblock and had to run through it, and got away from the guards in the roadblock. We figured we couldn't get out of the city, which we had planned to do, so we holed up in a house, which had been boarded up. We replaced the boards on the outside of the door-way, so it appeared no one had gone through there." (Smith, 1953)

Captain Locke: "I was told this by the three schoolteachers that helped us escape—that one group of four soldiers were caught that night trying to escape and were taken out into the schoolyard and shot." (Locke, 1953)

Lee Hae Do: "The two hundred and fifty prisoners were assembled and marched about two kilometers north of Pyongyang, where they were put on a train consisting of flat cars, coal cars and box cars."

Walt : "They loaded us into an open gondola."

Ed: "They herded us into them so tightly that we couldn't fall down if we wanted to. Some of the men panicked and screamed, clawing at each other's faces and throats. I thought I'd lose my mind from the screaming and the smell of our wounds and human waste."

Jim: "It was bitterly cold and the steel walls intensified it. We huddled together to keep warm. The car jerked, slamming us against the walls as the train moved."

Bob: "All night the train shifted back and forth. I don't think we made more than ten miles that night."

Ed: "Several of us had stuffed newspapers and old rags inside our shirts to help keep us warm. Every so often, the guards made us take them out and throw them away."

Valdor: "By this time, we were all very skinny and had dysentery. We were packed in so tight that if we moved, we had to move all together."

Bob: "They took us off the train in the morning. We walked to a ravine where we sat down and rested all day. That night, they put us back on the train again."

○○○

The men who had escaped hid in Pyongyang.

Lieutenant Smith: "We got into the house, and we found a big Korean jar about half full of water, some flour, and about a handful of rice. We took the flour and made paste out of it, and lived off of that for about four or five days." (Smith, 1953)

○○○

Captain Locke, Lieutenant Makarounis and Sergeant Kumagai huddled in their crowded hiding place at the school, praying that the teachers who set up their escape wouldn't turn them in—praying that they would bring them food and water as promised—praying that the North Korean guards wouldn't find them.

Captain Locke: "They walked all over our heads. They searched for us for about three days and never did find us." (Locke, 1953)

They had planned the escape for several days. In preparation, they ate only half their bread rations and stored the rest in their pockets. Two nights after they went into hiding, their caregivers brought them fried potato cakes and water. Two days after that, they brought rice and water.

Captain Locke: "We were actually getting more food during the six days that we were underneath the building than we had been getting during the previous two months." (Locke, 1953)

○○○

The men on the train were not so lucky. As the days passed, food became scarcer.

John Martin: "We traveled at night and stopped at open fields in the day time and we ate raw vegetables, such as corn and radishes that we stole."

The guards passed out dried millet. It was hard and gritty— the consistency of birdseed. The prisoners tried to eat it but it broke their teeth and made their tongues swell. It also made them terribly thirsty. When they couldn't find a stream, they dropped to their stomachs and lapped water out of puddles or scooped it from rice paddies fertilized by human waste.

Jim: "No man in his right mind would have dared drink that stuff, but we were so crazed that we didn't care about the after effects."

Valdor John had burial detail many times throughout the march.

Valdor: "At first, they let us bury the prisoners with their dog tags. Later they refused to let us mark the graves in any way."

Jim: "Whenever anybody died, the Major (McDaniel) held services. He always said a few words and said a prayer. He saw that they were buried. He wrote the man's name on a slip of paper and he put the paper in a bottle and buried it with the body."

The men were desperate for reassurance. Now that Captain Locke and Lieutenant Makarounis were gone, they turned to Major McDaniel—for encouragement and hope.

Jim Yeager went up to the major on the third or fourth day out from Pyongyang. "Sir, can I talk to you?"

"Yes, son." McDaniel was sitting up above the tracks, looking down at the troops around the train.

"Will we ever get out of this?"

"Keep going," the major said, "because I just don't know."

It was only a few hours from the end.

The men knew that Captain Locke and Lieutenant Makarounis were no longer with them.

Valdor: "I assumed that they had been shot."

Hope was ebbing. Captain Locke, Lieutenant Makarounis and Sergeant Kumagai were not the only ones to escape. After a few days on the train, others concluded that the bleak autumn countryside held more promise than the hell inside those boxcars.

George Snodgrass: "It was a pitch-black night. We couldn't see anything and then a couple of us realized the guards couldn't see anything either. I've never since seen anything as black as that night."

Lieutenant Blaylock, Corporal Stevens and George Snodgrass slid out the door of the boxcar, grabbed hold of each other and just walked away.

George: "We could tell there were weeds. We stopped and lay down. We heard the movement as the guards moved prisoners around."

The train started up—leaving the three men behind.

George: "We walked for three days. Finally, we saw a small plane. Blaylock said our troops were close. We stopped for the night and hid under some shocks in a field. Along the way, we found blankets off an oxcart. Blaylock talked in his sleep and Stevens had a bad cough. They both fell asleep but I was awake. I heard some North Koreans talking as they came toward the field. They stopped to eat, so close to us that I could hear their teeth as they bit into their food. One sat down right on the shock we were hiding under. He was actually sitting on my left shoulder. I was scared that Blaylock would start talking or Stevens would cough. I prayed myself to sleep. It seemed forever before the North Koreans left."

Thirty men were lost on the train ride north from Pyongyang. Some died of exposure during the freezing nights.

Others fell over dead while in the fields searching for food. The guards shot some who were trying to escape.

The other men buried their comrades.

Jim: "We had to use our bare hands to dig the graves."

All the while, American jets soared overhead—making the North Koreans more anxious as each day passed.

The train's configuration changed. Some of the men remember two trains—others believe that it was a single locomotive with cars being added and taken away. At one point, there was an accident.

Bill Henninger: "We ran into another train. One of the North Koreans was crushed between cars. We were transferred into other cars."

Sherman Jones: "I think it was Buck who was crushed between the trains."

It might even have been a railway worker who lost his life that night. (O'Brien, 2007)

Ed: "Later we switched trains and they put us on regular cars with seats in them. That's when I lost contact with Bob."

Bob: "We were in a regular passenger car. They picked it up after bumping into a deserted train which had been left standing on the tracks . . . I left Ed Slater in the rear of the car and crawled under the seats to the forward part to talk with Allen Gifford."

Allen and Bob were old friends. They'd been roommates in Japan.

Bob: "We talked for quite a while about old times in Japan and about the march. We talked about how hard it was to walk by the fields and orchards full of crops and fruit without being allowed to eat. We shared broken hearts over having seen pilots in planes who were within hollering distance of us and yet couldn't help us."

The reorganized train moved north—stopping to repair damaged tracks along the way and hiding in tunnels during the day.

Twenty-Seven — Massacres

"And in that bright October sun
We knew our childhood days were done." — Billy Joel

Lloyd Krieder: "So in the daytime we went right through Sunchon City. When we got on the other side of the city they took us off the train and took us to the other side of the field, and I figured they were going to shoot us. When the planes came over, they put us back in the train. We were so weak we could hardly run or stand up. It was impossible to stand up, and we couldn't escape. Some of the men were so sick in soul and heart they didn't care if they lived anyway. They would as soon be dead as to go through any more torture." (Krieder, 1953)

The train came to a tunnel—and stopped. The guards told the prisoners that they couldn't travel during daylight because of the American planes.

Lee Hae Do: "They were taken to the first railroad north of Sunchon, arriving at about 1900 hours, 20 October 1950. They stayed there until evening the next day."

Some of the men slept. Others searched for comfortable positions—trying to ignore their growling stomachs and the stench of illness and wounds.

Jim Yeager: "The engineer pulled the entire train far enough inside so that the last car was out of sight."

Lloyd: "We got into a tunnel near Sunchon and they put the train in the tunnel. It was the morning of the 20th of October. We were hungry. We made an S-O-S with our bodies lined up on the ground a few times. We saw a lot of planes going over that day and we figured they were planes going to send food, but it was one of the 187th Airborne drops at Sunchon." (Krieder, 1953)

Roy Sutterfield: "They unhooked the engine and moved us up into the tunnel early that morning—and left us there all day. So long about that evening, we were having five or six people die every day and I was helping my group sergeant carry out the prisoners that had died that day and getting their identification tags and everything to bury them." (Sutterfield, 1950)

Ed Slater: "We all thought things might get better and that we might make it to a camp."

Walt Whitcomb: "The guy next to me was a sergeant who'd lost his arm to gangrene. He talked all the time. He'd fought in World War II—and had been a prisoner of war then, too. He'd been married twice. He kept saying that there might be another war—and another prisoner of war camp, but he'd never have another wife."

Jim: "The men on the water and burial details got off the train and headed back toward a village."

Degraded and humiliated, the prisoners were dependent on their tormentors for the necessities of life. The last three months had taught them that something awful could happen—and they lived with the moment-by-moment dread that it might. The enemy had complete control over them. Therefore, in the end, the men didn't see it coming—although there were signs.

Bob Sharpe: "I noticed they allowed us to do things they hadn't previously permitted."

Jim: "The water and burial details didn't come back."

Lee Man Yung: "In the early afternoon, the men were promised their first meal in several days. Prior to this time, they had eaten only hard crackers doled out at various times along the way. A detail of fifteen men was selected to go to a village nearby to prepare the food. With these men went Major McDaniel, ranking US officer among the prisoners."

Allen Gifford: "After a while, Major McDaniel and a couple of other guys were taken back south with a guard named Johnny, a South Korean-turned-Communist. They left about one o'clock in the afternoon and were supposedly going to get chow."

Lee Hae Do: "At about 1300 hours, 21 October, fifteen US POWs, including an American Major (McDaniel), were taken from the train after being told they were going to prepare food. Major Chong Myong Sil, together with five guards, was in charge of this group. They were taken about five hundred meters from the tunnel where they were executed by fire from pistols, rifles and burp guns. I saw my Battalion Commander, Major Chong Myong Sil, firing a pistol at the above-mentioned prisoners."

After the first execution, the guards returned for the next thirty.

The men had gotten used to the routine—getting off the train a few at a time. They were so hungry that they obeyed without thought when they heard that they were going for food.

Allen: "About four o'clock, they told us to fall out with our bowls. They separated us into groups of about thirty each. I was with the first group that was taken off the train and lined up in the tunnel."

Bob: "I was with that group because I hustled to get that food. We were like ducks elbowing each other to get out first."

Allen: "Then we walked south about fifty yards, turned left and walked in a trench about thirty yards."

They went through the brush to a little ravine.

Allen: "They told us to sit down. I was about the next to the last in sitting down."

Valdor John: "After we sat down, they passed bowls around."

Those with dishes began cleaning them out.

Bob: "I heard a rifle bolt go home."

Allen: "Gale, the guy with the bullet hole through his head, was sitting up behind me. Bob Sharpe was beside me. Just as I sat down, I turned and looked up at this guard. He put a full clip of ammunition in his gun. There was one colored guy and a couple of sergeants. They got up as I was watching the guard loading his rifle."

A shot rang out.

Allen: "One sergeant said, 'They are shooting at us.'"

The black man and the sergeants started running.

Bob: "I took a dive immediately—and as I did, I saw a guy sitting above us on the side of the trench. The first shot hit him right between the eyes."

In that first moment of panic, people acted on instinct. Some ran—others played dead.

Bob: "From my position, I couldn't tell where the running guys were headed but for a few seconds it drew fire away from the group."

The executioners opened up with rifles and burp guns.

Allen: "I jumped down between a bunch of other GIs. I got hit three times by rifle—not by burp guns. The burp guns were down by the railroad tracks. I was pretty well covered with other GIs. I was hit in the wrist, shoulder and head. Sharpe was underneath me."

Bob: "Two guys fell on top of me. I was on my back—and they were on top of me. I think one of them was Gifford. No one is rational in times like that—it was mayhem for a while. The good Lord decided who would survive."

Valdor: "We didn't know what was going on right away. The men started falling down and I hit the dirt. I played dead then. They shot me in the arm."

A bullet hit the man next to Valdor in the leg. Blood splattered Valdor's face and head.

The shooting went on for several minutes. The men screamed and begged for mercy. They called on God to spare their lives. The North Korean soldiers raked the ground up and down, cutting the POWs to pieces.

Most of the men were shot at least once. Piled together on the ground, the bodies on top took the brunt of the continuing fire. Those on the bottom were soaked in blood—their own and that of everyone else. Some moaned in pain and quivered.

After the initial firing died down, the North Korean soldiers began the clean-up phase of their assignment. They walked among the bodies, bayoneting or clubbing those who were still moving.

Bob: "I prayed that it would come quickly . . . that I would be dead without any more suffering."

As the murderers continued their mission, the victims' cries echoed through the empty countryside.

Valdor: "They pounded on my back and stuck a bayonet into my side—but not very deep."

Valdor still didn't move.

Bob: "I was shot in the arms. One round took the hair off the side of my head. In fact, I took a couple rounds to the head."

Allen: "Sharpe was moving and I told him to lie still."

Bob: "I whispered for Allen to be quiet."

The executioners moved toward the pile of bodies where Allen and Bob lay tangled in the arms and legs of those who had died.

Allen: "Just before they came to me, they hit one guy who moaned and moved. He didn't moan anymore after that. They hit me and I didn't move at all. They shattered Sharpe's arm with a rifle butt.

134

Most of the rest were already dead except for one guy who was moaning."

Joseph Mistretta[26]: "In the confusion, I ran across a field. In the field, I picked up four radishes. I jumped into another gully and stayed there, eating the radishes. I heard the gooks shoot the other groups of prisoners." (Time, 1950)

Lee Hae Do: "I was one of about fifteen guards who shot them. I fired a burp gun. Also used were rifles and pistols. The officer in charge was a Major who was a Cultural Officer from another unit."

Valdor: "One of the Koreans hollered, 'pari pari[27]' which means to hurry up and then they took off."

Bob: "Finally, all the Koreans left but one. Then he, too, left and we were alone among the bodies of our friends."

After a few minutes, it grew quiet in the trench.

Allen: "I got up and found about seven others alive. Only five of us could get up. We left together. We went about three yards up in the trench under briars. One kid was crawling. He couldn't keep up and told us to go on. We left. I don't know if he ever made it out."

Bob: "Some of them were alive but we had to leave them behind. We were too weak to carry them."

The survivors couldn't go far.

Bob: "I ripped out a piece of my fatigue jacket and made a tourniquet for my arm. I managed to stop the bleeding in both my wounds—but I was so weak that I fell down and it started again. I couldn't stop it and I got weaker and weaker."

Allen: "We were cold and hungry."

---

26 Joseph Mistretta — another survivor who spoke to *Time Magazine* a few days later.

27 Valdor's spelling for Korean word is incorrect. Ppali Ppali means 'hurry hurry' or 'fast fast' in Korean. (Chong, 2007)

Valdor: "I lay there all that night."

○○○

The men waiting inside the tunnel heard gunfire.

Jim: "Toney asked me, 'What's going on?' 'I guess some poor devils tried to get away,' I said. Toney agreed."

John Martin: "I didn't think of them shooting the men. It never occurred to me because the Koreans were always firing their weapons anyway." (Martin, 1950)

Roy: "Someone said it sounded like they were having a gun battle down there. We thought the guards were shooting over the heads of someone who was in a garden or something." (Sutterfield, 1950)

The men in the train heard it, too.

Ed Slater: "We heard guns and screaming."

Walt: "The guards were always shooting at something."

Although they must have known on some level what was happening, each man focused on his own immediate situation.

Perhaps it didn't make sense to them—after all, the North Koreans had kept them alive for three months. Why would they rush them out of Seoul—and then Pyongyang, if they were going to kill them all?

Valdor: "I don't know why the North Koreans did this to us. Maybe because we were dying off so fast that they didn't want any more to do with us. Or maybe we were just holding up their progress northward." (Carlson, 2002)

○○○

The executioners turned their attention to the next group.

Jim: "Twenty minutes later, five guards came back to the tunnel and ordered our group to line up."

136

John Martin: "They told us that the house where we would get the chow was a small house and that was the reason we were being broken up into smaller groups." (Martin, 1950)

Jim: "The guards were nervous and hurried in their actions. It was the first time I had seen them like this. They were usually cocky and arrogant. Now they were quiet and sullen."

The guards marched this group of men, including Jim Yeager, John Toney, John Martin, Melvin Rookstool, Roy Sutterfield, Lloyd Krieder and Bill Henninger, outside the tunnel and down the tracks for about two hundred yards.

John Martin: "I had a hard time keeping up because of my foot." (Martin, 1950)

Roy: "Going down there in that second group I began to think about just taking thirty at a time. We didn't meet the first group coming back—and when we got down to where they had turned to the left, we turned to the right." (Sutterfield, 1950)

Lloyd: "We went down along the railroad track and turned to the right, along a ditch, and they told us to sit down and the food would soon be there." (Krieder, 1953)

Melvin Rookstool: "They ordered us to sit down." (Carlson, 2002)

The soldiers positioned themselves around the prisoners. Suddenly, the men realized that something wasn't right.

Jim: "I glanced out of the corner of my eye and saw a guard standing about five yards away on top of a little ridge, facing us. He cradled a burp gun in his arm. I recognized him from Pyongyang. He was a South Korean who had turned communist."

Jim and Toney were in the third rank, the farthest away from the guard on the ridge. Roy Sutterfield was the fourth man from the front in the center row. John Martin was on the far end.

The guard raised the burp gun—and began firing.

Jim: "The men in the front row slumped over, not uttering a sound. The others in the second and third rows, hit by the burp slugs, screamed and yelled with agony . . . Eight slugs ripped through the chest of the man in front of me. He died instantly. I pitched forward the moment he was hit and managed to crouch my head under part of his body. The blood from his wounds covered my head. It was hot and sticky. As it ran down my face, I clenched my fists and gritted my teeth to keep from vomiting."

Roy: "I saw what was about to happen and fell before they shot me." (Sutterfield, 1950)

Melvin: "The first shot hit me in the thigh—and I fell toward this bank that the guards were standing on while they shot us. I just shoved my head right up into the bank." (Carlson, 2002)

John Martin: "I dove for the embankment and hugged the ground—and did a lot of praying." (Martin, 1950)

Lloyd: "I fell down on my left side, another boy fell on top of me bleeding, and I believe that saved my life. They thought I was already dead because I laid still." (Krieder, 1953)

Bill Henninger: "The guards started firing from about a twenty-five-foot distance. Only seven of us (out of the thirty) survived. The men who fired at us were not the guards who had been with us regularly."

The dying men twitched and cried out for their mothers. The guard with the burp gun ceased firing—and then the rest of the execution squad began shooting with their rifles.

Melvin: "They shot me in the back of the head, but the bullet went in just a little ways and came out." (Carlson, 2002)

Jim: "They walked around us, prodding with their bayonets and rifle butts. Those who looked like they might still be alive were either shot in the head or bayoneted."

Melvin: "When this guard stuck a bayonet into my arm, it was the first time it really hurt. It went right into the bone. When he pulled out his bayonet, my arm went right up with it. So he kicked my arm off his bayonet. Goddamn, that hurt—but I didn't yell out." (Carlson, 2002)

Bill: "Only Jim Yeager and I remained uninjured."

A boy lying next to Jim was delirious—thrashing around. Toney whispered to the kid to lie still, but the convulsions continued. Another shot and the young soldier relaxed into death.

Jim: "I was breathing so hard that I was gasping, so I bit my lip until it bled to keep from uttering any sound."

A guard approached where Jim and Toney lay.

Jim: "I prayed. Oh God, how I prayed. I guess I had so much blood on me, the guard thought I couldn't possibly be alive."

Other men moaned. The guard killed them.

Roy: "I laid still." (Sutterfield, 1950)

It became quiet.

Moments ticked by.

Jim whispered, "Toney, Toney, you all right?"

"Quiet, dammit," Toney murmured, "or they will get us, too."

More time passed.

Finally Toney muttered, "I think they're gone, Jim."

The prisoners began to move—and look around.

Jim: "The men in the front row had literally been cut in half by the burp gun. The heads of some of them hung by small pieces of ragged skin."

Fifty yards away, a guard smoked a cigarette. He had his back to the pile of dead and dying prisoners.

Jim: "I ducked down and turned to Toney. 'There's one of them still out there.' He didn't answer. 'Toney,' I blurted out. 'You hit?'"

Toney nodded and motioned to his legs. He'd been shot twice—once in each thigh. Jim and Toney had been through so much together. Jim wasn't about to leave his friend there to die. He looked around. A bunch of millet shocks were stacked about one hundred yards behind them.

Jim: "We can't lie here forever," I told Toney, "or they might come back to make doubly sure all of us are dead."

Jim and Toney disentangled themselves from the pile of bodies. As they crawled over Bill Henninger, he decided to go with them. They inched forward for about twenty-five yards with Jim watching the movements of the last guard.

Without warning, the guard turned and looked over the bodies. Bill, Jim and Toney froze. Sensing no movement, the NKPA soldier dropped his cigarette and headed back toward the tunnel.

Jim: "Though it was colder than hell, the sweat dripped off my forehead like water out of a leaky faucet. My heart beat so fast that I thought the guard would hear it. We stayed in that spot for a full five minutes before gaining enough strength to move on."

They made it to the millet shocks. In the distance, they heard the burp gun again.

Jim: "Another group was getting it. Toney and I grimaced."

About thirty minutes later, they heard the train start up. The few prisoners who remained alive prayed that their tormentors were gone for good.

Bill Henninger: "After the guards left, Yeager and I tried to help those who were still alive—but there wasn't much we could do for most of them."

Jim created a shelter from the cold wind using millet shocks. Soon others joined them.

Melvin: "Every time I tried to stand up, I would just topple over backward. Two other fellows and I crawled under a shock of corn." (Carlson, 2002)

John Martin: "We laid there until I thought they had gone and I started to look around for somebody else that was alive. There were about six men left alive . . . we thought that they would be back with bayonets, so we crawled out of the ditch into the corn stalks and stayed there until morning." (Martin, 1950)

Roy: "We thought we were the only six out of the thirty, but there was another one down at the other end. There were seven out of the second group altogether." (Sutterfield, 1950)

Lee Hae Do: "After the execution of the third group, I ran away, changed into civilian clothing and was captured in Sunchon, Korea. My Battalion Commander, Major Chong Myong Sil, gave the order to execute the POWs as described above."

OOO

It was dark when the train started moving. For the one hundred and twenty-five men left in the railcars, nothing had changed. They couldn't see out. They didn't know where they were—or where they were going. Without food, they lost track of time. Only the gentle rocking of the cars on the tracks told them when they were moving.

Ed, Sherm and Walt had no idea that many of their buddies lay dead or wounded in the Korean countryside behind them—or that a new kind of horror awaited them a few miles away.

Friendly fire remained a threat. At one point, as the train emerged from a tunnel, American jets attacked it. The doors were shut and locked. There were two little windows on each end of the car. The guys who could see said that the guards were running back into the cave. Then the prisoners started screaming, "Airplanes are coming. They're ours! They're ours!"

The first rocket hit the train.

There was a stampede. Desperate men tore at the door.

Despite the danger from the planes swooping down over them, the North Korean soldiers set up machine guns and raked the terrified men as they jumped out of the cars.

Ed: "The ones the planes didn't get, the machine guns did."

Another rocket hit in the middle of a pile of railroad spikes that flew everywhere. It exploded just as Ed got to the door. The planes came around again and did nothing—reassuring the prisoners that the pilots had finally recognized them.

The scene that faced the prisoners as they got off the train was horrific.

Ed: "Body parts were everywhere. They told us all to get back on the train. They got a lot of them loaded even if most of the body parts were gone. Some guards shot the men still lying there. They moved the train back into the tunnel."

Walt: "The sergeant next to me was in pain. He'd been hurt again—and he moaned throughout the night and the next day."

Many of the men in that car died. That evening after dark, the North Korean soldiers moved the train out into the open again. This time, there were no planes. The train headed north. About thirty-five miles beyond Sunchon Tunnel, it slowed to a stop—not too far from the entrance to a tunnel south of Kujang-dong.

Sherman Jones: "I was asleep when it began."

The damaged train had reached the end of the line. There were few options. The soldiers ordered the men out of the cars. They could walk or die.

When the guards came for them this time, it was different. The POWs no longer trusted anyone. Some jumped out of the car and tried to run—others refused to move. For some, death was preferable to another march. For some, death was the only option.

The guards became more frantic and demanded that the men get off the train and follow them.

Ed: "The guard said, 'You no walk, we shoot.' Nobody moved—so the guard got into the car and started dragging men out, throwing them out the doors."

Flashes from the guns lit up the inside of the railway car. People screamed as bayonets pierced their bodies. A round hit Sherman Jones behind his right ear. It blew out just below his eye—ripping open a massive wound on the young man's cheek. Another bullet destroyed part of his foot. He was alive—but helpless.

Ed: "The only thing I could do was scoot along the wall on the floor and head for the door. When I got to the door, I fell out and rolled down an embankment. They threw bodies out on top of me."

People screamed and prayed.

Walt: "We were slow because we were weak. They pushed me out of the train and I fell on top of someone else."

A bullet went through Walt's left arm and ricocheted through his leg.

Walt: "It all happened so fast. Something fell on top of me—then I realized it was the one-armed master sergeant. He was yelling, 'Shoot again'—and I poked him and said, 'Shut up!'"

The executioners shot about fifteen to twenty men standing up outside the train. They also set the boxcars on fire to burn the prisoners who were still inside.

Walt: "I didn't see Slater or Jonesy until after I was out of the train. I watched the guard that we called Johnny shoot someone beside the road."

143

Bodies lay all around. Many had tried to run when the shooting started but didn't get very far. Some were sprawled on the bank. Most hit the ground and stayed where they fell.

Ed: "Some of the guards dragged them and set them on fire. I rolled my head to the side to see what was going on. I saw them throwing diesel oil on piles of men."

Walt: "They came along and stuck a bayonet through the guy on top of me. It missed my nose and went into the guy below me."

Ed: "The man on top of me had been shot and blood was dripping down in my face. I told him to lay still. I had no idea it was my buddy, Walter. He stopped moaning and didn't move. Something hit me in the head and I was out."

Sherman: "As I lay there bleeding, a guard came and peed in my face."

The North Koreans were in a hurry. They left thirty-three bodies lying alongside the burning train and marched the rest north. (O'Brien, 2007)

Throughout the night, Walt and Ed lay in the pile of stiffening bodies. Sherman was a few feet away. They were bleeding out. Hypothermia slowed their breathing and weakened their pulses. The smell of burning flesh and diesel oil enveloped them. They heard the footsteps of their executioners as they left the murder site. The blazing boxcars crackled for hours. They dared not move. Hurt, fear and outrage flickered in their hearts as they waited—for dawn, for death—for rescue. They drifted in and out of consciousness—praying for a tomorrow that held some promise of life.

Twenty-Eight — Task Force Rodgers

"If the weather had not delayed our departure, we would have intercepted the train and perhaps enfranchised our prisoners." — Samuel L. Clark, a member of the Rakkasans

As the pressure on Pyongyang increased, the North Koreans retreated, leaving the bodies of American POWs strewn behind them like breadcrumbs. US pilots harassed the enemy as they withdrew—attacking roads, bridges and railroad tracks in an attempt to slow or stop them.

Airdrop near Sunchon, October 20, 1950 *(National Archives)*

The 187th Airborne Regimental Combat Team (RCT)[28] had participated in the amphibious landings at Inchon. When the

---

28 A Regimental Combat Team (RCT) is an organizational group often used in the Korean War. It consists of an infantry regiment with a battalion of artillery and in some cases armor and engineer elements attached. Most were *ad hoc* put together for a particular operation. (Summers Jr., 1990)

Eighth Army crossed the 38th parallel and headed toward Pyongyang, General Mac-Arthur kept the 187th RCT in reserve at Kimpo Airfield near Seoul. Now he ordered them to conduct a parachute operation north of Pyongyang aimed at trapping the Communist troops and rescuing hundreds of priso-ners under enemy control.

On October 20, the 187th RCT attacked two points thirty miles north of Pyongyang—the towns of Sukchon and Sunchon. Twenty-eight hundred Rakkasans made the jump along with three hundred tons of equipment and supplies. The remaining North Korean troops in the area abandoned their positions—and UN forces took Pyongyang.

While the 1st Battalion, 187th focused on the town of Sukchon, the 2nd Battalion landed in Drop Zone Easy, two miles southwest of Sunchon. There was little resistance. Two companies established roadblocks south and west of the town while a third joined up with elements of the ROK 6th Division and took Sunchon itself.

General MacArthur flew to Pyongyang in triumph. However, the enemy had already withdrawn north of the jump zones. Civilians reported that the principal North

Korean government officials evacuated Pyongyang on October 12 and that rear guard soldiers removed most of the American and South Korean prisoners to a remote part of North Korea. These prisoners, some part of Task Force Smith captured in the first days of the war, were to become part of the infamous Tiger Death March. However, command had recent intelligence that a trainload of American prisoners, traveling only at night, was on its way north from Pyongyang. There was still hope that this group, which was the last to be hustled out of the city before it changed hands, might still be rescued.

The next day—October 21, the 1st Battalion, 187th blocked the main highway and established contact with the 2nd Battalion at Sunchon.

A new task force, formed around the 1st Battalion, 8th Cavalry Regiment, and a company of tanks, 70th Tank Battalion, started from Pyongyang to meet the airborne troops at Sunchon. Lieutenant Colonel William M. Rodgers of the tank battalion commanded the task force. It arrived at Sunchon at nine A.M. Along the way, they picked up five recently escaped American prisoners.

> **General Allen**
>
> Frank Allen was born in 1896. During WWII he served as a Brigadier General in the US Army, as Commanding Officer of Combat Command A and B of the 9th Armored Division and Commanding General of the 3rd Armored Division. He also served as Press Chief for General Dwight D. Eisenhower.
>
> Though a good combat officer, Allen's record as a P.R.O. does not inspire confidence in war correspondents. As press chief for General Eisenhower during World War II, he was blamed for holding up news of the German offensive at the Battle of the Bulge. He also held up the news of the German surrender and war's end until the A.P.'s Ed Kennedy defied the ban and broke the story.

From a plane, Brigadier General Frank A. Allen, Jr. and others watched Task Force Rodgers establish contact with the 187th RCT paratroopers. Satisfied, he returned to Pyongyang, climbed into his jeep and accompanied by his aide, his driver, and two war correspondents (Don Whitehead of the Associated Press and Richard Tucker of the *Baltimore Sun*), started for Sunchon. He got there about noon.

Twenty-Nine — Rescue

"Too late my brothers, too late, but never mind
All my trials Lord, soon be over." — Peter Yarrow

Even as the death squad shot the men outside Sunchon Tunnel, advancing American troops rescued Captain Locke, Lieutenant Makarounis and Sergeant Kumagai in Pyongyang as they emerged from hiding under the floor of the Fourth Grammar School.

Rescue of Lt. Makarounis, Captain Locke and Sgt Kumugai *(AP)*

Lieutenant Makarounis: "The space was only about two to three feet high, and there we stayed for six days and nights. The underground school teachers, one of them anyway, daily would come and bring us water, and a couple of times brought us rice and poached corn."

Lieutenant Smith: "On the fifth day as we were out of food, we figured we had better leave those quarters because they were fighting all around us all the time."

They were afraid that a shell might hit their hiding place— or that some Korean might find them. On the next day, the sixth day, one of the men noticed South Korean flags flying in the city.

Lieutenant Smith: "He called me over to peep through the crack and I saw it, and he asked what I made of it. I told him I couldn't

148

figure it out. I said, 'The city has not fallen, because I can still see North Korean troops.' I said, 'Evidently it is about to fall, and they are just turning sides again.'"

The men noticed that the natives in the area had two flags—a North Korean and a South Korean one. Whichever side was winning, they put that flag up. The South Korean flag was flying.

Lieutenant Smith: "We called to an old man, 'papasan,' I stayed in the background. There was a Nisei fellow there, myself, and three American GIs, Caucasians, and all of them had heavy beards. One of them had a big black beard. This man came up to this civilian and said, 'Rusky, Rusky,' and he said 'No, not Russian. American.' He said, 'American? Americans are down the road.'"

Sgt. Jones, Lt. Smith, Lt. Makarounis, Pfc Holcomb, Cpl Cerakowa, Sgt Kumagai, Sgt. Morris, Captain Locke *(AP)*

OOO

George Snodgrass, Lieutenant Blaylock and Corporal Stevens walked for three days after they slipped away from the train somewhere between Pyongyang and the Sunchon Tunnel. When they saw a small plane, Lieutenant Blaylock told his comrades that American troops must be close.

149

They were hopeful but the landscape remained forbidding—and the enemy was all around them. The three comrades grabbed food out of a field and stole blankets off of an oxcart. On the evening of the third day, they stopped for the night, hiding under some shocks in a field.

George Snodgrass: "Blaylock talked in his sleep and Stevens had a bad cough. They both fell asleep but I was awake. I heard some North Koreans talking as they came toward the field. They stopped to eat, so close to us that I could hear their teeth as they bit into their food. One sat down right on the shock we were hiding under. He was actually sitting on my left shoulder. I was scared that Blaylock would start talking or Stevens would cough. I finally prayed myself to sleep. It seemed forever before the North Koreans left."

The next morning when Lieutenant Blaylock stuck his head out of the shock, he saw another plane. George got up and looked around. He didn't see anyone so they started walking. Soon, they saw a column of trucks a few hundred yards away. It was the 1st Cavalry, on their way to liberate the prisoners.

George: "We were too weak to run. I had on Korean clothes and no shoes. They started shooting at us, but soon realized we were Americans, too. They took us back to the ammo truck and gave us each a case of C-rations and some clothes."

American soldiers took the weary men to the head of the column where General Allen questioned them.

General Allen: "On Saturday, 21 October 1950, while present with the Task Force Rogers 1st Cavalry Division at its junction with a battalion of the 187th RCT, I talked with a Lieutenant Blaylock and four other Americans who had been POWs of the North Korean Army but who had the day previously escaped from the railroad car bringing the prisoners to the North. He indicated that there were more than one hundred still remaining on the train, which he presumed was now close to the Manchurian border. I directed the commander of the Task Force Rogers to send these five returned prisoners to the airstrip at Pyongyang for prompt evacuation, which was done."

George: "Then they put us on a half-track and sent us back to Pyongyang."

OOO

Later that day, October 21, General Allen arrived in Sunchon northwest of Pyongyang.

General Allen: "I went in to visit the Batallion Commander of the 187th (Col Bolye) to inquire if the 1st Cavalry Division could be of any assistance to them. I was advised that they were in good shape and needed no assistance that their drop had been successful and supplies appeared adequate. I later went in to Sunchon to establish contact with the 7th ROK Regiment, 6th ROK Division, which had entered that city the night previously."

General Allen had only been there a short time when a Korean civilian came in and reported that the fleeing North Koreans had murdered about two hundred Americans the night before at a railroad tunnel northeast of town. Shocked, Allen decided to check out the veracity of this story at once.

"I'll never feel right about it," General Allen remarked, "if we don't do all we can to find out about this."

General Allen: "The individuals present with me were my aide, Lieutenant Jo Hodes, two newspaper men, Mr. Don Whitehead of AP, and Mr. Tucker of the *Baltimore Sun*, who had come up with me from Pyongyang, Major Fleming and Captain Olsen with the 7th Regiment ROK."

OOO

After the massacre on October 20, the survivors feigned death until the North Korean execution squads left. Then they began moving. Cold, bleeding and traumatized by the attacks, they helped each other crawl away from the heaps of bodies that were once their friends and fellow prisoners.

Allen Gifford: "When morning came, I heard voices. I ducked down and a briefcase fell on my head. I saw a Korean civilian and his daughter walking right on by the trench. They were talking. Whether or not they saw me, I don't know. I should have kept the briefcase but I threw it away. We took off another ten yards into a sugar cane field. We were trying to get to the middle of the field where we could settle in. We didn't make it. Two North Koreans were coming down the side of the ditch about ten or fifteen yards away. They were talking and laughing. We just lay down and started praying without making a sound. My back was facing them. I didn't look up. They never saw us."

Bob Sharpe: "When the sun came up, I was spitting up blood—and I was sure that I couldn't live through the day. We were all just about dead." (R. L. Sharpe, 1951)

About eight A.M., Allen and the others made it up into the mountains.

○○○

Lloyd Krieder found another survivor—a master sergeant who was too weak to walk.

Lloyd Krieder: "We stayed in a corn shock that night, it was so cold. Early the next morning I got up and saw a North Korean boy, about ten-years-old, walking by, and I yelled to him in Japanese that we wanted some food, but he didn't understand. They could speak Japanese from about fourteen-years- old up in that country, as they were under Japanese before. I don't believe he understood Japanese but he brought his dad out, an old man with a beard, and he came out and took us down to the house and gave us food and then he took us to Sunchon and turned us over to South Korean forces, and the South Koreans turned us over to the 187th, and the 187th to the 1st Cavalry." (Krieder, 1953)

○○○

General Allen's group stopped at the ROK 6th Division command post in Sunchon and an ROK colonel, an interpreter, and a driver in a second jeep joined them. Together, they drove to the tunnel arriving there at three P.M.

Several yards above a dirt road, the railroad tracks ran along a hillside cut and entered the tunnel. While General Allen and his companions waited on the road, the ROK colonel climbed the hillside and entered the tunnel. When he came back to the two jeeps, he told them that he had found seven dead Americans inside.

General Allen and the others now climbed to the tunnel. The seven bodies lay on straw mats beside the tracks. Scrawny, dirty and almost naked, these men had either starved to death or died from disease. Some had old wounds.

Don Whitehead:[29] "There were no identification tags or marks on them. All we found in their pockets was a handful of hard, dry crackers. Two of the youths huddled as though for warmth. One had his arms protectively around the other. Beards were heavy on their faces. Four of them were barefoot. One still had his GI boots but the soles were worn through. One wore tennis shoes—the same kind worn by North Koreans. For a few moments, we believed these seven dead were all there were." (Whitehead, 1950)

The ROK colonel walked on through the tunnel to explore the landscape on the other side. After a few minutes, he reappeared at the far opening and called that there were five Americans on top of the ridge.

Valdor John: "I was unconscious for quite a while. I guess it was the next day when I came to. I heard someone speaking English. They were on the hills looking around. I started yelling and they yelled back. One other guy and I were still alive in my group."

Wounded in his arms, legs, ribs, stomach and back, Valdor got up from where he'd been lying in the brush and staggered toward his rescuers. He shivered in the cold autumn air.

---

29 Don Whitehead — Pulitzer Prize Winning journalist for the AP

When General Allen put his own coat around him, Valdor sobbed that he was too dirty and lousy to wear it.

Valdor: "General Allen said, 'I'm promoting you to a one star general.'"

After months of mistreatment, the general's kindness overwhelmed Valdor. Then, he remembered, "They are over there." Following the devastated young man's shaking finger, General Allen saw seventeen dead Americans in a gully.

Don Whitehead: "For a moment in the shadows, it seemed that no one was alive. Then I saw a youth looking up at me. He was propped against the bank among the dead, weak and pale. His eyes were trying to smile. He was Corporal Dale Blake . . . He said, 'Oh God, so glad you came.' Tears coursed down his cheeks. 'I didn't think anybody would ever find us.' Tucker gave him a cigarette and told him to sit quietly and everything would be all right." (Whitehead, 1950)

The newsmen also found Private Ray Hanchey crawling through the weeds toward them.

Horrified by what he'd just found, Don Whitehead wandered across the railroad track into a cornfield. There, he saw a semicircle of fifteen more dead American POWs—shot as they sat on the ground with rice bowls in hand.

Don Whitehead: "The wind rustled the dry stalks about them." (Whitehead, 1950)

Melvin Rookstool: ". . . we heard a Korean running around hollering for us to come out because the Americans would be there soon. We figured it was a trick. Finally, we said, 'The hell with it.' We crawled out and this Korean ran up to us. We couldn't tell a South from a North Korean, but he had an American's second lieutenant's bar on his uniform. He was an ROK soldier." (Carlson, 2002)

Don Whitehead: ". . . out of the brushes came Privates John Martin . . . Melvin Rookstool . . . and Eugene Jones. Martin and Rookstool were helping Jones who was the weakest." (Whitehead 1950)

While the others took care of the three survivors, General Allen climbed the ridge to the Americans the ROK Colonel had seen.

Bob: "We heard a call, 'Americans, come on out. You're free.'"

Hurt and wary, the men feared it might be a trick.

Bob yelled, "Who is Betty Grable's husband?"

Someone answered, "Harry James."

Bob: "I was pretty well convinced that the folks we heard were Americans—but we were still cautious. I got up on my feet, feeling pretty dizzy, and hollered, 'If you guys are Americans, come up here.'"

They didn't have to wait long.

Bob: "I looked up and saw a massive Master Sergeant from the 1st Cavalry. It was the happiest day of my life."

Joyfully, they tackled the Master Sergeant.

Bob: "I'll never forget the look on that guy's face—or how grateful we were."

Allen: "We sat there until about three. Then some US troops came by and we were safe."

Bob: "The 1st Cavalry, 187th Airborne, had made a drop near us. They picked us up, gave us something to eat—don't remember what."

OOO

Jim Yeager, John Toney, Bill Henninger and the others were hungry and thirsty.

Roy Sutterfield: "We crawled to the top of the hill and stayed there that day." (Sutterfield, 1950)

Jim Yeager: "There was a village off in the direction where they killed Major McDaniel. There were whiskey bottles. I went down to figure out what was happening. My hair was curly and blonde. When I got down there, I met this old papa san and a younger man in his forties. I asked them for tobacco. They thought I was Russian. I said, 'No, I'm no goddamned Russian.' Then I saw that they were cooking rice. I tried to get them to give me some, but they wouldn't do that. However, they did offer me some water."

Roy: "That evening, this one boy went down to the bottom to a village and got us some water from a civilian Korean—and he gave him a little bowl of rice and he brought it back up and we all had a little rice." (Sutterfield, 1950)

Jim: "I went up a hill. The younger man had something under his shirt—a brass bowl full of rice. He dumps rice into a bag—I go back to the guys and give them the rice and water."

Roy: "And he came back up there and said something about Americans. We still didn't know Americans were close. We didn't see any Korean troop movements that day at all, but we didn't know they'd moved out that quick." (Sutterfield 1950)

Then they saw the trucks.

Jim: "I saw a Korean coming toward us. As he drew closer, the group prepared for the worst. I strained my eyes to get a better look. Behind the Korean was an American soldier. 'For Chris sakes,' I yelled to Toney and the others, 'it's a general.'"

The men who could get up ran toward the general. Several of them broke down and cried when they realized that their long ordeal was over.

Jim: "We tried to salute, but the general said, 'Forget that, boys. We're here to help you.'"

General Allen helped six emaciated, jubilant men down off the ridge. Four were wounded. The general's eyes were wet and he kept repeating, "It's a great day, boys. I just wish we could have been here soon enough to save the others."

Don Whitehead: "The six were Privates John Robert Toney, Rex E. Reed, Roy G. Sutterfield, James Yeager, Raymond Rindels and William Henninger." (Whitehead, 1950)

Jim Yeager and Bill Henninger after rescue

General Allen's group found three murder sites—one was also a mass grave. He engaged civilians from the surrounding community to carry the more seriously wounded men out on litters. The 7th ROK Regiment provided transportation for the ambulatory patients and those few who were uninjured. The US medical officer with the 187th RCT in Sunchon performed triage—transferring the worst cases to Pyongyang immediately, treating the others and sending them on to the airstrip for further medical evaluation on October 22.

Back in Sunchon that night, General Allen visited the survivors. By that point, they'd warmed up and eaten something. At least one of the men wanted vengeance.

Jim: "They'd captured a couple of gooks. They all had tennis shoes under their arms. I turned to the colonel and asked if I could have a weapon, but he wouldn't let me. I wanted to do something bad to the prisoners, so I made them throw their tennis shoes to the crowd. I still wanted to do them—everyone did."

The general told them that the Army would interrogate the guards and that they wouldn't be a problem again.

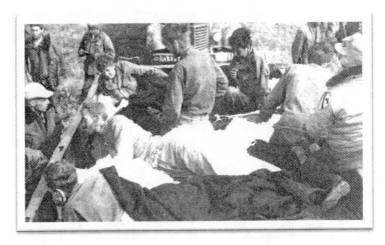

Survivors at airfield in Pyongyang awaiting a flight to Japan

Death still haunted them. Two of the men rescued that day, including the man who'd survived the massacre of Valdor John's group, passed on that evening.

There were sixty-eight bodies and twenty-three survivors discovered by General Allen's team the evening of October 20.

Relieved and overjoyed, the survivors began telling the rescuers about what happened to them. They talked about the five days on the train and about the five or six men who died and about the graves along the tracks between Pyongyang and the Tunnel outside Sunchon. They told about the men who'd escaped—and the POWs who disappeared up the tracks still packed into railway cars—and about the final horrendous moments with their captors.

L.D. Van de Voort, Commanding Officer F Company, 187th Avn. RCT.

To me it looked as if the POWs had been lined up in the erosion ditches alongside the railroad tracks and shot by someone standing on the banks of the ditches. They must have been shot at close range because shell casings were lying on the ground near the top edge of the ditches.

There were 73 dead in all.

Maurice A. Johnson, Jr., Infantry, Platoon Commander, 3rd Platoon, F Company, 187th Airborne HCT RCT, 24 October, 1950

Upon arrival at the tunnel, I inspected the area after having evacuated wounded American POWs. I saw four heaps of bodies of American soldiers. Three of these heaps were in erosion ditches, and the other was in a cornfield adjacent to the railroad tracks south of the tunnel. I examined the bodies and could see that the soldiers in the ditches had apparently been shot at from behind at close range, and from above as bullets had entered the bodies at a point higher than when they left them. There were empty shell cases strewn about on the ground at the edge of the ditches. The Americans, who were in the cornfield, had apparently been sitting down at the time they were shot. Most of the Americans, in the cornfield, had been shot through the head or the top part of the body. It appeared that they had been sprayed with small-sized 32 caliber bullets.

At the time I examined the bodies, they appeared to me to be extremely emaciated and were very poorly clothed. There were, however, three Negro soldiers in the group who appeared to be in somewhat better condition than the others.

In the southern entrance to the tunnel I saw the bodies of seven other Americans. These soldiers had not been shot. These bodies gave indication of extreme malnutrition and exposure. These soldiers were wearing native shoes, and some were clad only in underwear and in portions of fatigues.

There were still the one hundred and twenty-five men squeezed into the railcars. What happened to them? The 187th RCT spread out into the adjacent areas looking for answers.

OOO

Ed Slater, Walt Whitcomb and Sherman Jones were thirty miles away—still waiting for help. Ed and Walt remember their rescue differently.

○ Ed's Memory ○

"Every time I moved the pain went all through my body. My arms were stuck under the pile of bodies. I managed to get my left arm loose. I reached up to my head and there was a bayonet stuck in it. Walter was still warm so I knew he was alive. Rigor mortis had set in most of the bodies and I could hardly move. The fires from the cars felt warm and comforting although I was pinned under these bodies and scared to death. I couldn't think about anything but the guards coming back. I struggled for a long time and finally got loose.

Walter was out but he woke up when I shook him. I told him I was leaving. 'Don't leave me here,' he replied. I told him I would be back to get him. I didn't want to leave him, but I knew the guards were going to come back. I saw a train station a couple of miles back down the track, so I started back. When I got to it, there was no one close. The floor of the building was still warm so I knew someone had built a fire during the night. I lay down and went to sleep. I woke that afternoon to the sound of troops and army tanks. I had to get out of there and into the hills. There was a birdbath with old green water, but I drank all of it I could. The bank toward the hills was steep so I slid down on my butt again. When I reached the bottom, there was a small boy standing there. He told me to come and he would get me food and water. He said the GIs taught him English. I told him I didn't have enough strength to get up. He offered to help me. He took me to a house and told an old lady to get me some food. I sat on the warm floor and waited. She brought me some warm broth. I kept wondering how soon the guard would be back. Could I eat and get out of there? The boy said he'd be right back. While I was eating, I heard some talking outside and the door slid open. The biggest master Sgt I ever saw was standing there. He held out his hand and said, 'Let me take you home.'

I cried all the way back to the next village. He took me to see General Allen who asked me if there were any more alive. I told him there was one. He asked if I'd mind riding back in the jeep to show him where. Walter was still alive when we got there.

They put us in an ambulance. I told Walter, 'We're going home.' The General said, 'No, not yet. Not until we clean you up a little bit and feed you.'

I never did like tomato soup before, but that's what they gave us. It burned like hell in the cuts in my mouth but it was good. When the ambulance left, neither Walter nor I looked out the back window."

◯ Walt's Memory ◯

In the morning, Sherman Jones moaned. Walt said, "Are you okay?" and Ed answered, "Yeah."

The sound of Ed's voice—so close—made Walt jump.

Walt: "Slater's head was bleeding where the bayonet had hit him. Jonesy was helpless with bullet wounds up the side of his body and in his face."

The one-armed sergeant on top of Walt was dead. Walt pushed him off and got up. Then, Ed got up. Together, they went over to Sherman Jones who seemed to be the only other person still alive. It was one more horror for Walt. Sherm's wounds were massive—and obviously life threatening.

Walt: "There was nothing we could do for Jonesy—so we covered him up with some rice bags."

Walt and Ed walked down the tracks to a small substation. It was warm inside—and small, one room with a bench. They discussed dragging Sherm inside but they didn't have the strength to move him. They hid inside for several hours. During the day, they saw retreating North Korean troops hustling past the small building.

Walt: "Down the hill outside our window, we could see the roof of a house."

The next morning, more troops went by.

161

Walt: "Some of those troops were South Korean, but we didn't know it at the time."

They waited another hour, before the need for food and water forced them to emerge from the relative safety of the train depot. It was right around noontime. They walked along the tracks—and then down the hill to that little house.

Walt: "At this point, I wasn't worried about my wounds. They had stopped bleeding—but we were still in enemy territory and I was plenty scared."

The North Korean civilians in the house took them in. They had a big galvanized bucket—and they had chicken and rice—and water. Walt and Ed were eating when the door opened and they saw Korean soldiers. Walt assumed that the family had turned them over to the NKPA.

Walt: "I was sure that we were dead this time. Then a big American sergeant came in and said, 'Come on,'—and I said, 'You are the prettiest son of a bitch I've seen in years.'"

They'd been there four or five minutes.

Walt: "We told the sergeant about the massacre—and about Jonesy laying back there hurt so bad."

The sergeant wrapped them in blankets and put them in the back of a truck.

Walt: "I was busy talking and getting cigarettes. I didn't see Jonesy again while in Korea. I didn't figure he was gonna make it."

All that the officer in charge of transporting Walt and Ed had to eat was tomato soup and crackers. They rode back to a MASH unit and stayed there over night. Then, the next day they flew to Yokohama, Japan, and received treatment at the 28th Station Hospital.

○ Sherman's Memory ○

Sherm's memory was even more limited given the nature of his injuries. He was helpless. Riddled with bullets, he couldn't get up—so he lay as quietly as he could, praying that the soldiers would leave.

By morning, he was thirsty and very weak. He knew that he would die if he didn't get help soon. He hurt—and he was all alone in a field of corpses. As the sun rose the morning after the massacre, he moaned. Then he heard voices.

Sherman: "Walt and Ed found me—but they were hurt, too, and couldn't move me."

While they went to find help, Sherm lay in his own blood—drifting in and out of consciousness—trying to stay alive.

○○○

On Sunday, October 22, rescuers found Ed Slater and Walt Whitcomb near Kujang. They told General Allen about the pile of bodies near the burnt out train—and where to find Sherman Jones. They also told them about the remaining POWs who were being marched north to the Manchurian border. (Quinn, 1950)

The rescuers evacuated Sherman by helicopter from the site where the guards had burned the men in the railway cars. The others went south for medical care, rest and interrogation.

There was one sad piece of business yet to be addressed. General Allen asked the 187th to notify the Graves Registration Service to identify the bodies and arrange for burial.

○○○

The prisoners' loved ones had received little information about them. In the weeks following Jim Yeager's capture, his distraught father went to an old fortune teller. She told him,

"Your son is in grave danger, but you will hear that he is okay in three days, three weeks or three months."

That was the end of the session leaving Jim's dad to cling to that hope.

Three months to the day, the Yeagers were in church. The homily was about the return of the prodigal son. The preacher had just begun his sermon when the telephone in the office adjacent to the sanctuary rang. He tried to ignore it—but it kept ringing. The congregation looked at each other with raised eyebrows. Exasperated, the minister asked the head usher to answer it.

The usher disappeared. Everyone sat silently wondering what was so important to interrupt his or her Sunday services.

The usher hurried back into the sanctuary, shouting, "Jim Yeager has been found and he is okay!"

The congregation exploded with joy and thanksgiving.

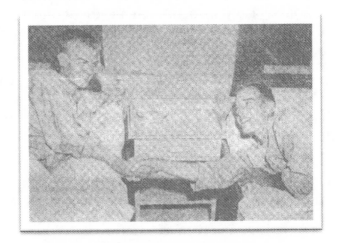

Jim Yeager and John Toney after rescue (AP)

OOO

After months of terror, the survivors were safe. There was food—and medical care. They were warm. They could rest—

and the only people trying to kill them lived in their nightmares.

Bob: "They flew us to Japan. Japanese were in the streets to welcome us. I was put in a hospital with curtains around me. Through a hole, I saw a Major about to go back. He pulled the curtains back and asked, 'Son, you goldbricking on me?' He could see I was in bad shape."

Ed: "The next thing I remember, I was in a hospital in Japan. They were trying to get all the lice off of me and care for my wounds."

Allen: "Before I went to Korea I weighed one hundred and seventy-nine pounds. When I was rescued, I weighed one hundred and fourteen."

Walt couldn't eat anything and keep it down. All they had was cold roast beef sandwiches and milk. Walt hadn't had milk since he was about sixteen. He tried—but it didn't work. He was dangerously underweight so they started trying to feed him whatever they could find.

The military allowed him to call home. The conversation with his family lasted only a minute or two. Walt didn't care.

Now that he was safe, the whole thing began playing in his mind—the last three months, the ugly interrogations, his buddies who died in Hadong—the ones who died of disease or wounds or starvation on the march north. He was afraid to close his eyes lest he see their faces in his dreams.

Walt: "Jonesy was in a bed across the room from me. I couldn't believe he was alive. I couldn't believe I was alive either. When I first saw Jonesy, I said, 'How ya doing?' and he said, 'I think I'm gonna make it.'"

Walt found the hospital bed too soft to be comfortable. Finally, he gathered up his covers and slept on the floor.

Most of them had an assortment of afflictions—from malnutrition to grotesque wounds. Exposed as they were to parasites and the elements, they fought a variety of diseases.

As soon as Valdor John reached the hospital, the dysentery started. The staff gave him bourbon before he ate each meal to cure the dysentery. Then, he contracted double pneumonia and slipped into a coma for several days.

Valdor John: "I remember regaining consciousness and fighting for air. A Grey Lady was sitting by my bed. She said she had been with me every day of the coma."

She wrote a letter to his parents for him.

As the military debriefed them, the survivors began to put their ordeal in context with what they were learning about the progress of the war.

Eugene Jones, Allen Gifford and John Martin after rescue *(AP)*

The massacres took place in two different locations miles apart. Most of the men never learned the fates of their buddies.

George: "We flew to Seoul to the 4th Field Hospital, then on to a hospital in Japan and finally to Letterman Hospital in California. My injuries included shrapnel wounds in my face. I had also been bayoneted after my capture, but mostly I suffered from beatings, malnutrition and dysentery."

Recovery was long and painful.

Sherman: "When they picked me up that day, they shipped me back to a field hospital and then on to Tokyo General. I arrived back in the States at Walter Reed Hospital on December 19, 1950 where I remained for almost a year."

Sherm's facial wounds required years of surgeries to correct. He also had to have part of his foot amputated.

Sherman: "I spent the years from 1952 to 1954 in a Dallas hospital. They'd do a surgery, keep me there a couple weeks and then send me home. After a month or so, they'd call me back."

Valdor was in Japanese hospitals about a month before shipping to Hawaii for four or five days. He stayed in a California facility for another month and then went on to Texas. In total, he spent about one and a half years in the hospital.

Valdor: "I'd been shot twice in the left arm and the muscles were all torn up. My arm was just a little piece of bone with a hand stuck to it . . . finally, one guy operated on it and put me on these exercises and my arm started filling out." (Carlson, 2002)

His Ordeal Is Over

Bob Sharpe after rescue in October 1950

Thirty — The Tiger

"Forgive your enemies, but never forget their names." — John F. Kennedy

What happened to the rest of the men who left Pyongyang on October 10? Actually, the story of the survivors of the massacres at the two tunnels—Sunchon and Kujang—is part of a much larger tale.

Beginning with the fall of Taejon on July 22, the North Korean Army gathered up captured American soldiers and marched them north. The enemy had already sent other prisoners from the first actions of the Korean War to Seoul. These first groups joined up in early August and continued on to Pyongyang in September. From there, they traveled by train north to Manpo on the south bank of the Yalu River.

Shorty Estabrook:[30] "On 11 September 1950, we arrived in the frontier town of Manpo-Jin,[31] North Korea."

These men made up the beginnings of the infamous "Tiger Death March." Along with military POWs, they included civilians—journalists, schoolteachers, priests and nuns, families, and children. Major John J. Dunn[32] was the ranking officer of this group.

The POWs involved in the Sunchon and Kujang massacres, Major McDaniel's men, were the second group of POWs the North Koreans sent north. At Seoul, the Security Guard Bureau, Home Affairs Ministry, led by Major Chong Myong

---

30 Shorty Estabrook – Korean War ex-POW and survivor of the "Tiger March."

31 The -jin at the end of a town's name means "near water." The -ri or -ni means "small place."

32 John Dunn retired as a full colonel. (Estabrook, 2007)

Sil, took charge of them. Major Chong had unlimited power of life and death—over the US prisoners and over his own men.

A lieutenant, who the men describe as "cruel," supported him. This officer told Lieutenant Makarounis that he'd recently killed twelve men. (Makarounis, Subcommittee on Korean War Atrocities, 1953) The UN forces captured Junior Lieutenant Lee Hae Do in Pyongyang shortly after the Sunchon Tunnel murders. The only other North Korean lieutenant mentioned by the survivors of the Sunchon death march was Junior Lieutenant Moon Myong Ho, NKPA, identified by Lee Hae Do in his testimony.

During the march from Seoul to Pyongyang, the men endured harsh treatment promulgated by the Home Security Guards and Communist interrogator Mr. Kim. By the time they reached Pyongyang, they were in bad shape. Several escaped. Some died in the attempt. They were in Pyongyang a few days when advancing UN troops forced the North Koreans to move them again.

Major Chong Myong Sil,[33] charged with getting the prisoners to the Manchurian border, was in a hurry. The men were exhausted from months of marching—and dysentery. They were depressed. They moved slowly. Their clothing was unsuitable for the weather, which was colder than normal for that time of year. The limited diet was insufficient to sustain them. They were underweight and suffering from a variety of vitamin deficiencies. A few of the POWs died every day. Many of the others were so miserable that they could no longer be bullied. The stronger ones were beginning to slip away. Planes harassed the train making it harder for the guards to accomplish their mission. North Korean troops were retreating and the major didn't want the line of battle to bypass them. They'd been traveling for five days and they still were only a few miles beyond the town of Sunchon. He knew of the 187th RCT paratrooper drop in the area. He was losing situational control. (O'Brien, 2007)

---

33 As identified by Junior Lieutenant Lee Hae Do in his testimony.

Lee Hae Do estimated that two hundred and fifty men boarded the train in Pyongyang. The prisoners themselves testified that four or five men died each day that they were on the train. George Snodgrass, Lieutenant Blaylock and Corporal Stevens escaped, as did several others. General Allen says that he met with five. The rescue party found seven corpses at the mouth of the tunnel. That left around two hundred fifteen prisoners on the train on October 20.

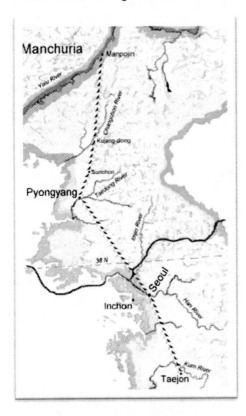

The route from Taejon to Manpo

Just south of Sunchon Tunnel, the major got rid of almost half of his problem. He murdered sixty-eight prisoners and left twenty-three behind. Possibly, one hundred and twenty-four men continued on toward Kujang where the rocket attack disabled the engine. At that point, without transportation, the guards rousted the men out of the cars to start the long march north. Those who re-fused—or could not walk—were expendable.

Rescuers discovered twenty-nine more bodies beside the abandoned train. Seven of them were covered with oil and burned. Another man was inside the train—dead of natural causes. Walt Whitcomb and Ed Slater were nearby—wounded and being tended to by North Korean civilians. Sherman Jones lay under a straw mat with part of his face shot away and the bone of his left leg exposed. (Chinnery, 2000)

That left about ninety-one men headed north with Major Chong and his men. Their fate is unknown. Only three POWs from the Sunchon group—Gilbert Van Nosdall, Ancil Roten, and Albert Mickelberg—made it the whole way to Manpo on the south bank of the Yalu River six days later.

How did the final three men survive to reach Tiger Group?[34] Apparently their guards, perhaps Christians, led them off as others were about to be murdered. They just kept walking, and finally reached Manpo, about the same time as the Tiger, but separately. (O'Brien, 2007)

The earlier group of military prisoners and a large contingency of civilians were camped just outside the town.

Shorty: "We had been kept in old Japanese Army buildings in town—when the Chinese entered the war, they commandeered the buildings. We were moved around and ended up in a cornfield about two miles out of town—the Chinese paid no attention to us."

The guards herded the three exhausted men to the larger group of POWs.

Shorty: "We never figured out why the guard brought them to us."

Gilbert Van Nosdall, a member of Signal Company, 1st Signal Battalion, 1st Marine Division, died at Hanjang on November 21, 1950.[35] Albert Mickelberg and Ancil Roten survived the war and provided information about their ordeal.

The new commandant arrived in Manpo on Halloween and took control of the whole group.

Shorty: "His record had preceded him and he was a very bad man. He had already killed a great number of people at a tunnel north of Pyongyang. We would later call him 'The Tiger.'"

---

34 The people involved in the Tiger March refer to themselves as the Tiger Survivors. (Estabrook, 2007)

35 As recorded by Johnny Johnson. See historical note in Appendix XI.

The survivors of the "Tiger March" believe that the Tiger was also in charge of the Sunchon Tunnel–Kujang Massacres.[36] One of the civilian prisoners, Father Phillip Crosbie, had met the Tiger before—in Pyongyang. (Zellers, 1991) Of course, Nosdall, Roten, and Mickelburg, the three men who began their ordeal as part of the McDaniel group, would have recognized the North Korean Home Security Guard major, too. The timing is right. If so, Major Chong Myong Sil arrived with almost two hundred fresh murders to his credit.

The Tiger brought five men with him.

Shorty: "I remember the names of three of them—Johnny, Pat, and Kim. Kim talked to Major Dunn and told him that Johnny was one of the guys who gave the orders at Sunchon."

Given the testimonies of the survivors of both groups, "Johnny" participated in the Tiger Death March in much the same role as "Johnny" did in the Sunchon–Kujang march. The men describe him as a guard without mention of his rank. Since Johnny is supposed to have given orders at Sunchon, it seems likely that he was a non-commissioned officer—a sergeant or master sergeant. Lee Hae Do names a master sergeant in his squad as Kang Myong Sik, 1st Company, 2nd Battalion, 316th Unit. The other possibility is Master Sergeant Cho Chang Ho, 2nd Battalion, 316th Unit.

Senior Sergeant. Kim Hak Chin, Squad Leader, 4th Squad is a possibility for "Kim." There are many people with the Korean surname of "Kim"[37] so the evidence that this might be the same person is circumstantial.

On November 1, the Tiger Death March began. It ended on November 9 at Chung-Gang. The Tiger and his men shot

---

36 The Tiger Survivors refer to Major McDaniel's group as the "Parallel Tiger March."

37 The man known as "Mr. Kim" by the men was not a guard. Other historical descriptions of Mr. Kim depict him as a Communist interrogator—a South Korean 'traitor' and a man of some education.

eighty-nine people during the march—including a nun and an elderly woman. On November 16, 1950, the Tiger's victims walked to Hanjang where another two hundred and twenty-two people died at the hands of their captors. Later they moved to Andong where fifty more died. In October 1951, guards separated military and civilian prisoners and sent the POWs to a Chinese Camp. Whereas the North Koreans found prisoners of war burdensome, the Chinese saw propaganda value in them. While being a POW is never pleasurable, their treatment improved. In August 1953, the Tiger's surviving victims came home.

Rescuers buried the victims of both the Sunchon and Kujang massacres beside the tracks where they were killed. Finding those who died on the marches was more difficult and time consuming, although the burial details as directed by Major McDaniel tried to leave identification with the men interred. A few days later, formal graves' teams exhumed the bodies near the Sunchon Tunnel and took them to a temporary cemetery in Pyongyang.[38] They intended to do the same with the dead near the Kujang site.

However, recovery was complicated when the Chinese entered the war. As the fighting developed, they retook the area including the city of Pyongyang.[39] Those graves not yet processed were lost.

In 1954, the North Koreans and Chinese returned many of the bodies during an exchange known as Operation Glory. (See Appendix XI) The military sent identifiable bodies home and reburied the rest in Hawaii.[40]

At present, all of the men who died at Sunchon are known by name, but those who died at Kujang—or on the long march north—are more difficult to identify. Also, unknown American bodies may still lie buried alongside Korean roads.

---

38 Pyongyang UN Military Cemetery

39 Seoul changed hands four times during the course of the war.

40 Punchbowl National Memorial Cemetery of the Pacific in Hawaii

As time passed, advances in DNA testing gave new hope to families with lost loved ones in Korea. The Defense Prisoners of War/ Missing Personnel Office (DPMO) exhumed some of the unknown bodies in Hawaii. However, a heavy preservative compound used to treat the remains prevented identification. They are following-up on options to enable DNA use.

In the meantime, the DPMO focuses on re-examinations and progressive elimination using emerging information about sites and dental work. So far, there are no confirmed, by-name IDs from Kujang proper because exactly who died there is unknown. They do have a few men from McDaniel's group who expired during the march since the North Koreans did return bodies from along the route. It's possible that one or two of these might be from Kujang, as opposed to somewhere above or below. The process of identifying remains and sending them home continues. (O'Brien, 2007)

What happened to Major Chong Myong Sil? Some of the Tiger March survivors reported being told that the Tiger had been imprisoned for stealing money given to him to feed his prisoners. (Zellers, 1991) Others say that high ranking civilians from the North Korean government told them that he sold prisoner food on the black market—and had been arrested for that. (Estabrook, 2007) Whether Major Chong and the Tiger are the same person or not, the fate of the man responsible for the Sunchon Tunnel and Kujang-dong massacres remains unknown at this time.

Thirty-One — They Came Home

"Nothing fixes a thing so intensely in the memory as the wish to forget it". —
Michel de Montaigne

Ed Slater has lived with his memories of Korea for over fifty years—and dealt with them as best he could. Some of those years were better than others. One day, he was in a library in Kansas City when he met Pat McGrath Avery—a writer and publisher of children's books. After a pleasant conversation, he said to her, "Why don't you write my story?"

Pat agreed and Ed began digging into the most painful time of his life again. His story became part of a book published by River Road Press, titled *They Came Home: Korean War POWs Tell Their Stories*. Pat also wrote several articles about Ed. Over a two-year period, veterans and their families began reading the book.

Then in early 2005, Ed received a phone call. Walt Whitcomb had tracked him down. Up until this point, Ed believed that the man who'd fallen on him during the massacre was his friend, Bob Sharpe. Now he learned that the man on top of him had, in fact, been Walt Whitcomb. He had to come to terms with the fact that memories are fragile.

After several phone conversations, Ed and Walt decided to meet. Walt came to Kansas City. Both he and Ed were nervous. How do you greet someone who shared the same brutal and horrendous experiences another lifetime ago? Could they connect?

The local press was present, taking pictures and asking questions. This helped the two of them in the beginning moments of their reunion. Soon they were sharing memories. However, the mind plays strange games in times of stress. They soon realized their memories didn't always jive. While each person sees an event from his own perspective, certain facts should be the same. This wasn't always true for them.

Walt Whitcomb and Ed Slater, May 2005 — Kansas City *(Photo by Authors)*

Both re-examined their own memories. Each thinks he remembers correctly. That's not surprising. Traumatic situations often result in memory impairment. (See Appendix — PTSD and Critical Incident Amnesia) Extreme stress causes physical and emotional arousal that changes how individuals experience an event.[41] Both Ed and Walt were wounded. Neither of them could walk very well. They were disoriented, cold, hungry—devastated. Their ability to store information would have been limited to what they could see or hear. Their debilitated state would affect what they saw or heard.

In addition, their ability to recall information might be compromised. They have been remembering what they remember for over fifty years—the images in their heads are

41 Grossman and Siddle, *Critical Incident Amnesia: The Physiological Basis and the Implications of Memory Loss During Extreme Survival Stress Situations*, 2000

their own personal realities now. They both have dealt with alcohol and other PTSD (See Thirty-three) related issues. They have read what others have said about the event. They each put their experiences into the context of history, as they knew it.

Joyce Faulkner, in researching her book, *In the Shadow of Suribachi*, about her dad's experiences during the battle of Iwo Jima, spoke with several veterans of that event. They, too, struggled with memory. One explained that he'd been troubled with alcoholism and depression for years. He didn't remember that his experience had been especially traumatic— although he had a bad feeling about it. His psychiatrist suggested that he get involved in "someone else's war" so he visited Gettysburg during the annual reenactment. As soon as the cannonade began, he became catatonic and had to be taken back to his hotel. As soon as he lay down in the air-conditioned room, the terrible images that he'd repressed came rushing back.

Ed and Walt spent several days together. They parted with mixed feelings. It was good to see each other, but a whole sea of thoughts rolled through their minds—ugly pictures of old friends and old enemies.

Several months passed.

Then in January 2006, while Ed was in a Home Depot store, he received a call on his cell phone. It was Sherman Jones—the third survivor of the massacre that took place near Kujang. Sherm wanted to thank Ed for trying to help him that day in Korea. Ed, normally blessed with the gift of gab, was speechless. He could not remember seeing Sherm after he disentangled himself from the pile of dead bodies alongside the railway tracks. The POW days were front and center again. One of the first things he wanted to do with Sherm was to check some of the facts surrounding the death march and massacre.

As they talked, Ed developed the idea of a reunion. There are eight living survivors of the massacre—Valdor John, Allen

177

Gifford, Bob Sharpe, Jim Yeager, Bill Henninger, Walt Whitcomb, Sherman Jones and Ed. Would they be interested in seeing each other again? He decided to ask them. Everyone but Allen Gifford agreed to meet in Branson, Missouri on Memorial Day, 2006.

Thirty-Two — Reunion

". . . if life is just a highway, then the soul is just a car
And objects in the rear view mirror may appear closer than they are." — Jim
Steinman

It was a beautiful day in May. Branson glittered in the warm sunshine. War was a blurry image in the rear view mirror.

The survivors checked into the Radisson Hotel. They were excited—but nervous. They came from different parts of the country—lived different lives. The only thing they knew they had in common was Korea. They'd presumed that the others must be dead. Now, they wondered—how does one recognize ghosts?

They settled into their rooms before venturing out to the lobby.

Jim Yeager was first. He sat in a straight-backed chair, chatting with the authors of this book. His wife and grandson had accompanied him to the reunion. He'd brought a written account of his Korean experiences with him—and photos of his various trips back looking for the remains of other soldiers. They were spread out on a glass coffee table.

John Toney died of a heart attack in 1970. Jim talked about his old friend and all the things they did together.

John Toney

Jim: "I told Toney that we'd be back home before Christmas—and we were." He tapped a faded newspaper photo of the two of them—young, scrawny, smiling—shaking hands across the narrow space between their cots. "Never thought it would be like that."

179

With a soft, wet intake of breath, Sherman Jones rushed across the lobby to hug Jim. Family members and friends swallowed back tears. Sherm muttered something into Jim's ear. Jim patted Sherm's back and nodded. For a few moments, conversation was stilted as if neither man knew what to say next.

Then other people began arriving—several men wore hats identifying them as ex-POWs.

Bob Sharpe and his grandson, Bill Henninger, Valdor and Linda John, Walt Whitcomb and his grand-daughter, Ed Slater—soon they were together again.

Sherman Jones and Jim Yeager reunite, May 2006 *(Photo by Authors)*

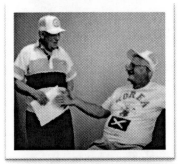

Bob Sharpe and Jim Yeager meet after fifty years, May 2006 *(Photo by Authors)*

Bill Henninger and Bob Sharpe greet each other in Branson, May 2006 *(Photo by Authors)*

Sherman Jones, Valdor John, Jim Yeager and Tom McDaniel *(Photo by Authors)*

Bob Sharpe, Sherman Jones, Walt Whitcomb, Jim Yeager, Valdor John and Ed Slater — Together Again, May 2006 *(Photo by Authors)*

Allen Gifford — 2007

Throughout the next few days, the men got to know each other again. They met several times to discuss what had happened to them—and to share how they dealt with their extraordinary status as ex-POWs and survivors of a brutal massacre.

Ed Slater led the conversation—explaining how he came to organize the event. He told them that health concerns had kept Allen Gifford away and that George Snodgrass couldn't attend either. Everyone was saddened to hear that Melvin Rookstool had recently died. He also introduced a special guest, an Air Force officer, Colonel Tom McDaniel, the son of Major William McDaniel.

George Snodgrass — 2007

Then they went around the room—reminiscing, sharing—catching up.

Ed: "There were bodies hanging in trees. That's when I realized that we were in war. We took some land—then the North Koreans took it back and then next day we took it back—then it went back to original position. We sat there until early morning—the land of early calm. At night, you can stand on one mountainside and talk to a guy on the other mountain. Fog settled in the valleys . . . we were overwhelmed . . . I was fourteen days behind enemy lines. Then I was captured."

Then Ed talked about his life since Korea.

Ed Slater — 2007
(*Photo by Authors*)

Ed: "One day, my brother said, 'You have to do something, your life is going to hell . . .' and I said, 'I don't know what to do.' My brother said, 'Come with me and I'll start you out in Fuller Brush.' I got a kit and put brushes and stuff inside. Then I went down one side of the street, and he took the other. I sold something to just about anyone so I got into sales—and I was in it for thirty-eight years."

He talked about his three marriages—and how he'd finally found peace with Phyllis, his third wife. He told them about volunteering at the VA and about helping other POWs. Then he sat down.

Each man followed suit, standing up and talking about the things that they could bear to discuss.

Clad in a colorful shirt, Valdor John leaned on a walker as he spoke. His eyes sparkled as he looked around the room—and then he looked down.

Valdor: "I was in Taejon. There were thousands slaughtered there. We were told that we had orders from General MacArthur to stay there to the last man. That's about what it ended up at."

He glanced at a pretty woman sitting beside him. She smiled.

Valdor John — 2006
(*Photo by Authors*)

Valdor: "I had this PTSD thing going on for a long time. Of course, I didn't know what was happening. I messed up my marriage. She went one way, I went another. I retired on April 1 and started work the same day for the State of Texas as a plant engineer. I had to go to six months transition school. I got a business degree—and along with that got licenses for heating and air conditioning. Big units. I learned about blueprints and reading schematics and the like. I started off pretty good."

Valdor lowered his voice and talked about the role of alcohol in his life. He talked about his relationship with Linda who started out as a drinking partner and later became his second wife. He talked about the jobs that he left for no reason and about the many visits to the VA trying to get his disability upgraded.

Valdor: "A woman there said, 'You come to the VA so much why not get job there? So I worked for the VA hospital there in Dallas—worked there five or six years. I stopped at Social Security office to look into retirement—and they offered a large amount so I retired. Then I went to see a counselor about my alcoholism. He helped me and introduced me to others who helped me. He took both Linda and me in hand—and stuck with us until we got over the tough part. We have been practicing ever since—next month I will be sober twenty-two years. I became part of the Imperial Chapter in Florida. I got to be a commander there by sobering up, acting my age."

Linda: "Almost."

Everyone chuckled.

Sherman Jones — 2007
(*Photo by Authors*)

Sherman Jones stood up. He licked his lips and began. He talked about how he and the Army and then the VA dealt with his ongoing disability.

Sherman: "In 1954, I found out I couldn't farm any more. That's when I realized I needed an education so I went to Lubbock, and said I wanted to get a high school diploma. They said that they'd send me to Amarillo College."

He stayed there until 1955 when he went to El Paso. He took a college entrance examination. He wanted to go to Abilene Christian College.

Sherman: "I went spring semester. Every three months, I had to go to Dallas for an operation. I had over sixty operations. When I came back to Abilene, they told me that I didn't have enough to finish my college degree—so they sent me to Business College in accounting. They said, 'In January of 1957, you can go back to Abilene Christian.' Then in February, they sent me to Amarillo to get my foot amputated so I couldn't go back to school. I got to Amarillo in January of 1958 and was going to Business College. On March 3, phone rang and my mother answered. She said that Oleta called and wanted to know if I'd like to join a disability organization. She invited me to play games. By the time I got back to Walter Reed, I had a drinking problem. My brother- in- law and sister- in- law had been studying with me. I couldn't study. After I met Leta—her husband had died in 1956 and I met her in March of 1958—on May 3, I asked her to marry me."

Sherman beamed as though reliving the joyful occasion.

Sherman: "On June 3, we got our rings and got married on October 3. I went back to Business College. When I got ready to take my CPA, I still had PTSD so I started driving a cab. Leta had osteomalitis when she was twelve so she was on crutches. In 1961, there was this guy in New Mexico. We could have a little white baby or Mexican baby. We started sending a pregnant girl so much a month for clothes and hospital, but she decided to keep her baby. So we got a baby boy. We had to get the money to pay the lawyer. We got the baby in Dallas and took him to a pediatrician. He said he was fine but he couldn't hold his head up. He couldn't walk or talk. In 1968, we went to Children's Hospital in Denver where he was diagnosed with Cerebral Palsy caused by separation of cord at birth. He lasted forty-three years and died last year."

Sherman fought with his emotions for a moment, before continuing.

Sherman: "March 1963, the doctor said I needed to go into the hospital. My right heel was bending back, so they lengthened the heel. In December of that same year, the employment office called and said we want you to put in your application for Merchants Bank. It turned out that the man's father was a double amputee so they put me to work as a cashier. Every time there was a raise, they'd give me a double raise. I was a driver's cashier. I worked there for twenty-four years and we adopted two little girls. In 1974, I started volunteering for the VA hospital. I did it for eighteen years."

Sherman had one more story to tell the group.

Sherman: "I read about how Korean War and Vietnam veterans could get their high school diplomas and I always wanted to have one—so I got it on December 16, 2005. Then I found out that they were going to close Spade High School. The kids who were about to graduate—the last Spade High School graduation ceremony— invited me to walk across the stage with them and pick up my diploma. I was so excited—and I said 'Yes.' Therefore, they give me a cap and gown and on May 19, 2006, I walked across the stage to get it. The congregation of my church came down to see me get my high school diploma—and then the next Sunday, the preacher called me down and gave me a card. When I opened it, there was a check for $1500."

Again, Sherman wiped at his eyes as he sat down. Everyone else did, too.

Bill Henninger gave his fellow POWs a belt buckle before beginning.

Bill: "You all know what happened in 1950. I was in Sasebo with

the 34th Regiment. They loaded us up on the 1st of July and the next morning, we were in Pusan. We went up to Osan and started doing our thing up there. I have arguments with the day that we started firing up there. I still swear it was July 4. We were a whole day ahead of what they were back here. It's all history now."

Bill Henninger — 2006
(*Photo by Authors*)

He sighed, as though happy he didn't have to go into details about Korea.

Bill: "When we got home, I got my discharge in 1952 and raised the family. I started out as a truck driver but then began working for the county as an ambulance driver for five years. My wife decided I wasn't making enough money. She wanted me to go overseas to make enough so that she could live comfortably—but the job fell through. I got up to New York, but New York wouldn't let us train up there for the overseas work. I might have ended up in Vietnam except that the French were over there at the time. My wife stayed with me until 1964—then she said she wanted to get a divorce. I started running around and started drinking again. I was remarried about 1970. She was a widow. I was with her for about twelve years. She died in 1982. I was working for a medical lab at that time and I stayed with them until 1988 until I retired. In 1997, I got married again . . ."

He blushed but his eyes twinkled.

Bill: "To my first wife."

The others laughed and shook their heads.

Jim Yeager: "My father had raised me to be a soldier. When I was a little fellow, I never had a teddy bear—I always had a cap pistol or a pop gun. The first time I fired an army rifle, I was five years old. My dad was too old during WWII. They activated the National Guard so they didn't have anyone to watch the utilities in Kansas. I learned how to take care of guns. I watched them doing close order drill. I made a point to take my bicycle, go down, and talk to the soldiers. I was ready to roll—as ready as the military was concerned."

Jim Yeager – 2007
(*Photo by Authors*)

Jim's father had always been an enlisted man. He didn't have a college education. In fact, he had a problem with college people. Consequently, when it was time for Jim to get ready for college, he didn't have the math skills. His mother held him back so he was older than the rest of the kids in the class. As a result, during his junior and senior year, he was running around with guys coming back from WWII.

Jim: "My dad always made sure that I was prepared to go into the National Guard. We went to a submarine encampment. I was proficient with submachine guns. Then I went to junior college. The kids that were in my class were sharing tests. I got ticked off so in October, 1949, I joined the Army"

Right off the bat, Jim met John Toney and they became friends.

Jim: "Right after we got to Korea, we headed out for Chinju. Lots of guys threw food to the poor folks along the way. When officers caught on to what we were doing, they offloaded us and we marched into Masan. It was so hot that day that tar came up around our combat boots. There was a school. A couple of guys went over for some water and heard officers in the schoolhouse talking with old Fat Chae. He was the one that wouldn't blow the bridge in Seoul until it was too late. He was floating around and unofficially assigned himself to our unit as a guide. We were eavesdropping. They were planning to make this push to Hadong. I found out after the fact that we weren't really going after guerillas but the whole Red Army."

Jim remembered that night well.

Jim: "It was calm—the moonlight reflected off the rice paddies. One driver fell asleep and went off the road, wrecking the jeep. Later on, there was some firing. Toney and I went up the hill. Just as I went over the military crest, Clyde, who was the 3rd platoon leader, pulled down on me with his carbine. He almost shot me. They were doing some firing. The observers were in the rice paddies. We kept moving on up. Kids were running out of water. Some were dipping canteens in rice paddies. The NCOs were telling them not to do that. When I ran out of water, I walked up to a hut, knocked on the door, and asked for water. She slammed the door on me, but came back and gave me a drink."

Jim talked about going on reconnaissance with Captain Mitchell and Toney and about the battle and about being captured. He told the group that he still found it ironic that on leaving San Francisco, he'd told his friend John Toney that they would be back before Christmas—and they were.

Jim: "After I came back from Korea and got out of hospitals, I ended up in Fort Benning, Georgia. I put in for OCS. I got tired of doing night assignments so got into the Motor Pool."

His back was in bad shape. He knew he was too badly injured to stay in infantry. However, he ended up in OCS for infantry. He got about three-quarters through OCS and changed his mind.

Jim: "I told myself that I became a prisoner of war because of bad leadership, so I handed in my letter of resignation. Two Korean War veterans turned down officers training at the same time. I went to machine gun committee until I got discharged. I thought about reenlisting but dad didn't want me to because of anxiety about the Korean War."

So Jim got a job—and in the process met a "beautiful little receptionist named Nadine," whom he married. Like Sherm and Valdor, he seemed amazed at his good luck in finding such a woman.

Still, life was complicated for Jim. He was angry—about what happened at Hadong, about what happened at Sunchon—about so many things. He struggled with health problems—and he drifted from job to job.

Jim: "I got hooked up with a guy who was in the Battle of Bulge. He was as squirrelly as I was. Turns out, I was the only person he'd been able to work with very long. That went bankrupt, too. My back got so bad that I went to Long Beach Hospital. It was filled with a bunch of druggies—people who'd gotten in trouble and they were treating them—kids coming back from Vietnam. They told me that I needed spinal surgery but there would be only forty percent chance of walking again."

The odds didn't seem good—so after walking him around a swimming pool for a while, they put him back on the street.

Jim: "I couldn't get a job anywhere so I went to Hughes Aircraft. I had to take a physical. The company doctor had me strip down to my shorts, turn around and touch the floor. He said, 'Okay, you can put your clothes back on.' I thought it was fine, but the doc said, 'You have a serious back problem. We can't use you.' So I went back to the Army and said I can still shoot a gun, but no go—so I became a security guard."

Jim talked about his work with Operation Freedom—his project to try to repatriate the remains of soldiers left behind in Korea—and about talking with a shrink and about his frustrations with the VA. He had one final story to tell.

Jim: "The pilot of the plane that flew us back was from my hometown of Grand Junction, Colorado. A Hispanic—quite a coincidence!"

Walt Whitcomb spoke next. He talked about his ambivalent feelings toward his parents—and about how much he liked the Army—until Korea. He told them about the drinking and the women and the fighting.

Walt Whitcomb — 2007
(*Photo by Authors*)

Walt: "While I was still recovering from the wounds I got during the massacre, I got into a fight in a bar. Some guy cut my thumb pretty bad—so they gave me time off."

After he left the Army, he worked in sales—and made a good living using a veteran's pitch. He got a job on the railroad, he worked as a Fuller Brush salesman, he went back to the railroad—he went to school on the GI Bill—Bryant and Stratton Business School in Buffalo.

Walt: "All the time, I was still drinking and fighting."

When he graduated, he got fired from the railroad again and went to work for General Tire.

Walt: "I worked my way up to general manager. I loved to dance and get drunk. Crazy thing was, I never had trouble getting jobs when I was drinking. Once I was sober, it wasn't that easy."

Like Valdor, Walt married a woman who drank with him—and fought with him. They had eight children in the course of their tumultuous relationship. She left him and died several years later—of alcoholism.

Walt: "I had a lot of heartache because of the losses—and I was angry. I wanted revenge. After I quit drinking—after I was sober four or five years, I was grateful that I was alive. I'm happy—as anyone can be. I live in California by the beach. I go to AA. I have a roommate. I have children and grandchildren and great grandchildren. I don't carry stuff with me anymore. I say what I feel. I no longer shut up and just take it. It's satisfying—but sometimes it's not good because I say the wrong thing at the wrong time to the wrong person—and I have to go back and apologize. Still, I try my best."

It was Bob Sharpe's turn to speak.

Bob: "It's been a great treat to see these folks breathing and living."

Bob glanced around the room. Several of the men smiled.

Bob: "I married a woman with six children. My rich aunt called to tell me that that wasn't too smart. My wife-to-be captured the telephone call on the other end. 'I don't know you,' she said, 'but I know Bob—and he'll make a great father.'"

Bob Sharpe – 2007
(Photo by Authors)

Bob's wife passed in November 2002.

Bob: "She wanted to go see her sister in Bakersfield. I said, 'Fine, I'll get us some tickets,'—but she said, 'Don't do that, get a Cadillac.'"

They spent twenty days enjoying the country. They came home on October 25. On November 8, she had a stroke.

Bob: "So I've been without her for awhile. Life has been something for me. When I was a kid, my father said, 'You have to help,' so I said 'Fine.' I had paper routes—first morning and then evening. My father always got me involved. I thought, well, I can get me a job downtown. Maybe I can do better as an usher in the theater. I had three jobs now. When I finished school and couldn't pay for education, I went to service to get an education, you see. By the time I got back from Korea, my health wasn't so good. I started hustling and got promoted."

Bob talked about training young men for Vietnam—and about making the decision to go with them even though his wife was expecting their first child.

Bob: "I began to really move in the service and retired after 26 years. Then I became a school teacher. When I got my Master's degree, I went to school with lots of folks who were in corrections. They told me, 'Your chances are slim and none for becoming a warden' and I was discouraged, but the deputy warden encouraged me. So I went back and my application was approved and within ten years, I was the warden."

It was a tough job.

Bob: "One side of the house will never accept you for anything other than the man. I was the warden of the prison near Andersonville. It's not like the military. Nothing will ever make them like you."

After a while, Bob decided to teach in college. He went to Georgia State and he really liked that.

Bob: "I'd start a war in the first class. I'd say, 'How many know anything about corrections?' Everyone would raise a hand. Then I'd ask, 'Where did you get your information?' Answers would be— *Cool Hand Luke, Brubaker,*—the problem is that movies show that the administration is the bad guy and inmates are the good guys. I know that when I was a prison warden that I made some accommodations with the devil—I'm sure everyone who's been in corrections has done something like that."

Then Bob changed gears and talked about how his father took care of him after he returned from Korea.

Bob: "All the time I was missing in action, there was no information for my family. My dad ran up and down the highway on weekends picking up soldiers bringing them back and forth to have some connection with me. Not sure why, but dad would not tell me about it. My mother told me. They notified my dad that I'd be coming home to Fort Bragg. My father got the family together and told them, 'Do not be emotional, don't make it tough on him.' However, it didn't work. When I came home in a wheelchair, everyone broke up and cried. Then dad and I had a discussion about the anatomy of Korean ladies—something to make me laugh."

Bob broke down at the memory. The room was quiet. He took out a handkerchief and wiped his eyes.

Bob: "I think that Colonel McDaniel's father should have the Medal of Honor."

The other survivors agreed—and turned toward the good-looking young man who sat quietly listening to their stories. Tom McDaniel had searched for information about his father for years—and planned on writing a book about him.

Bob: "He was older than the rest of us—in his thirties. He went up and down the lines busting his fanny for us. I first met Major McDaniel in Seoul after I was a prisoner. We were at a school for girls. We came in different times from different areas. The 21st Regiment was first. He was around to see how everyone was doing when each group came into the camp. On the march, I noticed that he had to struggle to get to see everyone. He was unwounded and he did more than twice what everyone else was doing. He stood up to Kim and demanded that something be done about what was happening. Locke would sass the guard for the morale of the group. The major had to put up Locke to escape but he himself refused to leave in Pyongyang."

Colonel Tom McDaniel — Son of Major William T. McDaniel *(Photo by Authors)*

Tom McDaniel smiled at Bob—and at all of the men who his father had tried to save. He'd been a small boy when they were ordered off the train near the Sunchon Tunnel. Their ordeal has been as much a part of his life as it has been theirs.

After Bob spoke, Sherman had one more thing to say.

Sherman: "There is this woman that called me. She says that she's my buddy's sister. She wants to know about Gene. I haven't called her back—I couldn't."

He licked his lips and fought back tears.

Sherman: "I didn't know what to tell her—but now, after this. I think I'll call her back."

Ed: "That's good, Sherman. Maybe it's time."

Sherman nodded—quick, abrupt movements of his head. "Yeah," he said. "It's time."

The others were quiet—remembering all the young men left behind in Korea.

Thirty-Three — Branson

"And in those times of trouble
When you are most alone
The memory of love will bring you home." — John Denver

The town of Branson, MO, is a magical place—especially for veterans. When Steve Weyher, Marlyce Stockinger and Arlen Lipper heard the story of the Sunchon Tunnel Massacre Survivors, they leapt into action. The Branson phone lines buzzed. Restaurants, entertainers and other businesses came together to create a supportive environment for these men who'd been through so much.

Bob Sharpe, Ed Slater, Valdor John, and Walt Whitcomb meet a young American at the Jim Stafford Theater in Branson, MO *(Photo by Authors)*

A long white limousine whisked them off to shows, dinners and meetings.

The first evening, the survivors went to the Jim Stafford show. Talented and funny, Jim played guitar, sang and joked around, as usual. Then, part way through his performance, he paused and read the story of the Sunchon Tunnel Massacre

195

Survivors. With a quivering voice, he asked the men to stand. Applause filled the theater. The seven veterans squared their shoulders and lifted their chins. Jim Yeager's cheeks flushed. Tears filled Sherman Jones' eyes. Individual members of the audience reached out to touch them—to shake their hands and to thank them for their service. Afterwards, in the lobby, parents thrust their children forward to greet them as heroes. For soldiers of the "Forgotten War," it was a special moment.

Another Branson celebrity, Shoji Tabuchi—a Japanese American immigrant and virtuoso violinist, introduced the Sunchon Tunnel Survivors to his audience. In honor of the men—and all veterans, he performed a dazzling patriotic act that moved everyone. His kindness extended beyond the show. After the theater cleared, Shoji came out and shook each old soldier's hand. He chatted with Sherman Jones and Jim Yeager, telling them that he had also performed "honey bucket" duty when he was a boy in Japan. The men were thrilled by Shoji's great talent—and his generosity.

Shoji, Sherman Jones, Walt Whitcomb, and Jim Yeager, Branson 2006
(Photo by Authors)

Toward the end of their time together, the seven men went to the see The Comets at the Dick Clark Theater. They clapped and cheered when the band broke into "Rock Around the Clock." Dressed in the oversized blue dinner jackets of the 1950s, the Comets performed several numbers from that era—songs that reminded the survivors of the good things from their youth. Like at the Jim Stafford and Shoji Tabuchi shows, one of the Comets read the story of the Sunchon Tunnel Survivors to the audience. The performers had come of age at the same time. They were shocked at the pain the survivors had endured—and the two groups spent time appreciating each other. Sherman Jones was a special fan. Comet Joey Ambrose arranged for Sherman to wear one of their jackets.

The Comets pose with the Sunchon Tunnel Massacre Survivors, The Dick Clark Theater, Branson, 2006 *(Photo by Authors)*

After dinner and being entertained by Allen Edwards at the Golden Corral, managed by Steve Weyher, the survivors attended a special program honoring them.

After an honor guard posted the colors, Branson's American Kids performed—and Lou Schaefer, the Mayor of Branson, welcomed the Sunchon Tunnel Survivors. Pat McGrath Avery told the audience why these men were special. Holding up a map of Korea, she plotted the route of their marches. Joyce Faulkner read an excerpt from Ms. Avery's earlier book about Korean War POWs.

Then, Bob Sharpe spoke.

He thanked the public for their interest—and the city of Branson for its hospitality. He talked about the joy he and the others felt at having found each other again. His voice rose with passion and dropped with sadness. In the end, he thanked God for their lives.

Valdor John, Bill Henninger, Sherman Jones, Walt Whitcomb, Jim Yeager, Bob Sharpe, Ed Slater, and The American Kids, Golden Corral, Branson, MO 2006
(Photo by Authors)

Thirty-Four — Conclusion

"Anything worth living for," said Nately, "is worth dying for." "And anything worth dying for," answered the old man, "is certainly worth living for." — Joseph Heller, *Catch 22*

There are all kinds of heroes—firefighters who climb into burning houses to rescue toddlers, astronauts who ride rockets into the unknown and doctors who cut into human bodies. There are generals and martyrs and pioneers—revolutionaries, idealists, and politicians. Throughout history, young men stood between danger and their homes. They did it for many reasons—passion, responsibility, adventure, patriotism, and obedience. In the past, their rewards were prosperity, security, and a sense of accomplishment. In the past, returning soldiers marched down main streets all over America to the cheers of their neighbors.

The survivors of the Sunchon Tunnel Massacre faced a ferocious and complex enemy. Captured within days of their arrival in Korea, they endured three months of murder, torture, and neglect. Their return was quiet and painful. In the end, their sacrifices slipped into history without much comment—in between the triumph of World War II and the national ambivalence over the Vietnam War. There were no ticker tape parades or pretty girls welcoming them with kisses. The country barely noticed when they came home.

Still, there's something heroic about survivors—although they usually deny it.

Walt Whitcomb: "I didn't deserve to live more than anyone else. I guess God wanted to keep me around—luck and God. I didn't do anything special—just clowned around and kidded with other guys to keep us all going."

George Snodgrass: "I did the best I could and God took care of me."

Bob Sharpe: "The good Lord interceded and brought me back."

Ed: "The good Lord took care of me day by day."

What magic kept them alive while others died? Providence (or luck) protected them from rockets, strafing planes and artillery rounds that blew their buddies to pieces. They took beatings like everyone else, but something inside them fought back—as though life itself was revenge. They starved like everyone else, but their bodies had just enough reserves to last until October 20. They marched like everyone else, but they had enough stamina to make it those last few miles. They were wounded like the others, but the maggots did their job and their infections healed. They had dysentery, pneumonia and malaria, but even disease couldn't kill them. They lost friends—and still they lived on.

In the end, they beat the odds once again—defying enemy burp guns, rifle butts and bayonets. Ed and Bob and Bill and Sherman and Walt and Jim and George and Allen and Valdor fought for life when others chose death. They clung to it when death was easier. Generations of children will see the world differently because they did. Perhaps that's what they were born to do.

Ed Slater, Bob Sharpe, Walt Whitcomb, Jim Yeager, and Sherman Jones — Branson, Missouri Memorial Day 2007 (*Photo by Authors*)

Epilogue

After the first reunion of the Sunchon Tunnel Massacre Survivors in Branson, in May of 2006, Sherman Jones made good on his promise to contact his good friend Gene Putzier's sister, Nancy Zeman. He cried and told her how Gene died in his arms in Pyongyang—and how Gene had called for his mother.

For Nancy, it was the first real information she'd had about her brother in years. His remains have never been identified. In October 2006, the authors of this book and Walt Whitcomb visited her in her home near San Diego—to learn about Gene, to look at photos and to remember that real people participate in historical events—and real families grieve.

201

Appendix I — Critical Incident Memories and PTSD

"And it's hard to believe after all these years
That it still gives you pain and it still brings tears." — Billy Joel

O Post Traumatic Stress Disorder (PTSD) O

The survivors of the Sunchon Tunnel Massacre have dealt with a wide assortment of lingering health issues—from the physical ramifications of old wounds to PTSD.

Veterans were a large percentage of the male population in the early 1950s—either of World War II or of Korea—or both. Horror had stamped its image on the souls of many. Even so, there was a cultural bias that made those suffering from "battle fatigue" try to hide their symptoms. Societal attitudes toward any kind of "mental problem" embarrassed and angered the afflicted.

However, in private, nightmares and/or insomnia besieged some combat veterans. The everyday sounds of civilization—bus backfires, the screech of trains, sonic booms—could trigger terrifying flashbacks or panic attacks. Some froze at any mention of the precipitating event, while others obsessed about their trauma—talking about it all the time, reading about it, thinking about it. They could be hypervigilent, a constant wariness often interpreted as paranoia. They found themselves taking offense at the slightest provocation—or experiencing feelings of shame or embarrassment. Many agonized over the unanswerable question—"Why am I alive when so many other good people are dead?" (Military Veterans PTSD Reference, 2006)

Other symptoms included irritability, depression, low self-esteem and feelings of detachment. Those caught in the loop tried to make themselves feel better—with alcohol or drugs or women. They felt that they were "blowing a second chance at life"—so they rode the Merry-Go-Round faster and with more intensity. Families were sympathetic in the beginning, but more than one wife tired of the behaviors eventually and insisted that it was time that their mates "get over it."

In the 1950s, people called the more extreme cases "nervous breakdowns" and doctors gave such patients "nerve pills" or "electric shock" treatments.

Veterans were not the only people exhibiting such symptoms. Concentration camp inmates and victims of disasters or assault also struggled to put their intense experiences in perspective. Doctors began seeing the similarities and evaluating possible treatments—but it took many years.

In the first edition of the *Diagnostic and Statistical Manual*, published in 1952, stress response syndrome appeared under the heading of "gross stress reactions." In 1968, *DSM-II* listed trauma-related disorders under "situational disorders."

Then, in 1980, the *Diagnostic and Statistical Manual of Mental Disorders (DSM-III)* recognized Post Traumatic Stress Disorder as a subcategory of anxiety disorder. In this book, a traumatic event was defined as a "catastrophic stressor outside the range of usual human experience"— things like war, torture, rape, genocide, natural and man-made disasters. For those dealing with the problem, this was an important change—their complaint now had a name—and with it came recognition that they weren't "crazy" or "weak" or "just drunks." For veterans, it led to recognition by the VA—and compensation. In the most current edition of *DSM-IV*, published in 1994, the Advisory Subcommittee on the subject classified PTSD as a new stress response category.

The change took away the stigma and encouraged more veterans to seek treatment. For POWs in general—and the survivors of massacres at Sunchon and Kujang-dong, in particular—knowing that they weren't alone with their frustrations was comforting.

Valdor John: "Thank God they identified PTSD and are able to treat it now."

Valdor John — 2007

The Sunchon Tunnel–Kujang Massacre survivors had a lot to overcome. They all had bouts of acute grief—for their buddies and for themselves.

Walt Whitcomb: "I think about watching all those guys get shot just before I was captured . . . the river . . . the river was full of blood. Those guys . . . I went through basic with them. I played pool with them. Hung out—and you know, even now, I forget and think about one of my friends—that I should give him a call—and then I remember . . . ."

As they tried to create new lives for themselves, they experienced feelings of betrayal, horror, rage—anxiety. They felt isolated and alone—after all, most people have never been lost in a strange land. Who could fathom what it's like to be shot or stabbed or beaten? Who would understand why small things set already raw nerves jangling?

Jim Yeager: "I became a security guard and I couldn't handle that—I worked with a chiropractor and wanted to kill my patients."

Bob Sharpe: "When I came back, it infuriated me to see some guy putting out a cigarette in his mashed potatoes. I wanted to beat him to death, but knew I couldn't."

Walt: "When I came back, it was like I'd never even gone—like I'd been out of town for a couple of days. I'd start fights—striking out at people whenever I got stressed."

Ed Slater: "It was a war—not a police action, not a conflict!"

Some of the men stayed in the Army. Bill Henninger and Walt Whitcomb served out their commitment and returned to civilian life. Valdor John, Bob Sharpe, Ed Slater and George Snodgrass all re-enlisted. Valdor, Bob and George fought in Vietnam. Sherman Jones, because of his severe injuries, never functioned as a soldier again—however, he received a military retirement rather than a discharge.

George Snodgrass: "I re-enlisted because I knew I could never adjust to civilian life. I needed the structured environment."

Valdor: "I had a lot of things wrong with me. The Army decided to discharge me for medical reasons, but I said,' No way, keep me in.'"

The military finally let Valdor stay in on a waiver—in fact, he stayed for twenty-six years on waivers.

Valdor: "Every three years, I had to get someone with power to help me renew these waivers."

Although some of the survivors felt that they needed the Army, some of them couldn't hold back their anger at the organization that had both lost them and saved them.

Walt: "I had a bad attitude about people. I stayed in the service, but they lied to me all the way and I stayed drunk all the time. Whatever they wanted me to do, I didn't want to do it. I did my thirty-seven months and got out."

Valdor: "I used the Army. I ran over the Army. I pulled a lot of raw deals on the Army—it was that PTSD thing, but I didn't know what was happening at the time."

Ed: "I was in the service for another eight years. I was a good soldier—in fact, I competed for soldier of the month—but it got to a point that I resented any orders from anybody. I had NCOs that I liked and I'd do what they said—but I resented officers. I knew I was doing it and tried not to . . . ."

Most of the men had trouble keeping a job.

Walt: "I had sixteen jobs in three months. Some jobs lasted eighteen to twenty minutes."

Sherman Jones: "I got a job at a cement company. I worked for them for three months and they said I was making too many mistakes. I'd put my application in someplace and they'd say, 'you draw 100% and we can't insure you,' so they'd not hire me—or they'd say they couldn't hire me cause I'm deaf in the left ear or because I was too nervous to concentrate."

Jim Yeager: "Everything I turned to, sooner or later things went sour. It got to the point where I couldn't stand to hear the phone ring."

Returning warriors often want a wife, a family and a home. This most natural of desires was difficult for some of the survivors. PTSD complicated their relationships and magnified the everyday troubles of ordinary life.

Ed: "I divorced my first wife. Later, I married a German woman who was an alcoholic and very jealous. Our daughter was born in Germany."

He got a boring job in a factory but his wife kept calling the office. He told her to get a job—and then he quit and began drinking and gambling himself. His marriage dissolved. Years later, he found happiness and peace with Phyllis, his third wife.

Walt: "I met my wife in a bar. We had eight kids. She drank as much as me. We had a rip-roaring marriage. She put up with me for twenty-two years and then she left."

Sherman: "Everything got on my nerves. Sometimes I drank and wasn't so nice to my family."

Bill: "I got my discharge in 1952 and raised the family. In 1964, we divorced. I started drinking and running around."

Valdor: "Finally I met Linda. She was going through her divorce and I was going through mine. We were good drinking buddies—we cried in our beer together."

Everyone feels the need to control their own environment. For those who have lost everything, the urge is stronger. However, it proved impossible for the survivors to manage wives, children, neighbors, fellow employees, bosses, customers—and this added to their frustrations.

Walt: "I had no control over anything. I started drinking to help me live in the world the way it was—the way I was."

These men went to Korea in good faith—to help the South Koreans. Most were captured before they had many good experiences with the people they were trying to save. At a young age, they faced chaos brought about by politics way beyond their ken. They dealt with "turn-coats," partisans, guerillas, security police—psychopaths. It was easy to focus their hatred on the Korean people as a whole.

Walt: "I took a job as a telemarketer. The girl that trained me was Asian. One day, I had to give her a check—and she said to make it out to Betty Kim. The minute she backed up against the stove because she was afraid of me, I realized that God had put her in my life—to teach me to understand other people. It was time to stop hating."

Given the nature of the Korean War and the fact that the men faced frequent interrogations, several of the survivors found themselves feeling defensive or paranoid.

Sherman Jones: "Questions about what happened to me sometimes feel like I'm being interrogated again."

Valdor: "I didn't like answering questions then—and I don't like answering them now."

Jim Yeager: "I try to stay away from people as best I can."

Like other combat veterans, many of the survivors had trouble sleeping—and many of the other symptoms of PTSD. One of the wives described her husband's frequent nightmares—waking to sheets that were soaked in sweat. Others talked about insomnia or erratic sleep habits.

Walt: "I had nightmares for years. My poor wife would wake up and I'd be on top of her with my hand on her throat with my fist ready to beat her up. I'd be sitting at the table and an airplane would come over and I'd dive under the table and the food and all would go sailing."

Allen Gifford: "I still get emotional and cry easily."

George: "I've had problems throughout my life."

Ed: "It had been thirty-eight years and I was having a terrible time. The nightmares began again. I was having them every other month."

Some of the men became fatalistic—engaging in dangerous behavior as a matter of course—as if they were daring angry gods to smite them.

George: "On my first trip to Vietnam, I was in the impact zone for machine guns when I headed across an open field in an advance on a VC position. A medic later said to me, 'Sergeant, I want to ask

208

you something. I don't understand how you can still be alive. I remember watching you stand up and start to run—bullets were hitting the ground in front of you and behind you. I don't know how they got there without going through you.'"

Their problems went untreated for many years. They just had to "live with it." Now that help is available, some of them have examined their feelings with doctors. Some confided in spouses or friends—others found solace with other veterans.

Walt: "There were no shrinks right after the event—they weren't offered for guys that were 'battle fatigued' or 'shell shocked.' Only time I talked to a doctor was back in 1999, when I got a POW protocol in veterans admin."

Ed: "I reported to the VA hospital. They wanted me to admit myself. They said, 'We have a clinic on the tenth floor'—and I said, 'No, you have a nut ward on the tenth floor.' I said 'No, I have to work.' They then suggested that I come in and visit—and they gave me Prozac. Ten days later, I was driving to work whistling. So I went back to see the doctor . . . ."

Valdor: "In Florida, the PTSD program was a good one. They took wives in, too—and separated folks into groups based on war served. People poured their hearts out. You have to let it all out. Keeping that stuff down and away from families hurts you more— and them, too. I did what they were telling me to do and passed it on to others."

Jim: "Eventually I talked to a shrink . . . ."

Some of them don't remember much about the other survivors. That, too, is a symptom of PTSD. Some events are too terrible to remember—and so some survivors avoid thinking about them as much as possible.

Ed Slater knows that he and Walt tried to take care of Sherman Jones. However, he has no memory of it—and was shocked when Sherman called to thank him for saving his life.

Bill Henninger remembers very little about the marches. Valdor doesn't remember his fellow survivors.

Valdor John: "Everyone I knew except for Lieutenant Makarounis died or was killed along the way."

Walt: "I tried to suppress those memories—I tried to stop going around looking for revenge. I was getting into fights all the time."

Some of the survivors, like Ed Slater and Jim Yeager, came to terms with their three months in captivity and the massacre, by learning as much about it as they can. They collect pictures, read reports, and seek out witnesses whenever possible.

George: "I still have trouble talking about my time as a prisoner of war. There's no fixing it and I can't forget. I have tried to accept it and I think I've done so. But when I think about it, I still cry."

Perhaps it's a natural progression, but after years of trying to "go it on their own," the men are reaching out to other veterans and participating in veteran and POW events.

Walt: "Now I have a great life. I belong to the VFW—I'm a Quartermaster. I go to meetings and march in parades."

Sherman: "I've volunteered at the VA hospital for eighteen years."

Ed: "I've been the Senior Vice Commander for the State of Missouri, and National Service officer for Ex-POW Organization and volunteer for the VA. I've helped veterans get the compensation that's due them for years now."

Jim: "I have worked with Operation Freedom for years—to find the remains of US soldiers and repatriate them."

○ Critical Incident Amnesia ○

There is considerable variation between testimonies that took place a few days after the rescue, what the first Americans on the scene reported—and what the men remember. This is to be expected. The differing reports do not invalidate each other—rather they show how personal memories can be.

Memory is a complicated concept under the best of circumstances. Until recently, juries considered eyewitness testimony sacrosanct. Since it's become available, DNA testing has freed dozens of innocent men convicted on the word of people who had no reason to lie. Some are mistaken identity cases—however, some are the result of the chasm between first person observations—and the memory of those observations.

Scientists are still studying how long term memories are created and stored. However, most agree on several issues.

First, the brain collects information from the senses—the item to be remembered must be seen or heard or felt or tasted or smelled.

A person better records those incidents on which he is focused. Two people going through the same episode may pay attention to different aspects—and thus remember different elements of the incident.

What an individual might focus on depends on a variety of elements—what interests him, what he recognizes from other incidents, what he believes in, what arouses him—what he fears. For example, one man might notice a woman's eyes—another will like her hair. When asked to describe her, each will elaborate on the feature that most attracted him.

Jim Yeager wanted to be a professional soldier. He viewed himself as a scout even after capture. He paid attention to all things military—and he talks about those things now. Ed Slater was horrified by maggots—he remembers them on others, on dead bodies, and in the wound of his own leg.

A man must be able to direct his attention in order to retain information about specifics. A healthy, alert person might see clues that something bad is about to happen. A depressed, hungry man like Bob Sharpe might only hear that he is about to be fed. A man drifting in and out of consciousness like Sherman Jones cannot focus at all.

Second, memories are stored when the brain creates a physical connection between neurons. Ill health or injury could interfere with the process. Low blood sugar or other chemical imbalances in the brain, as well as head wounds and/or concussions, make cognitive judgments difficult.

Third, there might be problems retrieving memories. A wounded man might be given medicine to dull pain or relieve anxieties—however, those same drugs might make it more difficult to recover stored images. Sherman Jones underwent dozens of operations to repair his face and leg. He remembers some of his ordeal clearly—such as when his friend Gene Putzier died in his arms in Pyongyang. Other events are hazy for him.

Over time, memories fade—and as the mind collects information from other sources, it fills in the gaps with generally "known" facts. The events described in this book took place over half a century ago. Since 1950, the survivors have had many other experiences. They hold the faces of lovers, children, grandchildren, and other family members in their hearts. They held down jobs that required them to learn other things. Current events captured their attention. They liked Ike and loved Lucy and dreamed of Jeanie. They lived through the Kennedy Assassination and the Murrah Building bombing and the 911 attacks. Allen Gifford may not "remember" that the massacre outside the Sunchon Tunnel took place on October 20, 1950, but he "knows" that is the date.

Memory problems are symptomatic of PTSD. Sufferers either have upsetting flashbacks or they try to forget or they obsess about the event. These recollections are filled with "what if" anxieties—what if I'd not reacted when I heard the rifle bolt go home. What if I'd been first in line to be interrogated and not fourth? What if they'd left me buried in that hole? Such thoughts are often filled with remorse and sorrow. Wrenching back a sense of personal control is an important part of recovery. Daydreams about the situation—where the outcome is more acceptable—are inevitable. Sometimes fantasies and memories get mixed up during the recall process.

Fourth, one can learn from others—and that information can become intertwined with first person data causing confusion. For example, if an individual sees an accident and an interviewer asks, "Was the light red or yellow?" The witness may be unsure if his initial perception is the correct one. Later memories will reflect this uncertainty.

Finally, memories combine facts with emotions and belief. Who you are to begin with impacts how you experience an event. A young man confronted with bestial behavior remembers that the perpetrator looked like an animal.

Allen: "The guard looked like an ape and he had big buck teeth."

Who you become influences how you remember it. For example, a religious person may incorporate his faith into his recall.

Jim: "I prayed. Oh God, how I prayed."

Bob: "The good Lord decided who would survive."

Anytime the brain perceives a threat, the body is suffused with stress hormones, which prepare an individual for "flight or fight." This causes the blood vessels in the eyes to contract creating the effect known as "tunnel vision." It limits a person's ability to appreciate or recognize events taking place outside the "tunnel." It also reduces the eye's ability to focus which results in a loss of depth perception (D. Grossman, *On Combat*, 2004)

During each of the shootings, the men being shot were overwhelmed with images—sounds, smells, sights. Their hearts pounded. Their blood pressures skyrocketed. Unable to focus on everything, they "fixated" on a particular aspect of the event. Both Allen and Bob saw their friend get shot between the eyes in the opening salvo.

For Allen and Bob, that first shot is the pivotal moment in the event for them. The excitement is so intense that the mind can't absorb anything else—the rest of the barrage is secondary to that first image.

Bob: "It's burned into my mind."

Lieutenant Colonel David Grossman: "If the visual system is disrupted or narrowed, the amount of information to collate a complete picture will be incomplete . . . [Soldiers] will fixate on major threat cues, but cues on the periphery of the visual system may not be processed into memory. This explains why individuals sometimes fail to remember "seeing" individuals or cues immediately adjacent to the threat."

During the rest of the massacre, they lay beneath a pile of bodies wounded and pretending to be dead. Bob's description of what happened next lacks detail—and moves through two days of suffering in five short sentences.

Bob: "One guard hit me with his rifle butt. This was October 20. A few of us still alive crawled into a nearby field. The next day, we heard a call, 'Americans, come on out. You're free.'"

Bill and Jim were not wounded—and they are the only ones who are mobile. Jim's recollections are more detailed—especially of the events following the shooting. He remembers hollowing out the shocks to create a shelter—and a village not too far away from the murder site—and a whiskey bottle. Small details that imply Jim was continuing, even under the most stressful of situations, to view his environment with the eye of a scout.

Jim: "I'm watching the village right down below us so I go down to figure out what was happening. My hair was curly and blonde. I get down there and see this old papa-san and a younger man in his forties. I asked them for tobacco. They thought I was Russian. I said, 'I'm no goddamned Russian.' Then I could see that they were cooking rice and I tried to get them to give me some. They wouldn't do that but they offered me some water."

By the time, the final shooting began in the railway cars near Kujang, Ed, Walt, and Sherm knew what was coming. During the massacre, all three received serious wounds. They lay in their own blood all night long. Sherm had been shot in the head. His ability to collect and store information was compromised—and he is not able to provide much detail. On top of that, he lay several yards away from the others. His ability to see was limited.

Walt and Ed's memories are remarkably consistent about the murders themselves. They both recall the rocket attack on the train, the North Korean soldiers machine-gunning the men as they came off the train—and the burning railway cars. However, after that, their stories diverge.

For over fifty years, Ed believed that the man who'd fallen on top of him was his close friend Bob Sharpe. When Pat McGrath Avery interviewed him for her book, *They Came Home: Korean War POWs Tell Their Stories*, he had no reason to doubt that the picture in his mind was correct.

Ed: "The man on top of me had been shot and the blood was dripping down into my face. I had no idea it was my buddy Bob . . . He was still warm so I knew he was alive . . . Bob was out, but when I shook him, he woke up. I told him that I was leaving and he said, 'Don't leave me here.' I told him that I'd get back to him." (Avery, 2004)

That Ed mistook Walt Whitcomb for Bob Sharpe is understandable. Throughout most of the marches, he and Bob stuck together. They'd only been separated a few days before the massacre. In the chaos of the moment, men dashed for the door of the train without paying attention to who else might be wrestling their way to the same exit. Then they were shot—and it was nighttime. Significantly, Ed was bayoneted in the head—and lapsed into unconsciousness for several hours.

Lieutenant Colonel David Grossman: "The greater the trauma, the greater the impact of post-incident amnesia is likely to be. Key factors, which will increase the stress, include the perception of threat or danger, the suddenness of the threat and the available time to respond or prepare, the amount of sensory input needing to be processed, and the degree of physical effort (aerobic and anaerobic output) that was engaged in during the incident. If the individual is physically wounded or injured the effect will be even greater, and the effects of post-incident amnesia will be greatest if the wound or injury results in unconsciousness." (Grossman and Siddle, *Critical Incident Amnesia: The Physiological Basis and the Implications of Memory Loss During Extreme Survival Stress Situations*, 2000)

When they awoke the next morning, Ed and Walt describe activities that sound similar. Each realized that the man next to him was warm—and therefore, alive. They spoke to each other. Then, their recollections deviate.

Ed remembers getting up and leaving Walt at the murder site. Walt remembers that he and Ed tended to Sherman. Ed remembers hiding in the train station by himself. Walt remembers wandering around the countryside with Ed. Ed remembers being alone when he met the Master Sergeant who rescued them. Walt remembers being with Ed in the North Korean home, eating rice and chicken. Ed remembers riding in a jeep and an ambulance, Walt remembers riding in a tank.

Both Walt and Ed were in deep shock. Trauma caused their confusion about this period.

Appendix II — The Geneva Conventions
"In war, there are no unwounded soldiers." — José Narosky

Several of the men in this story expressed outrage that their guards ignored the provisions of the Geneva Convention. A few remember Major McDaniel and the other officers castigating Mr. Kim for disregarding its principles. Certainly, the prisoners were mistreated. Their captors took their clothes and shoes. There wasn't enough food and the quality of the food they did receive was abysmal. They marched hundreds of miles with insufficient protection from the elements. Their wounds weren't treated. Their declining physical condition made them vulnerable to disease. The guards shot and bayoneted them, murdered their comrades, stole their belongings and disrespected them. Mr. Kim subjected them to both verbal and physical punishments.

War creates conditions where atrocious acts are committed as a matter of course. Prisoners are an unwelcome resource drain on any army. Captors must guard them—to prevent escape or liberation. They need medical care. They require food, shelter and clothing. Transporting POWs uses facilities needed by fighting units. Routing them around battlefields and other obstructions takes time and manpower. Still, it is hard to imagine how human beings could treat other human beings the way that Allen, Bob, Bill, Ed, George, Jim, Sherm, Valdor, and Walt were.

Most people don't need a commandment to tell them that killing other people is unacceptable. It's hardwired into human beings. When faced with situations where one person must kill another, most individuals experience some degree of psychic damage. The greater the space between killer and victim, the easier it is to kill. Since soldiers must be willing to take life in support of their comrades and to achieve the goals of war, they use various devices to create distance. (D.

Grossman, *On Killing: The Psychological Cost of Learning to Kill in War and in Society*, 1996)

Technology allows people to kill remotely. Bombs dropped from airplanes, artillery, gas, and bio-weapons kill great numbers while protecting those manning such weapons. For soldiers who must attack the enemy in a more "up close and personal manner," it is necessary to create psychic distances. It's easier to eradicate "vermin" than it is to execute people. Gooks, Ragheads, Japs, Krauts, Devils—such derisive names reduce the enemy to a group identity that is inherently different, inhuman, and evil.

Unfortunately, the physical and cultural differences used to make it easier to kill the enemy also make it easier to abuse noncombatants and prisoners of war. Throughout history, the brutality of war went unchecked. Then, through a series of treaties and agreements, the global community began to discuss issues like legality, suitable combatant behaviors and the appropriate treatment of prisoners.

As these conversations progressed over time, it became clear that the concept of "war crimes" required definition. For example, diets, which are livable for Asians, starve larger peoples like Americans and Europeans. On the other hand, should a country deny their own citizens in order to feed prisoners of war?

The Third and Fourth Geneva Conventions defined humane treatment of prisoners of war. Of course, it was binding only to those countries who were party to the agreement. The document that applied to World War II was signed in 1929 and went into effect in 1931. At the time, Korea was occupied by the Japanese who were not signatories.

After the excesses of the 1930s and 1940s, a Diplomatic Conference met to update international conventions to protect victims of war. It convened on April 21 and ended on August 12, 1949. The agreement took effect in October 1950—the same month as the Sunchon Tunnel and Kujang-dong massacres.

It included agreements, which if followed, would have prevented many of the deaths and abuses committed against these POWs. At the time of the Korean War, neither of the Koreas were signatories. North Korea did not sign until 1957, South Korea not until 1966. Russia, China, and the United States did sign in October 1949, but the decision was not ratified until long after the hostilities in Korea were over.

However, on the day after the fighting in Korea began, the International Committee of the Red Cross informed the Secretary General of the United Nations that it had sent messages asking the authorities of both North and South Korea to observe the appropriate Geneva Conventions.

A few weeks later, the Secretary General of the United Nations sent a telegram to the Foreign Ministers of both North and South Korea urging both sides to support the Conventions throughout the war. (O'Brien, 2007)

General MacArthur, in his Third Report to the Security Council, wrote, "I have extended the proclamation I issued as Commander-in-Chief of all United States forces in the Far East with regard to the treatment of prisoners so that now it applies to all forces of the United Nations Command."

Then, on July 13, 1950, North Korean Foreign Minister, Pak Hen Yeun, sent a telegram. "In reply to your telegram of July 12, I have the honor to inform you that the People's Army of the Democratic Republic of Korea is strictly abiding by the principles of the Geneva Convention in respect to prisoners of war."

However, although all sides claimed to be observing the conventions, there were no means implemented to enforce the agreements. The North Korean government refused neutral visits for inspection of prisoner-of-war camps.

It's not clear how much any of the Korean combatants in this conflict knew about the Geneva Convention. The captors ranged from NKPA troops to local guerillas to civilian guards. The interrogators were both officers and enlisted men. They could be local militiamen or trained Communist operatives.

The American officers knew about the Third Geneva Convention in some detail.

The enlisted men provided their interrogators with name, rank and serial number as prescribed by the agreements. The prisoners did expect fair treatment and they found Korean antipathy both puzzling and hurtful.

The "brainwashing" efforts, coming as they did during the height of American hostility toward the ideology, did little more than annoy the prisoners—and give them a focus for their resentment. The Communist propaganda program, however embarrassing, wasn't personal—it was politics and the men knew it.

However, even if one presumes that there was little food to be shared and that the men passed through the hands of several different Korean political entities, the harsh treatment they experienced was personal.

Within hours of his capture, Jim Yeager witnessed the murder of a man who did not provide the information his questioner required. Valdor John's interrogators pulled off his fingernails. Guards threw Sherman Jones to the ground and pressed bayonets into his back. The men who captured George Snodgrass buried him alive—several times. Ed Slater's captors stomped on his feet—and made him think they were going to shoot him.

Such brutish behavior was excessive given that the men were subdued and not trying to escape. They weren't causing trouble—and their offenses were minor. One explanation might be that North Koreans had more prisoners than they could manage—and the guards wanted total control over the men.

Psychologically, there are three elements to control—dependency, degradation, and dread—the three Ds.[42] In some cases, it's a deliberate strategy—drill sergeants use it to this day. It seems unlikely that the majority of the people involved with the POWs were educated in such things (although some sources report that Mr. Kim claimed to have a degree in psychology (Deane, 1977))—but it doesn't take a degree in psychology to realize that starving, terrorized men are more manageable than bold, healthy ones.

In later years, the VA presumed that the non-signatory status of the enemy in the Korean War might have compounded POW mistreatment. Prisoners of war during the Korean War are assumed to have been subjected to lengthy solitary confinements, repeated threats of death, constant interrogation and starvation, physical and psychological abuse, lack of medical treatment, non-recognition of rank, lack of protective clothing and rations, poor accommodation—and an almost total lack of communication with home and family. (Veteran's Entitlements, n.d.)

Therefore, even though North Korea agreed to abide by the Geneva conventions, there were many reasons why they didn't. By the time Mr. Kim, Buck, and Johnny took charge of the prisoners in Seoul, the POWs had already faced significant trauma at the hands of a variety of unknown parties. From the testimony of Junior Lieutenant Lee Hae Do, a member of the execution squad, the last part of their ordeal was the work of the Security Guard Bureau, Home Affairs Ministry, which was the North Korean national police. Despite the findings of the tribunal at Nuremberg after World War II, there was and continues to be a conflict between personal responsibility and the obligation of soldiers to follow the orders of their superiors. Regardless, Major Chong Myong Sil and his men bear the responsibility for the carnage at Sunchon and Kujang.

---

42 Three D's of control/torture — dependency, degradation and dread.

Appendix III — Code of Conduct

The Code of Conduct for U.S. Armed Forces was first published by President Dwight D. Eisenhower in Executive Order 10631 in 1955. It was later amended by President Carter in 1977. It outlines the basic responsibilities and obligations of all U.S. service members to the United States.

ARTICLE I.

I am an American, fighting in the forces, which guard my country and our way of life. I am prepared to give my life in their defense.

ARTICLE II.

I will never surrender of my own free will. If in command, I will never surrender the members of my command while they still have the means to resist.

ARTICLE III.

If I am captured, I will continue to resist by all means available. I will make every effort to escape and aid others to escape. I will accept neither parole nor special favors from the enemy.

ARTICLE IV.

If I become a prisoner of war, I will keep faith with my fellow prisoners. I will give no information or take part in any action, which might be harmful to my comrades. If I am senior, I will take command. If not, I will obey the lawful orders of those appointed over me and will back them up in every way.

ARTICLE V.

When questioned, should I become a prisoner of war, I am required to give name, rank, service number, and date of birth. I will evade answering further questions to the utmost of my ability. I will make no oral or written statements disloyal to my country and its allies or harmful to their cause.

ARTICLE VI.

I will never forget that I am an American, fighting for freedom, responsible for my actions, and dedicated to the principles which made my country free. I will trust in my God and in the United States of America.

Appendix IV — Names on Blackboard in Seoul

"Will you remember me?" — Tim Buckley

HQ Special Troops, 8th US Army Korea, War Crimes Section, 6 Jul 1952. Following is info found on blackboards in MOO HAK Girls High School, Seoul SK by 441st CIC Team.

1st Marine Division

Infantry - 19th; 21st; 24th; 29th; 34th; 5th

Air Force - 35th Fighter Squadron

Cavalry- 5th; 8th; 7th

Artillery - 11th; 13th; 63rd

Service QMC (graves registry)

ARRIVAL: 8.21.50 — 9.20.50

Other units were also represented.

Only LAST names were written on twelve different chalk-boards (presumably where they slept). They have been alphabetized here for your convenience. Since last names only were handwritten, spelling is the best interpretation. One man was shot trying to escape from this school.

Name	STM	Status	Other
Abbott, Chas L		Glory	
Adams, John Q	X		
Adkins			(2)
Aitken, Virgil E	X	Glory	
Aki, Clar Hal	X	D	
Aldridge	X	Glory	
Allbritton, Ray L			
Ambrose, Thom	X	Glory	
Arakawa		Not Missing	Misspelling?

223

Name	STM	Status	Other
Baily, Paul R	X	Glory	
Baily, Clair E			
Baker			(3)
Ball, Mathis O			
Barber			(2)
Bartholomew, G			
Bell, Elbert B			
Bell, Jos T	X	Glory	
Bevilock, Ersel	X	Glory	
Blair, Elzie	X	Glory	
Black, Dale	X	Survivor	
Blalock		Not Missing	Blaylock?
Boggs, Bish			
Bomberry, R	X	Survivor	
Bond, Elihue, Jr			
Boydston, J L			
Bradley			(2)
Brady		Not Missing	Misspelling?
Brogna, Robert L		Not Missing	Misspelling?
Bullard, Bradley		Not Missing	Misspelling?
Bull, Clifford G			
Bussiere, Paul J			
Buster, Johnnie J			
Cain, Edmund H			
Cagle		Survivor?	Cables, MA
Carrouth, Ralph			
Carter, Doug E			
Castana, Pete	X	Glory	
Castle, Robert E			
Catchings		Not Missing	Misspelling?
Charles, Ray M			
Cherry, Richard F		D	Recovered
Christman, Harry			
Church, Har Curt			
Cisneros, Rud	X	Glory	
Clark			(3)
Clemons, Chas Ed			
Clifford, Clyde R			
Cook, Charles W			?
Correa, Jesus D			
Cozad, Kenneth L			
Craig		Not Missing	Misspelling?
Crawford			(3)
Dahms, Don E			
Davis, Geo T	X	Survivor	
Davis, Joseph L			

Name	STM	Status	Other
Davis, Henry L	X	Glory	
Deanda, Marc C	X		
Dick, Will L			
Dorsey, Harold R	X		
Dove, Leroy J			
Drown, Harold E			
Dutton		Not Missing	Misspelling?
Elias, Daniel A			
Ellis		Not Missing	Misspelling?
Ellison, John Y	X	Glory	
Emerick, How W			
Eyer, Gordon L			
Feeney, Patrick J			
Feyereisen, R F	X	Glory	
Filler, Clemond D	X	Glory	
Finn, Howard	X	Glory	
Fisher			(3)
Fleming			(2)
Franco, Julio P	X	Glory	
Freeman, Har W			
Galvin, Osvaldo R			
Garcia, Ernesto	X	Glory	
Garcia Leonard P	X		
Gifford, H Allen	X	Survivor	
Gillette, Robert L			
Gill, Wayne B			
Goad, Eual			
Gossar, Edward			
Gosnell Albert A			
Granberry, Carl	X		
Grant			GR?
Gregser, AG			Gresser?
Grenier, Donald T			
Gresser, Arnold G			
Haas, Buster			
Hadnot, Carles D			
Halcomb		Not Missing	Misspelling?
Hall, Hedry D	X	Glory	
Hall, Ray Earl	X		
Hallokib		Not Missing	Misspelling?
Hanchey, Ray	X	Survivor	
Harman		Not Missing	Misspelling?
Harmon, Hubert			
Harnage, Lawr A			
Harpster, Fred W			
Harrison, F E			

Name	STM	Status	Other
Harry, Edward S			
Hassel, Lamar F			?
Hayes, Cor E			
Heath			(2)
Henderson, And J	X		
Hephner		Not Missing	Misspelling?
Hester, Will H			
High, Carlis E			
Hill, Wyne W	X		
Hines, Leonard	X	Glory	
Hodge, Will M			
Hogan, Ken A			
Holt, Crenshaw			
Hoogacker, Phil T			
Hull, Leo C			
Hunsicker, Ken	X	Glory	
Hutchins, Amos R			
Jarvis, Donald R			
Jerome, Richard			
Jester			(2)
Juiko			(Jinks, Leon W)?
John, Valdor W	X	Survivor	
Johnson			(7)
Jones, Eug G	X	Survivor	
Jones, Frank L			
Jones (7)			
Justice, Alvis	X	Glory	
Kalama, Herbert			
Kanoru			(Kamoku,B)?
Kamoku, Benj	X	D	
Kenny		Not Missing	Misspelling?
Kerns, John A	X	Glory	
King, Ralph	X	Glory	
KIrwin, John W			
Kitt, Peter			
Knapp, Donald W	X	Glory	
Koch, Kermit Karl			
Kreider, Lloyd	X	Survivor	
Krygowski, Fran J			
Kumagai		Survivor	Escaped
Lagoni, Ditlef J			
Landers		Not Missing	Misspelling?
Larioz, Lopez			
Latanation, Mike	X	Glory	
Levesque, N R			
Linebaugh, O F			

Name	STM	Status	Other
Locke		Escaped	
Lopez, Jos Benny			
Lopez, Fernando			
Loving, Charles R	X	Glory	
Lucik, Paul			
Lundberg, Ken			
Luty, Edw J			
Lynch, Harold M	X	Glory	
Maher, Frank X			
Makarounis, A		Survivor	Escaped
Malanga, A S			
Martin, John E	X	Survivor	
Masters, Louis R			
Mattingly, Don L			
Maylor			Naylor?
McDaniels, Will T	X	Glory	
McDowell		Not Missing	Misspelling?
McKittrick		Not Missing	Misspelling?
Mesa, Rudy Fel	X		
Metowski, Edw			
Michael, Marion	X	Survivor	
Michaelbury		Not Missing	Misspelling
Mickelberg		Survivor	Tiger
Mikesell, Har Eug	X		
Miller			
Miller			(4)
Mireles, Mcacario			
Moore, Claude	X	D	
Moore, James	X	D	
Morris, Milton	X	Glory	
Mounce	X	Survivor	
Mulock, Art F			
Murray, Bern M			
Musser, Alvin D	X		
Myers			(2)
Naylor, Clifford	X	Glory	
Nearwood		Not Missing	Misspelling?
Newman		Not Missing	Misspelling?
Nichols			(2)
Norris, Adin C			
O'Brien			(2)
Ortega, Jose	X	Survivor	
Parenti, Glendon	X	Glory	
Parks, Ralph L			
Parsell		Not Missing	Misspelling?
Parsons		Not Missing	Misspelling?

Name	STM	Status	Other
Patterson, Ith T	X		
Pattison, Orlando	X	Glory	
Paytes, John Lee			
Perry, Edw Fred			
Peters		Not Missing	Misspelling?
Peterson			(2)
Phillips, Howard	X	Glory	
Pilcher, Melvin		Not Missing	Misspelling?
Pixley, Geo A			
Powell, Sam B			
Preas, Curlous M			
Putzier, Gene A			
Rarick, Rolan D			
Reese, Jodie S	X		
Reeves, Geo R			
Renneburg, Anth			
Richey, Aggie L			
Riley		Not Missing	Misspelling?
Rindels, Ray M	X	Survivor	
Rivera, Floyd	X		
Roden, Tracy R			
Roney		Not Missing	Misspelling?
Rookstool, M D	X	Survivor	
Roop, Donald H			
Roten, Teddy E			
Rowlette, Louis	X	Glory	
Royer, Chas B			
Ruffato, B P	X	Survivor	
Ruiz, John G			
Salvie, Robert J	X		
Samolinski		Not Missing	Misspelling?
Sanchez, Ken L			
Segura, Geo P	X		
Scholes			(Sholes, Erwin)?
Shaffron, Paul	X		
Sharpe, Rober L	X	Survivor	
Shepard, H R	X		
Sherman, Earl W			
Sherry			(2)
Shibao, Hiroshi			
Shinde, Robt M	X	Glory	
Sholes, Ervin S			
Sidler		Not Missing	Misspelling?
Stiler, Stinky		Not Missing	
Slater, James A			
Smith			(4)

Name	STM	Status	Other
Smith, Franklin			
Snodgrass, Geo		Survivor	Escape
Sorrentino, AT			
Speicher, Chester			
Spence, Rover G	X	Glory	
Springer, Will L			
Stamper		Not Missing	Misspelling?
Stancil		Not Missing	Misspelling?
Stakry, Clyde M	X	Glory	
Steler		Not Missing	Misspelling?
Stencel		Not Missing	Misspelling?
Stevens		Not Missing	
Stevenson, Rob E			
Stidham		Not Missing	Misspelling?
Stockman, Rich			
Sutterfield, RG	X	Survivor	
Szczepanski, Anth			
Tabor, Stan Eug			
Teager			Yeager?
Terry		Not Missing	
Thomas, Mitch		Survivor	Escaped
Tish, Clarence A			
Toney, John R	X	Survivor	
Toole, Arnold E			
Torigian, Frank W	X		
Treece, Will Al			
Trembley, Aurel	X	Glory	
Triggs, Greg Wil			
Triplatt		Not Missing	Misspelling?
Tugman, Rich J			
Valenzuela			(2)
Van Dike		Not Missing	Misspelling?
Van Harn, HnryW	X	Glory	
Voltoro, Sylvestre	X	Survivor	
Voyles, Eug R	X	Glory	
Vranic, Anthony			
Walk, Arnold E	X	Glory	
Wallen, James A			
Ward			(2)
Watt, Lawr John			
White			(2)
Whited		Not Missing	Misspelling?
Wilcosky, Thom R			
Williams, Johnny	X	Glory	
Winkler, Marv J	X		
Wirt			(Wirtz)?

Name	STM	Status	Other
Wirtz, Harold D			
Witcorz		Not Missing	Misspelling?
Withor			Witherell?
Witherell, Franc K	X		
Wood, Lyle Edw			
Wooldridge, Clau	X	Glory	
Worley, Donald B			
Wright			(2)
Yeager, James W	X	Survivor	
Yeter, Corbett J			
York, Ray Arnold			
Young, John M	X	Glory	
Zawacki, Frank J			
Ziemer, Jack R			
Zirbel, Ronald M			

(Source: O'Brien, 2007)

Appendix V — Victims of Sunchon Tunnel Massacre

"Pain makes man think, thought makes man wise—and wisdom makes life endurable." — John Patrick

There are several lists available—each with different information. This is a compilation of the names of all those POWs who were taken off the train outside Sunchon Tunnel and shot. The bodies of those who died were buried beside the tracks after the massacre. They were exhumed on November 1, 1950 and moved to a Pyongyang cemetery. Bodies were exhumed again in 1954 and brought home in Operation Glory (See historical notes.) However, some bodies could not be fully identified. Those marked missing may be buried in the Punchbowl in Hawaii or may not have been returned at all. (O'Brien, 2007)

Ackerman, Jack M	Operation Glory	
Adams, John Q	Missing	
Aitken, Virgil F	Operation Glory	
Ambrose, Thomas	Operation Glory	
Bailey, Paul R	Operation Glory	
Bass, William T	Operation Glory	
Bell, Joseph T	Operation Glory	
Bevelock, Ersel	Operation Glory	
Blair, Elzie	Operation Glory	
Blake, Dale D	Survivor	Mentioned in this book
Blanton, Emory M	Operation Glory	
Bomberry, R O	Survivor	
Cables, Myles A	Survivor	
Castana, Pete	Operation Glory	
Cisneros, Rudolph	Operation Glory	
Counts, Woodr W	Missing	
Davis, George T	Survivor	
Davis, Henry Lee	Operation Glory	
Deanda, Marcello	Missing	
Dorsey, Harold R	Missing	

Ellison, John Y	Operation Glory	
Feyereisen	Operation Glory	
Filler, Clemond W	Operation Glory	
Finn, Howard	Operation Glory	
Franco, Julio P	Operation Glory	
Garcia, Ernesto Jr.	Operation Glory	
Garcia, Leonard P	Operation Glory	
Gifford, H Allen	Survivor	Interviewed for this book
Granberry, Carl	Missing	
Hall, Hedrey D	Operation Glory	
Hall, Raymond Earl	Missing	
Hanchey, Ray	Survivor	Mentioned in this book
Henderson, Andrew	Missing	
Henninger, William	Survivor	Interviewed for this book
Hill, Wayne W	Missing	
Hines, Leonard	Operation Glory	Mentioned in this book
Hodges, William E	Operation Glory	
Hunsicker, Kenneth	Operation Glory	
John, Valdor W	Survivor	Interviewed for this book
Jones, Eugene G	Survivor	Mentioned in this book
Justice, Alvis	Operation Glory	
Kamoku, Benjamin	Missing	
Kerns, John A	Operation Glory	
King, Ralph	Operation Glory	
Knapp, Donald W	Operation Glory	
Kreider, Lloyd	Survivor	Testimony used
Loving, Charles R	Operation Glory	
Lynch, Harold M	Operation Glory	
Martin, John E	Survivor	Testimony used
McDaniel Will T	Operation Glory	Highest Ranking POW
Mesa, Rudy V	Missing	
Michael, Marion	Survivor	
Mikesell, Harold	Missing	
Mistretta, Joseph	Survivor	Quoted in this book
Moore, Claude	Missing	
Moore, James	Missing	
Morris, Milton	Operation Glory	Mentioned in this book
Musser, Alvin D	Missing	
Naylor, Clifford	Operation Glory	
Ortega, Jose	Survivor	
Parenti, Glendon	Operation Glory	
Patterson, Ithal T	Missing	
Pattison, Orlando	Operation Glory	

Phillips, Howard	Operation Glory	
Reese, Jodie S	Missing	
Rindels, Raymond M	Survivor	Mentioned in this book
Rivera, Floyd	Missing	
Rookstool, Melvin D	Survivor	Testimony used
Ross, Leo C	Survivor	
Ross, Robert P	Survivor	
Rowlette, Louis	Operation Glory	
Ruffato, Barn P	Survivor	
Ruthstrom, Carr O	Missing	
Salvie, Robert J	Missing	
Segura, George P	Missing	
Shaffron, Paul	Missing	
Sharpe, Robert Lee	Survivor	Interviewed for this book
Shalwver, James A	Operation Glory	
Shepard, Har R	Missing	
Shinde, Robert M	Operation Glory	
Spence, Rover G	Operation Glory	
Starkey, Clyde M	Operation Glory	
Stone, Oliver	Operation Glory	
Sutterfield, Roy G	Survivor	Testimony used
Taylor, Oscar	Operation Glory	
Toney, John R	Survivor	Mentioned in this book
Torgian, Frank	Missing	
Tremblay, Aurel	Operation Glory	
Van Har, Henry W	Operation Glory	
Volturo, Sylvestre	Survivor	
Voyles, Eug R	Operation Glory	
Walk, Arnold E	Operation Glory	
Williams, Johnny	Operation Glory	
Willis, Doyle D	Operation Glory	
Winkler, Marvin J	Missing	
Witherell, Francis	Missing	
Wooldridge, Claude	Operation Glory	
Young, John M	Operation Glory	
Yeager, James W	Survivor	Interviewed for this book

(Does not include names from Kujang-dong.)

Appendix VI — McDaniels' POW Group/TF Casey

Tim Casey is a retired Army Command Sergeant Major who has spent a great deal of time compiling a list of POWs who were in the second march north. Some died along the way. Some were murdered at Sunchon and some at Kujang-dong, some disappeared as they marched north from the burning train near Kujang-dong—and survived. Here's an excerpt from Mr. Casey's list.

Name	St		Regt	Div	MIA		Status	Location
Ackerman, Jack	MI	PVT	29	24	07.24.50	10.20.50	Murdered	Sunchon
Adams, John Q	AZ	PVT	29	24	07.24.50	10.20.50	Murdered	Sunchon
Adkins, Clifford	WV	PFC	34	24	07.20.50	10.05.50	Murdered	
Aitkens, Virgil F	IL	PVT	5 C	1 C	08.16.50	10.20.50	Murdered	Sunchon
Alberty, Estell C	WV	PVT	21	24	07.11.50	07.11.50	Murdered	
Ambrose, Thomas	NC	CPL	19	24	07.16.50	10.20.50	Murdered	Sunchon
Arakawa, Jack C	HI	CPL	19	24	07.16.50		Escaped	Pyongyang
Aulds, Opal D	LA	SGT	21	24	07.11.50	07.11.50	Murdered	
Baer, Donald L	WI	PFC	34	24	07.20.50	12.03.50		
Bailey, Paul R	PA	PFC	34	24	07.20.50	10.20.50	Murdered	Sunchon
Barfield, David D	AL	PFC	21	24	07.11.50	07.11.50	Murdered	
Barrick, George	WV	1LT	21	24	07.12.50	11.07.50	Murdered	
Bass, William T	NC	PFC	29	24		10.20.50	Murdered	Sunchon
Bedell, Norman C	MI	PVT	29	24	07.27.50		POW-MIA	
Bell, Joseph T	PA	CPL	29	24	07.27.50	10.20.50	Murdered	Sunchon
Beller, James E	CA	PVT	29	24	07.27.50		POW-MIA	
Bernal, Joe M	CA	PFC		1 C	07.29.50	10.21.50	Murdered	
Bessemer, Rob	MI	CPL	5 C	1 C	07.25.50		POW-MIA	
Bevilock, Ersel	WV	SFC	19	24	07.16.50	10.20.50	Murdered	Sunchon
Billigmeier, Milt	ND	CPL	29	24	07.27.50		POW-MIA	
Blair, Elzie L	FL	PFC	29	24	07.27.50	10.20.50	Murdered	Sunchon
Blake, Dale D	PA	CPL	3Eng	24	07.27.50		Survived	Sunchon
Blaylock, Doug	FL	LT	26AAA	24	08.10.50		Escaped	Before Sun
Blanton, Emory	FL	PFC	29	24	07.27.50	10.20.50	Murdered	Sunchon
Bomberry, Rob O		SGT	63 FA	24	07.14.50	10.24.50	Escaped	
Boydston, James	CO	2LT	3Eng	24	08.20.50	10.08.50	Murdered	
Bracken, Russell	CA	SFC	3Eng	24	07.19.50	07.19.50	Murdered	
Bradford, Ed	MA	PVT	29	24	07.20.50		POW-MIA	

Name	St		Regt	Div	MIA		Status	Location
Bradford, Leon G	CA	SGT	38	2	09.01.50	06.20.51	POW-MIA	
Bradley, George	AR	CPL	29	24	07.27.50		POW-MIA	
Brady, Thomas L		PFC	29	24	07.27.50	10.21.50	Escaped	Before Sun
Brower, William J		PFC	29	24	07.27.50	08.20.50	Murdered	
Brown, Donald C	NY	PFC	34	24	07.20.50	10.20.50	Murdered	Sunchon
Bussiere, Paul J	NY	PFC	34	24	07.20.50	10.17.50	Died	
Cables, Myles A	WA	PFC	34	24	07.20.50	10.20.50	Survivor	Sunchon
Castana, Pete	CA	PVT	29	24	07.27.50	10.20.50	Murdered	Sunchon
Catchings, Junior		SGT	29	24	07.27.50	10.20.50	Survivor	Sunchon
Cerino, Joseph Jr		PFC	29	24	07.27.50	10.20.50	Survivor	Sunchon
Cisneros, Rudolph	TX	PVT	29	24	07.27.50	10.20.50	Murdered	Sunchon
Counts, Woodrow	OH	CPL	29	24	07.27.50	11.04.50	Murdered	
Cox, Boyd E	KY	PFC	21	24	07.05.50		Died	
Cozad, Kenneth L	IN	CPL	19	24	07.30.50		POW-MIA	
Craig, Arlton B		CPL	19	24	07.27.50	10.21.50	Escaped	Bef ore Sun
Dahms, Donald E	NJ	PFC	5C	1C	07.25.50		POW-MIA	
Davis, George T		CPL	5C	1C	07.25.50	10.21.50	Survivor	Sunchon
Davis, Henry L	NC	PFC	19	24	07.19.50	10.20.50	Murdered	Sunchon
De Sau, Lawr	PA	PVT	5C	1 C	07.25.50		POW-MIA	
Deanda, Marcalo	TX	PFC	34	24	07.20.50	10.20.50	Murdered	Sunchon
Dick, William L	IN	PVT	5C	1C	08.15.50		POW-MIA	
Dorsey, Harold R	OH	PFC	29	24	07.27.50	11.04.50	Murdered	
Dove, Leroy	MI	PFC	29	24	07.27.50		POW-MIA	
Dulyea, Harold B	MI	PVT	5C	1C	07.25.50		POW-MIA	
Eggen, Burdett			29	24	07.24.50	10.24.50	Att Mur	
Ellias, Daniel A	PA	PVT	29	24	07.27.50		POW-MIA	
Ellison, John Y	IL	SFC	29	24	07.27.50	10.20.50	Murdered	Sunchon
Ewing, John D	MO	PFC	21	24	07.31.50		POW-MIA	
Fetzer, Leo E	OH	PFC	19	24	07.31.50		POW-MIA	
Feyereisen, Rob	CO	CPL	15 FA	2	08.11.50	10.20.50	Murdered	Sunchon
Filler, Clernod W	CA	PFC	29	24	07.31.50	11.05.50	Murdered	
Finn, Howard W	KY	PVT	29	24	07.31.50	10.20.50	Murdered	Sunchon
Fisher, John A	WV	PVT	29	24	07.27.50	10.16.50	Died	
Franco,Julio E	CA	PFC	19	24	07.31.50	10.20.50	Murdered	Sunchon
Frasher, Donald	CA	PVT	29	24	07.27.50		POW-MIA	
Garcia, Ernesto		PFC	29	24	07.27.50	11.04.50	Murdered	Sunchon
Garcia, Leon P Jr	LA	CPL	29	24	07.27.50	11.04.50	Murdered	Sunchon
Gifford, Allen J		PFC	21	24	07.17.50	10.21.50	Survivor	Sunchon
Gossar, Edward	OH	PFC	34	24	O7.27.50	10.31.50	Murdered	
Granberry, Carl J	FL	PFC	34	24	07.19.50	07.19.50	Murdered	Sunchon
Grenier, Donald	NJ	PVT	29	24	07.27.50		POW-MIA	
Gresser, Arnold	MT	PFC	5C	1C	07.25.50		POW-MIA	
Hadnot, Charles	FL	PVT	29	24	07.25.50		POW-MIA	
Halcomb, Edw G		CPL	29	24	07.27.50	10.20.50	Escaped	Pyongyang
Hall, Hedry D	AL	PFC	19	24	07.30.50	10.20.50	Murdered	Sunchon
Hall, Raym Earl	TN	PVT	29	24	07.30.50	10.20.50	Murdered	Sunchon
Hamilton, Ray DL		PVT	29	24	07.27.50	10.17.50	Released	
Hanchey, Ray H		PVT	19	24	07.16.50	10.20.50	Survivor	Sunchon
Harding, Tho Jr	MA	PFC	29	24	07.27.50		POW-MIA	

Name	St		Regt	Div	MIA		Status	Location
Harmon, Herbert	WV	PFC	29	24	07.27.50	08.30.50	Died	Mistreat
Harmage, Lawr A	GA	PFC	19	24	07.29.50		POW-MIA	
Harry, Ed S Jr	AR	PVT	29	24	07.27.50		POW-MIA	
Hartlieb, Lawr	IN	PVT	29	24	07.31.50	09.26.50	Murdered	
Hassel, Lamar F	WI	PFC	29	24	08.01.50	10.20.50	Murdered	Sunchon
Haynie, Robert E	CA	PFC	29	24	08.02.50		POW-MIA	
Henderson, Andr		PFC	19	24	07.20.50	10.24.50	Att Mur	
Hendricks, Chas	MI	PFC	19	24	07.18.50	10.20.50	Murdered	Sunchon
Henninger, Will C	MN	PFC	34	24	07.20.50	10.21.50	Survivor	Sunchon
Hill, Wayne W	IL	PFC	34	24	07.20.50	10.20.50	Murdered	Sunchon
Hines, Leonard	PA	SGT	24	25	07.26.50	10.20.50	Murdered	Sunchon
Hodge, William	IN	PVT	24	25	07.26.50		POW-MIA	
Hodges, William	AZ	PFC	29	24	07.27.50	11.04.50	Murdered	
Hoefeler, Geo M	MO	SGT	19	24	07.20.50	10.20.50	Died	
Hogan, Kenneth	WA	PVT	29	24	07.27.50		POW-MIA	
Holt, Crenshaw A	NY	1LT	34	24	08.13.50		POW-MIA	Esc Seoul
Hoogacker, Phil T	MI	PVT	29	24	07.27.50		POW-MIA	Seoul
Hull, Leonard C	NY	CPL	34	24	07.20.50		POW-MIA	Seoul
Hunsicker, Ken P	OH	CPL	5 C	1 C	07.25.50	10.20.50	Murdered	Sunchon
Jarvis, Charles E			34	24	07.20.50	10.22.50	Escaped	
Jerome, Richard	MD	PVT	7C	1C	07.30.50		POW-MIA	
Jinks, Leo WE	IN	PFC	19	24	07.16.50		POW-MIA	Pyongyang
John, Valdor W	WI	PFC	34	24	07.20.50	10.21.50	Survivor	Sunchon
Jones, Eugene G		PVT	29	24	07.31.50	10.21.50	Survivor	Sunchon
Jones, Marvin W		CPL	5C	1C	07.25.50	10.30.50	POW-MIA	
Jones, Sherm Lee	TX	PVT	29	24	07.27.50	10.23.50	Survivor	Kujang
Justice, Alvis	KY	PVT	29	24	07.27.50	11.04.50	Murdered	
Kalama, Herbert	HI	SGT	34	24	07.20.50		POW-MIA	Pyongyang
Kamoku, Benj S	HI	PVT	34	24	07.20.50	10.20.50	Murdered	Sunchon
Kerns, John A Jr	NY	CPL	34	24	08.08.50	10.20.50	Murdered	Sunchon
King, Ralph	OH	PFC	29	24	07.31.50	10.20.50	Murdered	Sunchon
Kirwin, John W	LA	PVT	5C	1C	08.16.50	10.20.50	Died	Sunchon
Knapp, Donald W	MI	PVT	19	24	07.16.50	10.20.50	Murdered	Sunchon
Kreider, Lloyd D		PFC	34	24	08.20.50	10.21.50	Survivor	Sunchon
Krygowski, Fran J	MA	PFC	29	24	07.27.50		POW-MIA	
Kumagai, Takeshi	HI	SGT	34	24	07.20.50	10.20.50	Escaped	Pyongyang
Lagoni, Ditlef J		SFC	26AAA	24	08.10.50		POW-MIA	Seoul
Laroiz, Martin		SFC	5C	1C	08.15.50	10.22.50	Escaped	
Latanation, Mike	IN	SFC	34	24	07.20.50	10.20.50	Murdered	Sunchon
Linebrough, Orv	CA	PVT	19	24	07.27.50		POW-MIA	
Locke, William D	NC	CPT	35 F	USAF	08.17.50	10.20.50	Escaped	Pyongyang
Loving, Charles R	VA	PVT	19	24	07.20.50	10.20.50	Murdered	Sunchon
Lynch, Harold M	MN	CPL	29	24	07.20.50	10.20.50	Murdered	Sunchon
Makarounis, Alex	MA	1LT	29	24	07.27.50	10.20.50	Escaped	Pyongyang
Malanga, Angelo	NJ	CPL	5C	1C			POW-MIA	Pyongyang
Martin, John E		PVT	29	24	07.31.50	10.21.50	Survivor	Sunchon
Masters, Louis R	PA	PVT	29	24	07.27.50		POW-MIA	Pyongyang
Mattingly, Don L	OK	SGT	34	24	07.29.50		POW-MIA	Pyongyang
McDaniel, Will T	GA	MAJ	34	24	07.22.50	10.22.50	Murdered	Sunchon
Menges, Robert		CPL					Murdered	
Mesa, Rudy V	NM	PVT	29	24	07.27.50	10.20.50	Murdered	Sunchon

Name	St		Regt	Div	MIA		Status	Location
Michael, Marion		MSG	27	25	07.27.50	10.21.50	Survivor	Sunchon
Mickelberg, Al		PFC	5 C	1C	07.25.50	08.25.53	Survivor	Tiger
Mikeskell, Har E	IL	PFC	29	24	07.27.50	11.04.50	Murdered	
Miller, Donald G	CA	PVT	29	24	07.27.50	10.20.50	Died	Sunchon
Miller, Robert B	CA	2LT	5 C	1C	07.25.50	10.20.50	Murdered	Sunchon
Mireles, Macario	TX	PFC	29	24	07.27.50		POW-MIA	Pyongyang
Mistretta, Jos L	MA	PFC	29	24	07.31.50	10.20.50	Survivor	Sunchon
Monscevitz, Jos T		PFC	3Eng	24	07.20.50	10.24.50	Survivor	
Moore, James R	KS	PFC	5C	1C	07.25.50	10.20.50	Murdered	Sunchon
Morris, John C		CPL	19	24	07.31.50	10.08.50	Died	Strafing
Morris, Milton Jr	AL	CPL	24	25	07.26.50	10.20.50	Murdered	Sunchon
Morris, Robert L		SGT	29	24	07.27.50	10.14.50	Escaped	Pyongyang
Morris, Russell L			29	24	07.27.50	10.17.50	Escaped	Pyongyang
Mounce, Aaron		SGT	29	24	07.27.50	10.21.50	Survivor	Sunchon
Mulock, Arthur F	MA	2LT	34	24	07.20.50	08.31.51	POW-MIA	Camp 3?
Musser, Alvin D	MI	CPL	29	24	07.27.50	10.20.50	Murdered	Sunchon
Naylor, Clifford	MI	PFC	29	24	07.27.50	10.20.50	Murdered	Sunchon
Nearhood, John	IL	CPL	34	24	08.08.50		POW-MIA	Sunchon
Newman, Geo R	OH	PFC	34	24	07.19.50	10.20.50	Murdered	Sunchon
O'Brien, Don P	PA	PVT	34	24	07.20.50		Died	
Ortega, Jose H		PFC	5C	1C	07.25.50	10.19.50	Survivor	Sunchon
Parenti, Glendon	AR	SFC	34	24	07.10.50	10.20.50	Murdered	Sunchon
Parks, Jack F	NY	PFC	21	24	07.11.50	07.22.50	Murdered	
Parsell, John A		SGT	29	24	07.27.50	10.22.50	Mistreat	
Parsons, Auvil Jr			29	24	07.27.50	10.21.50	Escaped	
Patterson, Ithal T	NM	PVT	29	24	07.27.50	10.20.50	Murdered	Sunchon
Pattison, Orl R	MI	PVT	5 C	1C	07.25.50	10.20.50	Murdered	Sunchon
Paytes, John Lee	OH	PFC	19	24	07.16.50	10.20.50	Murdered	Sunchon
Perry, Edward F	MI	MSG	34	24	07.29.50		POW-MIA	
Peterson, Lyle E	WA	PVT	29	24	07.27.50		POW-MIA	
Phillips, Howard	GA	CPL	34	24	08.06.50	11.20.50	Murdered	
Poole, Jack E	IL	PFC	5C	1C	07.25.50	10.30.50	Died	Mistreat
Preas, Curious M	TX	PFC	26 AAA	24	08.08.50		POW-MIA	
Pryor, George T	KY	PFC	29	24	07.31.50	10.10.50	Murdered	
Putzier, Gene A	CA	PVT	29	24	07.27.50	10.14.50	Died	Pyongyang
Rarick, Rolan D	MI	SGT	34	24	07.20.50	11.02.50	Died	Mistreat
Ratcliffe, Griff III	PA	SGT	19	24	07.16.50	10.14.50	Murdered	
Reese, Jodie S Jr	OK	PVT	15 FA	2	08.11.50	10.20.50	Murdered	Sunchon
Reeves, Clifford	KS	SGT	3Eng	2	07.20.50	10.20.50	Murdered	Sunchon
Reeves, Emmet J	LA	1LT	5 AF		09.30.50		Died	Pyongyang
Reid, Max E			29	24	07.27.50	10.20.50	Survivor	Sunchon
Renneburg, Anth	CA	PVT	29	24	07.27.50	10.11.50	Died	Pyongyang
Richey, Aggie L	CA	PVT	29	24	07.27.50		POW-MIA	Pyongyang
Rindels, Ray M			19	24	07.31.50	10.26.50	Survivor	Sunchon
Rivera, Floyd	CO	PVT	29	24	07.31.50	10.31.50	Murdered	
Roden, Tracy R	AR	PVT	15 FA	2	08.11.50		POW-MIA	
Roney, Gordon R		PVT	5C	1C	07.25.50	10.22.50		Mistreat
Rookstool, Mel		PFC	29	24	07.27.50	10.21.50	Survivor	Sunchon
Ross, Leo C		PFC	29	24	07.27.50	10.20.50	Survivor	Sunchon
Ross, Robert P Jr		PFC	29	24	07.27.50	10.20.50	Survivor	Sunchon
Roten, Ancil A		PFC	5 C	1C	07.25.50	08.26.53	Survivor	Tiger

Name	St		Regt	Div	MIA		Status	Location
Rowlette, Louis	KY	SGT	29	24	07.27.50	10.20.50	Murdered	Sunchon
Royer, Charles B	TX	CPL	34	24	08.11.50		POW-MIA	
Rozear, John M	PA	CPL	34	24	07.29.50		POW-MIA	Pyongyang
Ruffato, Barney P		MSG	34	24	07.20.50	10.20.50	Survivor	Sunchon
Ruthstrom, Carr	TX	PVT	5C	1C	07.25.50	10.20.50	Murdered	Sunchon
Salvie, Robert J	MI	CPL	34	24	08.08.50	10.20.50	Murdered	Sunchon
Samolinsky, Stan	IL	PFC	29	24	07.27.50	10.30.50	Died	Mistreat
Segura, George P	AZ	PVT	29	24	07.27.50	10.20.50	Murdered	Sunchon
Sewell, William G	CA	PVT	29	24	07.27.50	07.27.50	Murdered	
Shaffron, Paul	PA	PVT	29	24	07.27.50	11.05.50	Murdered	
Sharpe, Robert L		PVT	19	24	07.17.50	10.21.50	Survivor	Sunchon
Sharver, James A		CPL				10.20.50		Sunchon
Shepard, Harold	NC	PVT	29	24	07.27.50	10.20.50	Murdered	Sunchon
Sherman, Earl W	MD	MSG	34	24	07.20.50		POW-MIA	
Shinde, Robert	CA	MSG		1 C	07.25.50	10.20.50	Murdered	Sunchon
Slater, Edward N	IL	PVT	21	24	07.12.50	10.23.50	Survivor	Kujang
Smith, Harold E		PVT	5C	1C	07.31.50	10.22.50	Died	Mistreat
Smith, Howard C	CA	2LT	15 FA	2	08.11.50	10.03.50	Escaped	
Smith, James Bry	OH	1LT	24	25	07.26.50	10.20.50	Escaped	Pyongyang
Snodgrass, Geo			7C	1C	07.31.50	10.21.50	Escaped	
Spence, Grover	AL	CPL	7C	1C	08.01.50	10.20.50	Murdered	Sunchon
Springer, William	NJ	PFC	29	24	07.27.50		POW-MIA	
Stamper, Theo			29	24	07.27.50	10.22.50	Escaped	
Staric, William F	OH	PFC	5C	1C	07.25.50	09.16.50	Murdered	Seoul
Starkey, Clyde M	MD	MSG	34	24	07.20.50	10.20.50	Murdered	Sunchon
Steger, William H	OH	PFC	29	24	07.27.50		POW-MIA	
Stevens, Victor S		CPL	5C	1C	08.16.50	10.21.50	Escaped	
Stidham, Henry	KY	CPL	19	24	07.18.50	10.20.50	Murdered	Sunchon
Stockman, Rich		PFC	29	24	07.29.50	10.15.50	POW-MIA	
Stone, Oliver	CA	PVT	34	24	07.20.50	10.20.50	Murdered	Sunchon
Sullivan, Peter	MA	CPL	19	24	07.18.50	07.18.50	Murdered	
Sutterfield, Roy		PVT	5C	1C	08.02.50	07.21.50	Survivor	Sunchon
Sweat, Leonard B		CPL	19	24	07.30.50	07.20.50	Survivor	Sunchon
Tabor, Stanley E		1LT	19	24	07.20.50	10.08.50	Died	Mistreat
Takahara, Sam O	NY	1LT	34	24	07.20.50		POW-MIA	
Taylor, Oscar Leo	CA	PVT	29	24	07.27.50	10.20.50	Murdered	Sunchon
Thomas, Mitchell	AL	2LT	29	24	07.27.50	08.31.50	Escaped	Seoul
Tish, Clar A Jr	FL	PFC	5C	1 C	07.25.50 ·		POW-MIA	
Toney, John R		PVT	29	24	07.27.50	10.20.50	Survivor	Sunchon
Toole, Arnold	IL	CPL	9	2	08.11.50		POW-MIA	
Torogian, Frank	SD	SGT	19	24	07.20.50	10.20.50	Murdered	Sunchon
Tremblay, Aural	NH	SFC	19	24	07.30.50	10.20.50	Murdered	Sunchon
Tucker, Lloyd L	TX	PFC	15 FA	2	08.11.50		POW-MIA	
Van Dine,Don F	NJ	SFC	34	24	07.20.50	10.31.50	Died	
Van Harn, Harry	WA	PVT	29	24	07.27.50	10.20.50	Murdered	Sunchon
Van Nosdall, Gil	NY	CPL	1 Sig	1Mar	09.20.50	11.21.50	Died	Tiger
Voltuno, Syl S		PFC	29	24	07.27.50	10.21.50	Survivor	Sunchon
Voyles, Eugene R	IN	PFC	5C	1C	08.16.50	10.20.50	Murdered	Sunchon
Vranic, Anthony	WI	PFC	15 FA	2	08.11.50		POW-MIA	
Walczak, Cas F	IL	PVT	5C	1C	08.17.50		POW-MIA	
Walk, Arnold E	IL	CPL	29	24		10.20.50	Murdered	Sunchon

Name	St		Regt	Div	MIA		Status	Location
Wallen, James A	KY	PFC	5C	1C	07.25.50		POW-MIA	
Warren, Leo A		PVT	29	24	07.27.50	10.20.50	Escaped	Sunchon
Whitcomb, Walt	NY	PVT	29	24	07.27.50	10.23.50	Survivor	Kujang
White. Elvis J	AR	PFC	19	24	07.20.50	10.20.50	Murdered	Sunchon
Whited, Roy N	MO	SGT	19	24	07.16.50	09.26.50	Die	Mistreat
Williams, Johnny	OK	PFC	9	2	08.11.50	10.20.50	Murdered	Sunchon
Willis, Doyle D	CA	PFC	5C	1C	07.25.50	10.20.50	Murdered	Sunchon
Wilson, Richard L	IN	CPL	29	24	07.27.50		POW-MIA	Seoul
Winkler, Marvin J	PA	PVT	29	24	07.27.50	10.20.50	Murdered	Sunchon
Wirt, Fredrick B	IL	CPT	3Eng	24	07.20.50	10.20.50	Murdered	Sunchon
Wirtz, Harold D	CO	PVT	35	25	07.22.50	10.30.50	Died	Mistreat
Witherell, Fran	NY	CPL	34	24	08.29.50	10.20.50	Murdered	Sunchon
Wood, Lyle E	IA	CPL	5C	1C	08.16.50	10.20.50	Died	Pyongyang
Woolridge, Cla	CA	PVT	29	24	07.31.50	11.04.50	Murdered	
Yeager, James W	CO	PVT	29	24	07.27.50	10.21.50	Survivor	Sunchon
Young, Russell V	CA	PVT	29	24	07.27.50		POW-MIA	
Zawacki, Frank J	OH	PVT	5C	1C	08.16.50		Died	

Depart Taejon, September 5, 1950

Arrive Seoul, September 11, 1950

Depart Seoul, September 23, 1950

Arrive Pyongyang, October 10, 1950

Depart Pyongyang, October 17, 1950

Sunchon Tunnel Massacre, October 20, 1950

Kujang-dong, October 22-27, 1950

Appendix VII — Chronology of Principal Events

UNCLASSIFIED

CHRONOLOGY OF PRINCIPAL EVENTS RELATING TO THE

KOREAN CONFLICT

OCTOBER 1950

Foreign Policy Studies Branch

Division of Historical Policy Research

Department of State

UNCLASSIFIED

October 20

Military   7,000 enemy prisoners were taken bringing the total to 82,000. The 187th Regimental Combat Team made an air drop in the Sukchon–Sunchon area against little opposition (Oct. 20, 2:00 P.M. Korean time). The R.O.K. 6th and 8th Divisions were advancing west of Songchon toward Sunchon. Mopping up operations in the Pyongyang and Wonson sectors Maj. Gen. Edward M. Almond, Commanding General, Tenth Corps, assumed command of U.N. forces in the Wonsan-Hamhung area. He coordinated plans for a rapid advance in the east coast area. 10th Corps troops were moving north from Poson-Bong, Oesang, and Puchang. The people of Pyongyang greeted U.N. forces enthusiastically.

Atrocities   Three liberated Americans said their comrades had died like flies in a forced march from Seoul to Pyongyang. Maj. Gen. Chung Il Kwon, R.O.K. Commander in Chief, said that eighty political prisoners had been burned alive with flaming gasoline only three days ago.

Military   13,000 enemy troops were captured bringing the total number of prisoners to over 95,000. The U.S. 1st Cavalry entered Chinnampo. A task force from this division advanced north and contacted airborne elements in the Sunchon–Sukchon area, where a second drop of 1,800 men was made. The 27th British Commonwealth Brigade also reached this sector. A tank-infantry task force from the R.O.K. 1st Division raced fifty miles north of Pyongyang against little opposition. The R.O.K. 6th Division advanced north of Unsan. It was reported (Oct. 21 Korean time) that the bodies of sixty-eight American prisoners massacred by enemy guards Oct. 20 (Korean time) had been found in a railway tunnel ten miles north of Sunchon.

Appendix VIII — Most Deadly Battles of Korean War

Battle	Combat Fatilities	Dates
Pusan Perimeter	3,603	Aug 4–Sep 16,1950
Chosin Reservoir	1,641	Nov 27–Dec 9, 1950
Kunu-Ri	1,194	Nov 29–Dec 9, 1950
Naktong Breakout	834	Sep 16–27, 1950
Hoengsong	773	Feb 11–13, 1951
Taejon	638	Jul 19–20, 1950
Heartbreak Ridge	616	Sep 13–Oct 15, 1951
Kum River	490	Jul 13–16, 1950
Unsan	454	Nov 1–2, 1950
Soyang River	406	May 17–20, 1951
Chochiwon	405	Jul 10–12, 1950
Triangle Hill	393	Oct 14–25, 1952
Seoul	382	Sep 20–27, 1950
Bloody Ridge	341	Aug 18–Sep 5, 1951
Hadong	306	July 27, 1950

Appendix IX — Korean War Memorials — Not Forgotten

Korean War Memorial — Washington, D. C.

South Korean Memorial at Hadong (*Photo by J. H. Chung*)

Note: Additional memorial pictures are available on the companion CD for this book.

Appendix X — Branson Supporters

Allen Edwards — www.AllenEdwards.com

At Your Service Limousines — Box 213 Reeds Spring, Missouri 65737 — (417) 230-3602

Branson.com — www.branson.com

Branson Veterans Taskforce — www.bransonveterans.com

Celebration City

Dick Clark Theater — www.dickclarksabbranson.com

Dixie Stampede — www.dixiestampede.com

Golden Corral

Hard Luck Diner

Jim Stafford — www.jimstafford.com

Joe Bryant, National History Project

Korean War Veterans Association

Linda Ward, PR-Pro

Mayor Raeanne Presley

Mayor Lou Schaefer

Nancy Smith, Branson Daily Independent

Paradise Grill

Pierce Arrow Theater

POW Network

Radisson Hotel — 120 South Wildwood, Branson, Missouri 65616

Sharon Robinson, Singer

Shoji Tabuchi — 3260 Shepherd of the Hill, Branson, Missouri 65616 — (417) 339-7200

The American Kids — www.AmericanKids.com

Vietnam War Veterans Association

Appendix XI — What was happening back home

Many times, it's difficult for folks at home to appreciate what's happening to our servicemen when they are in faraway places. Our lives go on as usual. Here's a "Time Capsule" to put the events chronicled in this book into context.

In 1950, President Truman authorized production of the hydrogen bomb. Eight million homes in the United States had television sets. Senator Joseph McCarthy began his persecution of Communists. The Great Brinks Robbery took place in Boston. The United Nations Building in New York City was completed.

In 1950, new houses averaged $8,450 and new cars $1,150. Gas was $0.18 per gallon.

Top movies of the day were *Cinderella*, *The Asphalt Jungle*, *Born Yesterday,* and *Father of the Bride*. Top songs were "Rudolph the Red Nosed Reindeer," "If I Knew You Were Coming, I'd Have Baked a Cake," "The Tennessee Waltz," and "Mona Lisa." People were reading *The Cardinal* by Henry Morton Robinson and *Across the River and Into the Trees* by Ernest Hemingway. *Betty Crocker's Picture Cookbook* and *Kon-Tiki* by Thor Heyerdahl topped the non-fiction bestsellers' list.

While the men in Major McDaniel's group of POWs were suffering in Korea, back in the USA, Steve Weyher, Jim Stafford and Pat McGrath Avery were in grade school. Joyce Faulkner and Marlyce Stockinger were toddlers. Shoji Tabuchi was in grade school in Japan. He studied the classical violin but it would be the mid-60s before he saw Roy Acuff and found a new dream to come to America.

Bill Haley and His Saddle Men recorded their first record. Two years later, they changed their name to Bill Haley and the Comets. Marshall Lytle joined the band in 1951, Dick Richards and Joey Ambrose in 1953.

On September 7, while the POWs were in Taejon, back at home, the *Truth or Consequences* game show debuted on TV. On Sept 19, while the men were scrawling their names on a blackboard in Seoul, George C. Marshall became Harry Truman's third Secretary of Defense. As the men marched from Seoul to Pyongyang, the first *Peanuts* comic strip by Charles M. Schultz appeared on October 2 and the front cover of *Time Magazine* featured poet Robert Frost on October 9. The FCC issued the first license to broadcast TV in color, while Jim, Walt, Sherm, George, Bob, Ed, Allen, Bill and Valdor dreamed of food in the schoolhouse in Pyongyang. On October 18, while the men were crammed into a train headed toward Sunchon, Connie Mack retired from the Philadelphia Athletics after a fifty year career as their manager. On October 19, 1950 in the United States—the day of the Sunchon Tunnel Massacre (October 20 in Korea), President Truman signed an act formally ending World War II. While Ed, Walt and Sherm lay bleeding in the darkness near Kujang-dong, the Fourth Geneva Convention took effect.

Appendix XII — Historical Notes

Army versus Prison — The military did not get directly involved when a young man was offered "jail or the military." The police would have to say that the young man had no record or anything pending before the military could take him. A police report was always requested on new prospective service members. Anything less would require a waiver.

Black Soldiers — President Harry Truman signed an executive order in 1948 integrating the United States Army. However, during the first chaotic months of the Korean War, the process was incomplete. Three US Army infantry divisions—the 25th, the 2nd and the 3rd contained black combat organizations. Among the 25th Division's three infantry regiments was the Army's last black 24th Infantry, the largest black unit to serve in Korea.

The 24th Infantry was the Army's only three-battalion regiment in action during initial weeks of the war. The 159th Field Artillery Battalion and the 77th Engineer Combat Company, both black units, accompanied them to Korea. They arrived on July 13. By July 20, the 24th's 3rd Battalion, reinforced by a battery of the 159th and a platoon of the 77th, was the first 25th Division element to go into action at Yechon. They are credited with recapturing the town.

As the war progressed, white combat units took heavy casualties. Military commanders traditionally replaced lost white soldiers with other whites. However, necessity forced integration to proceed faster and black troops began filling in the gaps. Given their heavy involvement in combat, black soldiers joined whites as POWs. Like Valdor John, an American Indian, they were singled out for intense interrogations. After he became separated from his unit but before he was captured, Ed Slater came upon North Korean soldiers torturing a black man. An admired officer, who worked with Major McDaniel to provide leadership and hope to the prisoners as they marched north, Lieutenant James Bryant Smith, was black. He escaped in Pyongyang shortly before the men boarded the trains there. At least two of the victims of the massacre at Sunchon Tunnel were black men—Sergeant Leonard Hines and Private

Milton Morris, Jr. (O'Brien, 2007). Five black soldiers and one sailor were awarded the Medal of Honor during the Korean War. (Summers Jr., 1990)

DPMO — Department of Defense — Prisoner of War/Missing Personnel Office. This office was created to lead the national effort to account for personnel missing as a result of hostile action and establish the most favorable conditions to recover those who become isolated in harm's way." (Department of Defense Prisoners of War and Missing Personnel Office, 2007)

Johnnie Johnson's List — Wayne Archer "Johnnie" Johnson, L Company, 21st Infantry Regiment, 24th Infantry Division, became a POW and a member of the Tiger Group on July 11, 1950. Struck by the possibility that the families of the men dying around him might never know what happened to their loved ones, he decided to document their passing with as much information as was available to him in those difficult circumstances. Commonly known as "Johnnie Johnson's List", it is often the only way to determine the date of death for many of the Tiger's victims. Johnson risked being shot for this activity. Because of Johnson's efforts, he was awarded the Silver Star Medal at a reunion of former American POWs, Korean War, in Chicago on August 3, 1996. Due to the efforts of many, the complete Tiger Survivors roster is now on the Internet. Every Tiger Survivor is accounted for. (Department of Defense Prisoners of War and Missing Personnel Office, 2007)

No Gun Ri — Some number of South Korean civilian refugees were killed by confused, exhausted, and jittery American troops of the 7th Cavalry near the village of No Gun Ri, South Korea, between July 26 and July 29, 1950. Historians and veterans of the action disagree on the number killed and some of the circumstances. Survivor George Snodgrass was separated from his unit and captured the morning of July 26 and did not participate in this incident. (The Korean War, 2006)

Operation Glory — The Korean War Armistice Agreement required the exchange of military war dead on both sides. To facilitate this, members of the US Graves Registration Division met with UN and Eighth Army officials to work out the details. The exchange of deceased personnel began on September 1, 1954 and continued daily, except Sundays, until September 21, 1954 when North Korean representatives told UN graves registration officials that there were no more to be delivered. The United Nations group continued delivering enemy deceased a few more weeks. A final accounting revealed that 4,023 UN deceased personnel had been received from the North Koreans, and that 13,528 had been delivered to them.

Project Freedom — In the late 1970s, Jim Yeager and other ex-POWs participated in an effort to recover the bodies of US soldiers left in Korea. Project Freedom for All American POWs and MIAs was a non-profit corporation. The Government spent $250,000 on a recovery operation in South Korea. (J. Yeager, Survivor, n.d.)

Senator Charles E. Potter — Charles Potter was the senior senator from Michigan in the 1950s. He was a veteran who lost both legs during World War II. In the early days of the Korean War, the North Koreans captured a large number of young American soldiers. Before long, word of atrocities committed against US servicemen by Communist forces reached Washington, DC. The job of documenting the torture, murder, and brutalization of American POWs fell to a Congressional committee headed by Senator Potter in December of 1953. He called twenty-nine witnesses, with twenty-three of them being either victims or eyewitnesses. A formal report came out on January 11, 1954. Hundreds of photographs documenting this abuse that were presented at the Potter hearings came from the files of MacArthur's War Crimes Division. Much of this evidence was presented at the Potter hearings.

Seoul City Sue — A radio personality that read off the names of dead US servicemen from their dog tags. Her real name was Ann Wallis. She was a former Methodist missionary married to a Korean educator Mr. Suhr (Suh). Some say she was forced to broadcast for the North Koreans after her capture in 1950. Some people feel that she and her husband may have been executed by the North Koreans as later broadcasts under her name sounded distinctly different. Her voice on the original broadcasts was immediately recognized by those who knew her as well as her family. Ms. Wallis' 'nom d' broadcast' conjures up ill feelings among former POWs and servicemen from the wartime period. (Estabrook, 2007)

T-34 tank — These 32-ton, armor-plated, metal monsters were the workhorses that stopped the German blitzkrieg outside Moscow in World War II. Each tank had an 85-millimeter gun, and one of its few vulnerable points was the engine grating in the rear where the armor was thinnest.

Bibliography

Alexander, Bevin. How Wars Are Won: The 13 Rules of War—From Ancient Greece to the War on Terror.

—. *Korea: The First War We Lost*. Hippocrene Books, 2003.

American Psychiatric Association. Diagnostic and Statistical Manual of Mental Disorders (3rd Edition.). Washington, DC, 1980.

American Psychiatric Association. Diagnostic and Statistical Manual of Mental Disorders (4th Edition.). Washington, DC, 1994.

American Psychiatric Association. Diagnostic and Statistical Manual of Mental Disorders. (2nd Edition.) . Washington, DC, 1968.

American Psychiatric Association. Diagnostic and Statistical Manual of Mental Disorders. Washington. Washington, DC, 1952.

Appleman, Roy E. *South to the Naktong, North to the Yalu*. Department of the Army, 1998.

Armstrong, Charles. *The North Korean Revolution: 1945–1950*. Cornell, NY: Cornell University Press, 2004.

Avery, Pat McGrath. *They Came Home: Korean War POWs Tell Their Stories*. Branson, MO: River Road Press, 2004.

Badsey, Stephen. Korean War. New York: WH Smith Publishers Inc., 1990. *Korean War*. New York: WH Smith Publishers Inc., 1990.

Biewen, John, and Stephen Smith. *"Korea: The Unfinished War." A documentary film. American RadioWorks*. www.americanradioworks.publicradio.org/features/korea/full.html.

Blair, Clay. *The Forgotten War*. Anchor, 1989.

Bryant, Joe, interview by Pat McGrath Avery. *Korean War Correspondent*

Carlson, Lewis H. *Remembered Prisoners of a Forgotten War.* New York: St. Martin's Press, 2002.

Chinnery, Philip D. *Korean Atrocity! Forgotten War Crimes 1950–1953.* Annapolis, Maryland: Naval Press Institute, 2000.

Clark, Samual, interview by Pat Avery. *Rakkasans* (2007).

"Conflict & Consequence: The Korean War and its Unsettled Legacy display." Truman Presidential Museum and Library, 2003.

Critical Incident Stress Management. www.criticalincidentstress.com/acute_stress_disorder.

Deane, Philip. *I should have died.* Atheneum, New York: Halliday Lithograph Corporation, 1977.

Ent, Brigidier General Uzal W. *Fighting on the Brink: Defense of the Pusan Perimeter,* Turner Publishing Company, 1998.

Estabrook, Shorty. "THE TIGER SURVIVORS STORY: Capture and Beyond," 2007.

Evanhoe, Ed. *The Inchon Landing & Pusan Perimeter Breakout: Sep 15 to Sep 30, 1950.* November 2002. www.korean-war.com/TimeLine/1950/09-15to09-30-50.html.

—. *WITHDRAWAL TO THE PUSAN PERIMETER: Jun 25 to Aug 3, 1950.* November 2002. www.korean-war.com/TimeLine/1950/06-25to08-03-50.html.

Faulkner, Joyce. *In the Shadow of Suribachi.* Red Engine Press, 2005.

Fehrenbach, T.R. *This Kind of War: The Classic Korean War Story.* Dulles, VA: Potomac Books, 2001.

Flanagan, Lt. General E.M. *The Rakkasans.* Novato, California: Presidio Press, 1997.

Gifford, Allen, interview by Pat Avery. *Survivor*

Grossman, Dave, and Bruce K. Siddle. ""Critical Incident Amnesia: The Physiological Basis and the Implications of Memory Loss During Extreme Survival Stress Situations." *The Firearms Instructor: The Official Journal of the International Association of Law Enforcement Firearms Instructor*, 2000.

Grossman, Dave, and Bruce K. Siddle. *Psychological Effects of Combat.* Academic Press, 2000.

Grossman, David. *On Combat.* PPCT Research Publications, 2004.

—. *On Killing: The Psychological Cost of Learning to Kill in War and in Society.* Back Bay Books, 1996.

Halbersham, David. *The Fifties.* New York: The Random House Publishing Group, 1993.

Halberstam, David. ""Korea – A Fresh Perspective." ." *AARP Magazine,* July/August 2003.

Hastings, Max. *The Korean War.* New York: A Touchstone Book, Simon & Schuster, 1987.

Heefner, Wilson A. *Patton's Bulldog: The Life and Service of General Walton H. Walker.* Shippensburg, Pa.: White Mane Books, 2001.

Henninger, William, interview by Pat McGrath Avery. *Survivor*

Hickey, Michael. *The Korean War: The West Confronts Communism.* Woodstock, NY: The Overlook Press, 1999.

John, Valdor, interview by Pat McGrath Avery. *Survivor*

Johnson, CB. "The Story of Hadong." *Graybeards,* November/December 2003.

Jones, Sherman, interview by Pat McGrath Avery. *Survivor*

Kaufman, Burton I. *The Korean Conflict.* Westport, Conneticut: Greenwood Press, 1999.

Kim, Chom-gon. *The Korean War, 1950–1953.* Seoul, Korea: Kwangmyong Publishing Company, 1980.

Kim, Chung Un, interview by KWC76. *Testimony* (1951).

Kim, Young Sik. *Eyewitness: A North Korean Remembers,* 2004. www.kimsoft.com/korea/eyewit17.htm.

Know, Donald and Coppel, Alfred. *The Korean War: Uncertain Victory*. New York: Harcourt Bruce Jovanovich, 1988.

Korea Bulletin Staff Members and Office Files: Selected Records, Department of State, Document File Subseries, Truman Presidential Library. Document File Subseries, Truman Presidential Library.

Korea: Its History and Culture. Korea Overseas Information Service, Seoul, Korea: Korea Overseas Information Service, 1996.

Krepps, Vincent, interview by Pat McGrath Avery.

Krieder, Lloyd, interview by Senator Potter. *Subcommittee on Korean War Atrocities (Part I)* (1953).

Lech, Raymond B. *Broken Soldiers*. Urbanna and Chicago: University of Illinois Press, 2000.

Lee, Hae Do, interview by KWC76. *Testimony* (1951).

Locke, Captain William, interview by Senator Potter. *Subcommittee on Korean War Atrocities* (1953).

MacDonald, Callum A. *Korea: The War before Vietnam*. New York: Macmillan, 1996.

Mack, Richard E. *Memoir of a Cold War Soldier*. Kent, OH: Kent State University Pres, 2001.

Mahoney, Kevin. *Formidable Enemies: The North Korean and Chinese Soldier in the Korean War*. Novato, CA: Presidio Press, 2001.

Maihafer, Harry J., and Donald M. Goldstein. *The Korean War: The Story and the Photographer*. Potomac Books, Inc.

Makarounis, Alexander. ""I Survived the Korean War Death March."." *Argosy Magazine*, March 1951.

Makarounis, Alexander, interview by Senator Potter. *Subcommittee on Korean War Atrocities* (1953).

Martin, Affidavit of John E., interview by WOJG, USA Kenneth E. Washington. *Survivor* (October 31, 1950).

McCullough, David. *Truman*. New York: A Touchstone Book, Simon & Schuster, 1992.

Military Veterans PTSD Reference, Manual. "Military Veterans PTSD Reference Manual," 2006. www.ptsdmanual.com/.

Montejo, Victor. " "A Study of Prisoners of War in the Twentieth Century"." *Thesis submitted to Baruch College*. New York, NY: The City University of New York, 1997.

Moskin, J. Robert. *Mr. Truman's War*. New York: Random House Inc., 1996.

Muccio, John J., Ambassador to Korea, 1949 – 1952, interview by Jerry N. Hes Richard D. McKenzie. *Oral History Interviews; February 11 and 18, 1971*, (December 7, 1973).

O'Brien, Phil, interview by Pat McGrath Avery and Joyce Faulkner. *Analyst, DPMO* (July 2007).

Quinn, Joe. "29 PW Massacred in Brutal NK Atrocity." *UP*, October 24, 1950.

Report of Review of Veteran's Entitlements, Prisoners of War. www.veteransreview.gov.au/report/chapters/ch18.htm.

Sharpe, Robert L. as told to Bill Currie. "God Saved My Life in Korea", *Saturday Evening Post*, 1951.

Sharpe, Robert, interview by Pat McGrath Avery. *Survivor*

Slater, Ed, interview by Pat McGrath Avery. *Survivor*

—. "Written Account.", 2002.

Smith, Lieutenant James Bryant, interview by Senator Potter. *Subcommittee on Korean War Atrocities (Part I)* (1953).

Snodgrass, George, interview by Pat McGrath Avery. *Survivor*

Spiller, Harry. *American POWs in Korea*. Jefferson, NC: McFarland and Company, Inc., 1998.

Staff. "Barbarity." *Time Magazine*, November 9, 1953.

Stueck, William. *Rethinking the Korean War: A New Diplomatic and Strategic History*. Princeton: Princeton University Press, 2002.

—. *The Korean War*. Princeton University Press, 1997.

Summers Jr., Harry G. *Korean War Almanac*. New York, NY: Facts On File, 1990.

Sutterfield, Roy, interview by Kenneth Washington. *KWC76* (November 2, 1950).

The Enemy Flanks the Eighth Army in the West. www.army.mil/cmh-pg/books/korea/20-2-1/sn13.htm.

The Korean War. www.korean-war.com/.

The Korean War. www.kmike.com/CMH%20MilitaryHistory/Poster%20Narratives.htm.

The Korean War. 2006. www.rt66.com/~korteng/SmallArms/nogunri.htm.

The Korean War Educator. www.koreanwar-educator.org.

The Korean War Timeline. www.rt66.com/~korteng/SmallArms/TimeLine.htm.

The Korean War: Remembering Our History. korea50.army.mil/history/index.shtml.

The Truman Presidential Library and Museum . www.trumanlibrary.org/whistlestop/study_collections/korea/large/index.htm.

Time. "Death Train." *Time*, October 30, 1950.

—. "The Tough Prisoners." *Time Magazine*, September 21, 1953.

Van Zandt, James E. ""You are about to die a horrible death" Korean War." *VFW Magazine*, February 2003.

Varhola, Michael J. *Fire and Ice: The Korean War, 1950 - 1953*. Woodbury Publishers, 2000.

Veteran's Entitlements, Prisoners of War. *Report of Review of Veteran's Entitlements, Prisoners of War.* www.veteransreview.gov.au/report/chapters/ch18.htm.

VFW Magazine. "War in Korea, A 50th Anniversary Remembrance," 2003.

Whelan, Richard. *Drawing the Line: The Korean War, 1950-1953.* Boston: Little, Brown and Company, 1990.

Whitcomb, Walter, interview by Pat McGrath Avery and Joyce Faulkner. *Survivor*

Whitehead, Don. "Reds Murder 68 Yanks." *Kansas City Star*, October 23, 1950.

Wilson, Arthur W. *Red Dragon. Faces of War II.* Portland, OR: Artwork Publication, Inc., 2003.

Yeager, James. "My Trip to Hell and Back." *Written Account.*

Yeager, James, interview by Pat McGrath Avery. *Survivor*

Yeager, James W. ""Hadong: The truth about what really happened at Hadong, South Korea." ." *The Graybeards*, January/February 2004.

Zellers, Larry. *In Enemy Hands: A Prisoner in North Korea.* Lexington, Kentucky: The University Press of Kentucky, 1991.

Zeman, Nancy, interview by Pat McGrath Avery and Joyce Faulkner. *Sister of Gene Putzier* (October 2006).

Index

Sherman Jones and Ed Slater, Veterans
Day, 2006 — Branson, Missouri
(*Photo by Evelyn Harless*)

Sherman Jones, Ed Slater,
Paul Harless — Korean War
Jeep — Veterans Day, 2006
— Branson, Missouri
(*Photo by Evelyn Harless*)

Penny Gilley with Jim Yeager,
Veterans Day, 2007 — Branson,
Missouri

Printed in the United States
111446LV00003B/88-156/A

9 780978 515812